Reformed Theology

"Doing Theology" introduces the major Christian traditions and their way of theological reflection. The volumes focus on the origins of a particular theological tradition, its foundations, key concepts, eminent thinkers and historical development. The series is aimed readers who want to learn more about their own theological heritage and identity: theology undergraduates, students in ministerial training and church study groups.

Titles in the series:

Catholic Theology – Matthew Levering
Anglican Theology – Mark Chapman
Lutheran Theology – Steven Paulson
Reformed Theology – Michael Allen
Methodist Theology – Kenneth Wilson
Baptist Theology – Stephen Holmes

Reformed Theology

R. Michael Allen

t&t clark

Published by T&T Clark International
A Continuum Imprint
The Tower Building, 11 York Road, London SE1 7NX
80 Maiden Lane, Suite 704, New York, NY 10038

www.continuumbooks.com

British Library Cataloguing-in-Publication Data
A catalogue record for this book is available from the British Library

ISBN 13:   978-0-567-03429-8 (Hardback)
ISBN 13:   978-0-567-03430-4 (Paperback)

Typeset by Newgen Imaging Systems Pvt Ltd, Chennai, India
Printed and bound in Great Britain by the MPG Books Group

For Dad and Mom

Contents

Contents

Acknowledgments

Family, friends, and churches have made this book possible, and it must suffice to thank only a few. Wesley Hill, Geoff Ziegler, and Michael White helped refine my thinking in conversation and by reading sections of the manuscript. Mike Horton and John Webster read through and offered useful feedback on the manuscript; for that, as well as the ways in which they model contemporary Reformed theology at its best, I am immensely grateful. Dan Treier faithfully and wisely combed through a penultimate draft, offering advice and encouragement. His generosity continues to be a blessing. As always, my wife, Emily Jane, proved to be my most regular and most devoted conversation partner. Not only did she allow me the freedom to write, but she delighted in my process of discovery and expression, celebrating every step with me.

Again, Tom Kraft and the entire staff at T&T Clark proved themselves capable and enthusiastic. I am glad to have worked on this project, my second with them, and I look forward to future partnership over the years to come. Jason Paugh, a Reformed pastor-theologian in training, graciously prepared the index.

Much of this material was presented in spring 2009 as an adult education class at Immanuel Presbyterian Church in Warrenville, Illinois. For their comments, questions, and encouragement, I am grateful to those who participated. That church and the Reverend George Garrison, in particular, have provided a church home and a community of love and much grace. Over the years, various church communities have exemplified the faith and practice of the Reformed tradition for me: Trinity Presbyterian Church in Jackson, Mississippi; Second Presbyterian Church in Memphis, Tennessee; Immanuel Presbyterian Church in Miami, Florida; Coral Ridge Presbyterian Church in Fort Lauderdale, Florida; and

Park Cities Presbyterian Church in Dallas, Texas. Theology is best done by those living in the body of Christ, and I hope that my reflection on this common faith honors the witness of these churches and the rich love of their Lord.

Finally, I dedicate this book to my parents, Rob and Carrye Allen. Among the many things they taught me were the great truths cherished by the Reformed faith and the lively praise and witness voiced by the Reformed churches. For this, as well as all their love, I thank God for them.

Abbreviations

ABR   Shirley Guthrie, *Always Being Reformed: Faith for a Fragmented World* (Louisville, KY: Westminster John Knox, 1996).

BC   Constitution of the Presbyterian Church (USA), Part One: *Book of Confessions* (Louisville, KY: Geneva, 1996).

CD   Karl Barth, *Church Dogmatics* (4 vols.; ed. Geoffrey W. Bromiley and Thomas F. Torrance; Edinburgh: T&T Clark, 1956–1969).

FWERD   Amy Plantinga Pauw and Serene Jones (eds.), *Feminist and Womanist Essays in Reformed Dogmatics* (Columbia Series in Reformed Theology; Louisville, KY: Westminster John Knox, 2005).

ICR   John Calvin, *Institutes of the Christian Religion* (Library of Christian Classics XX and XXI; ed. John T. McNeill; trans. Ford Lewis Battles; Philadelphia, PA: Westminster, 1960).

Inst   John Calvin, *The Institutes of the Christian Religion* (4 vols.; Library of Christian Classics; ed. John T. McNeill; trans. Ford Lewis Battles. Louisville, KY: Westminster John Knox, 2005).

PRRD   Richard A. Muller, *Post-Reformation Reformed Dogmatics* (4 vols.; Grand Rapids, MI: Baker Academic, 2003).

RCSC   Arthur C. Cochrane (ed.), *Reformed Confessions of the Sixteenth Century* (Louisville, KY: Westminster John Knox, 2003).

RD   Herman Bavinck, *Reformed Dogmatics* (4 vols.; ed. John Bolt; trans. John Vriend; Grand Rapids, MI: Baker Academic, 2002–2008).

ST   Charles Hodge, *Systematic Theology* (3 vols.; Grand Rapids, MI: Eerdmans, 1968).

WJO   Works of John Owen (22 vols.; Edinburgh: Banner of Truth Trust, 1966).

What Is Reformed Theology?

This is a book about Reformed theology. Two things must be said about this claim. First, this book is about theology: reflection about God. Second, this book addresses one strand in the larger cord of Christian theology: the Reformed tradition. Each of these statements deserves greater explication.

First, this is not a sociological or historiographic study about particular persons or churches, even if they may be termed "Reformed." No, this book is about theology, thinking about God, and history is brought in only for the sake of examining this tradition of ideas and beliefs. Thus, whatever historical analyses arise within its pages will tilt toward the contemporary conversation known as intellectual history. At times, episodes or events will be described at some length, precisely because thinking does not occur in some sort of disembodied ivory tower (oxymoronic and nonexistent all at once) but in the midst of concrete, messy history. History, context, and actions affect thinking. But my attention to historical events will always be for the sake of better understanding the thinking of Reformed theologians and Reformed churches.

Presbyterian theologian George Stroup has written an essay entitled "Reformed Identity in an Ecumenical World," trying to describe what it means to be "Reformed." He presents five ways in which commonality might be viewed: according to its (1) polity and church structure, (2) essential tenets, (3) themes and emphases, (4) habits, and (5) cultural-linguistic patterns.[1] Stroup points to dangerous reductionisms tied to thinking of belief-sets as encompassing Christian identity in a particular tradition, and his concerns go far in helping us identify Reformed churches and Christians in a holistic way. Particularly in an era when theological pluralism

1

marks churches that claim the name "Reformed," investigations like that of Stroup are of great need; however, his concerns about ecumenical methodology are beside the point here, in as much as this book solely addresses doctrine.

Second, this book is about Reformed theology and not any other sort of thinking about God. What is Reformed theology? The question begs answering at the beginning of a book bearing this title. W. B. Gallie has suggested that democracy is an "essentially contestable concept," which simply cannot be protected from heated debate about definition. Is democracy inherently populist? Is it necessarily direct in its involvement of citizens in government? Is it egalitarian or tilted toward the poor? The very idea of democracy from the ancient Greeks to modern Europeans to today has always involved contests regarding visions for this theory and practice. So it is with "Reformed theology." As with many terms in the realm of theology, "Reformed" means many things to many people. Yet we can note some basic definitional hints. This book appears alongside other volumes in a series on Doing Theology: Lutheran, Anglican, Methodist, and Roman Catholic. Each of these other volumes describes the thinking about God related to a particular church or communion of churches. Thus, our expectation should be that Reformed theology is also a way of thinking about God related to a particular ecclesiastical body, in this case the Reformed churches.

Of course, this is simply to push the question back one level. We no longer ask "what is Reformed theology?" but now ask "what churches are Reformed?" Again, external examples may clarify. When asked to define pornography, a savvy politician begged off the question by saying "I know it when I see it." In so doing, he was following the self-awareness of St. Augustine made evident when faced with the question regarding the nature of time: "What, then, is time? If no one ask of me, I know; if I wish to explain to him who asks, I know not."[2] Like time, then, "Reformed"—whether affixed to "theology" or "churches"— remains an "essentially contestable concept." Fear not, however, for this book will actually provide an argument regarding the nature of Reformed theology, in as much as certain core emphases are to be found at the heart of all Reformed churches (albeit in varying contexts, combinations, and circumstances). Admitting a variety of manifestations within its compass, nevertheless this book provides an alternative to certain ways in which Reformed theology ought not be defined.

We ought to note the most common use of the term "Reformed" in contemporary church life and theological discussion. Frequently, the term "Reformed" is a synonym for "Calvinist," and both terms really refer to a person's predestinarian beliefs about Christian salvation.[3] A "Reformed" view of pre-destination involves affirmation that God unconditionally chooses who will be saved and who will be damned, prior to those individuals doing anything of (de)merit. This doctrine is accompanied by others, such as the belief that Christ effectively died to save these elect and that their salvation cannot be lost. This whole belief set is oftentimes shorthanded by the acronym "TULIP," a breezy way of describing the so-called five points of Calvinism as affirmed by the Reformed "Canons of Dordt," ecclesial affirmations made in the early seventeenth century. These beliefs are also frequently called the "doctrines of grace" as they highlight the free nature of God's salvation, the undeserving plight of the recipient, and the limitless sovereignty of the Christian God.

This contemporary use of the terms "Reformed" and "Calvinist" will not be followed in this book. While many theologians and churches self-identify in this way, a theological analysis cannot be satisfied to take them at their word and, instead, must push further toward greater clarity in noting affinities, trajectories, and dependencies. Without attempting to dismiss this typical meaning, I want to suggest that two problems attend such a definition as a helpful analysis of Reformed identity.

First, the term "Calvinist" ought to be dropped entirely.[4] A name which attaches certain beliefs or practices to a particular figurehead (in this case, John Calvin) requires strong footing lest it seem historically and logically idiosyncratic. Thus, such a term should be employed for those who (1) found a movement or initiate some belief or institute some practice, or (2) definitively shape the development of some movement, belief, or practice. With regard to the doctrine of predestination, John Calvin fails to fit the bill in either regard. In fact, he affirms the doctrine in the same fashion as Augustine of Hippo, a millennium earlier. In Calvin's own day, Martin Luther exhibited greater interest and deeper argument for the sake of clarifying the "Augustinian" view of predestination. With regard to predestination and the "doctrines of grace," Calvin is both unoriginal and not all that definitive. That is not to demean Calvin, who will be cited many times in the pages to follow, but rather to locate him within a broader theological movement. Most importantly, Calvin is one of several luminaries within the Reformed universe. His brilliant, faithful witness is accompanied by that of John Owen, Jonathan Edwards, Francis Turretin, Peter Van Mastricht, Johannes Cocceius, Peter Martyr Vermigli, and others. In fact, Calvin was a second-generation reformer, following in the footsteps of, not only Luther, but especially Ulrich Zwingli and Martin Bucer. Thus, we must learn to think of Calvin as an incredibly influential thinker best viewed alongside Bucer, Zwingli, Heinrich Bullinger, and others, rather than the founder of some new church. Thus, as Calvin is neither the founder of these doctrines or these churches nor one who definitively shapes them, "Calvinism" is less than accurate.

Second, "Reformed" cannot mean adherence to only these doctrines of grace. This is not to say that Reformed theologians and churches deny these doctrines; it is simply to say that affirmation of these tenets or themes is not distinctive to Reformed theology. Richard Muller of Calvin Theological Seminary has wisely noted that the major confessions of the Reformed churches are united on the five points in response to the Arminians, but they "also stand in substantial agreement on the issues of the baptism of infants, the identification of the sacraments as means of grace, and the unity of the one covenant of grace from Abraham to the eschaton."[5] Muller goes on to show common agreement on the roots of Christian assurance in both Jesus Christ and the internal witness of the Holy Spirit, as well as the identification of the millennium from Rev. 20 with the present era. His point, to be followed in this volume, is that the contours of Reformed theology are coherent. Adjusting one wall of the theological structure likely shifts weight across the whole. Reformed theology is systematic, not in the excessive sense of teasing out some "first principle" deductively but in the modest sense of showing the compatibility and lovely fittingness of all Christian teaching drawn from the one Word of God.

Muller determines that Reformed theology speaks to virtually the whole of Christian dogmatics. That is, there is a Reformed perspective on the future just as there is a Reformed angle on the person of Christ. This is not to suggest that there is strict uniformity in every area, to be sure, but to note that there is extensive interest in issues across every topic of dogmatics. Historically, Reformed theology is best identified by looking to confessions of the Reformed churches. These confessions engage issues ranging from the place of preaching in worship to the doctrine of the Trinity to the nature of Christian freedom. As exemplified paradigmatically in the Westminster Confession of Faith and the Savoy Declaration, Reformed churches confess a whole theology. And this is not merely the arid nature of some old scholasticism, as many detractors might claim, for the mainline Confession of 1967 issued by the United Presbyterian Church of North America (now the PCUSA) also addresses issues from theology proper to bibliology to eschatology (though, admittedly, with much greater brevity than the Westminster Standards).

So then, while most laypersons (and many professional theologians in certain circles) use the terms "Calvinist" and "Reformed" to label someone as opposing Arminian views of soteriology and predestination, this lacks the historical and theological specificity needed for a study of this sort. While such use of the term "Reformed" may be very handy in certain settings (e.g., differentiating predestinarian Baptists from other Baptists), it cannot be allowed to serve as the primary meaning. As the term will be used in this book, then, one cannot be both baptistic and identified as "Reformed" in as much as baptistic ecclesiology depends on a sharp distinction between Israel and the church, thereby disagreeing with the Reformed way of affirming the unity of the covenant of grace. Issues like the constitution of a church and the nature of biblical worship are integral to Reformed identity, alongside soteriological emphases more widely known. Again, this is not meant to suggest that in intramural discussions of predestination amongst baptistic churches the term would never be helpful. In such situations, though, it is best to say with regard to what doctrines one is laying claim to identifying with the Reformed or with Calvin.

To remedy these conundrums, a terminological distinction will be employed throughout this book. One could name a broader movement "Reformational theology," which includes the specific object of this book, "Reformed theology." Therefore, one can be "Reformational" without being "Reformed," though one cannot be "Reformed" (or at least coherently so) without also being "Reformational." By "Reformational," we speak of those churches and persons who affirm the five *solas* (*sola Scriptura*, *solus Christus*, *sola gratia*, *sola fide*, and *soli Deo Gloria*), the five points enumerated by the Reformed Synod of Dordt regarding the doctrine of predestination, and the importance of penal substitution as a crucial (though not exclusive) understanding of the atonement (an emphasis gleaned from Scripture especially by the magisterial Reformers and their followers). Eschatology, ecclesiology, and sacramentology are not addressed by this term "Reformational," though similarities may hold there as well.

The distinction between "Reformed" and "Reformational" should not be taken as a criticism of cooperative efforts involving parties in the latter category. Yet cooperation is best encouraged by honestly regarding each party's identity, history, and passions. Co-opting other churches into the "Reformed" camp necessarily minimizes the importance of any contested issues. That this follows in practice can be gleaned from the recent history of neoevangelicalism and Reformed churches. In cooperative efforts with baptistic and nondenominational Christians, ecclesiology and sacramentology are typically not discussed at any length. The effect has been to foreshorten drastically cogent analysis of either Reformed or evangelical ecclesiology; in short, it hurts all parties involved by narrowing their vision of Christian truth. Difference should not be overlooked, even as it should also not preclude cooperation in a number of avenues. For a historical exemplar, we can look to another cooperative effort, the Alliance of Confessing Evangelicals, as a group composed of members from a variety of ecclesiastical backgrounds (e.g., Anglican, Baptist, Presbyterian). Ecclesiology and sacramentology have not been minimized, however, because the group has celebrated its agreement on "Reformational" issues while continuing to debate vigorously and charitably its contested issues (e.g., baptism of infants, church polity). The definitional reforms are not intended to foreshorten such ecumenical efforts, but simply to promote intellectual specificity as we try to describe "Reformed theology" in a book series alongside Lutheran, Anglican, and other ecclesial theologies.

Such terminological comments are merely preparatory. This book proceeds to sketch the contours of "Reformed theology" across the major topics of Christian doctrine. Each chapter will deal with a major area of concern for Reformed theology, pointing out historic debates, major emphases, and lingering challenges. Hints at proposals for future development will also appear, though the constructive side of my argument will be relatively minimal. What is Reformed theology? We have considered what it is not, at least formally. We have pointed out how there is a Reformed perspective on all the major doctrines (even though it does share many commonalities with other ecclesial theologies). Each of the following chapters will now tease out what the Reformed confess about a number of major doctrinal *loci*, along the following lines.

The Word of God has been a consistent concern for Reformed confessions, theological systems, commentary, and preaching. In fact, Reformed confessions and dogmatics led the way in formalizing the Reformational principle of *sola Scriptura* ("Scripture alone") by tending to the doctrine of God's Word at their outset. For example, both the Ten Theses of Berne and the Westminster Confession of Faith, separated by a century and a channel, begin by attesting the singular authority of the speech of God. One negative point can be paired with two positive comments by way of summary. First, the Word of God is decisive precisely because humans left to their own devices are prone to idolatry, fashioning "God" according to their own conventions. Second, the misery of idolatry is met and conquered by the self-revelation of God, the divine Word; thus, sinful failure to meet the noetic demands of the law ("know the LORD") is not the final episode, but is met by the good news of God's communication to us. Third, this divine self-manifestation functions now through the witness of Holy Scripture, wherein the testimony of the prophets and apostles is recorded for posterity's sake in a true and authoritative manner. Chapter 1 will describe the way in which Reformed theology seeks to be based and renewed always by the Word of God.

"Reformed theology is covenant theology," according to John Hesselink. His slogan highlights the covenant theme as the way in which Reformed theologians have described the unity of the biblical witness. From Genesis to Revelation, a lengthy story of God's fellowship with humanity unfolds, taking various forms throughout redemptive history. In the sixteenth and seventeenth centuries, the so-called federal theology developed as a way to catalog these covenants under two broad headings: "covenant of works" and "covenant of grace." Thus, Reformed hermeneutics take covenantal form, even amongst those who, following the lead of Karl Barth, wish to criticize the bicovenantal shape of the federal theology. Chapter 2 will describe the shape of the federal theology, note Barth's critiques, and describe ways to reconceive this issue today.

As theology, of course, Reformed doctrine speaks of the triune God revealed most fully in Jesus Christ. The Reformed churches maintain the teaching of the ecumenical councils on the Trinity and the person of Christ. Nevertheless, Calvin, Owen, and others in the Reformed tradition have extended such beliefs in distinctive ways. Chapter 3 articulates the ways in which the Reformed doctrines of God and Christ build on and extend further the classical Western tradition of Christianity. For example, the humanity of Christ has been developed in robust ways by Owen, in particular, who accented the work of the Spirit upon the faithful Son. Similarly, Calvin extended reflections on the divinity of the Son by calling him "autotheotic," divine from himself, just as the Father is also autotheotic. In such moves, Reformed churches are trying to tease out the full implications of the full humanity and full divinity of the Son. In all these extrapolations, however, Reformed theologians have affirmed the classical doctrine of God, even as some revisionists have attempted to reconceive the divine attributes.

Though the so-called five points of Calvinism by no means encompass the content of Reformed theology or identity, the Reformed tradition has passionately addressed the issues of sin and grace. Chapter 4 teases out the ways in which sin and grace are conceived by Reformed theologians, especially noting the way in which they affect one another, that is, how one's view of the human plight shapes the understanding of its solution (and vice versa). First, the doctrine of sin must affirm that Adam's fall affects us all, in so far as death and depravity flow from this federal head to his posterity. Debate arises regarding the mechanics of this flow, to be sure, and the question of whether or not humans are personally guilty for the actual sin of Adam. Second, this depravity turns the desires and passions and thought-processes of humans away from obedience to God. Thus, third, humans must be transformed by the regenerative work of the Spirit, if they are going to respond rightly to the word of the Gospel. Here the effective work of the Spirit must match the proclamation of the Word if persons are to be converted.

As part of the broader Reformational movement, the Reformed churches have insisted that salvation is *sola fide*, "by faith alone." Indeed, justification has remained a key emphasis of Reformed theology, in many cases serving as the primary form in which salvation is understood. However, Reformed approaches to justification do not rest content to speak of the justified believer, but always insist that the faith which alone justifies is never alone in the believer. Justification is always followed by sanctification and, thus, Reformed theology has a strong horizontal or ethical emphasis. Indeed, it was this ethical impulse that so drew Karl Barth to Reformed, rather than Lutheran, theology in the early twentieth century. Pertinent to understanding Reformed ethics, however, is the way in which it is always founded upon justification by faith alone, so that the good news of Christ actually fuels obedience. Chapter 5 focuses on the place of justification within this wider setting of Reformed doctrine.

Reformed theology guides Reformed churches, particularly in their worship of God. In fact, Reformed theology is largely for the sake of rightly reforming worship by the Word of God. The Reformed practices can be located between the Roman Catholic and the Anabaptist, in as much as the former sees thoroughgoing continuity between Old Covenant and New Covenant worship while the latter focuses on the sharp discontinuity between these two eras. Against both emphases, Reformed worship manifests a continuity in discontinuity with the worship of Israel before the coming of Christ. This affects the sacramental practice of the church, as well as the formality and regularity of her gatherings. Chapter 6 describes some of these forms and their theological meaning.

The Reformed tradition has forged a distinctive confessional identity, by offering a *via media* with regard to issues of authority in the church. To grasp the way in which the church exercises authority, one must begin by thinking about how the Spirit is promised to guide the church and what means are employed to that end. Thus, ecclesiology is based upon wider beliefs about the economy of God's grace and guidance for the church. Human's authority must be traced back to divine disclosure. Chapter 7 will address this issue, as well as the relativism of authority in the Reformed churches. In so doing, issues of confessional identity will be addressed, noting the dangers of antinomianism and traditionalism.

Culture and politics have been a major component of Reformed history, in as much as both American and Dutch Reformed churches have instigated significant social development. Finally, therefore, Chapter 8 addresses the way in which Reformed theologians have viewed human society and cultural work in light of eschatology (and the rest of Christian doctrine). A brief analysis of Reformed eschatology will be offered, paired with a survey of redemptive history as it affects social and political activities. In addition, interesting case studies (e.g., the Southern Presbyterian opposition to abolitionist preaching in the nineteenth century) will provide a pathway to seeing how Reformed churches have distinguished between the individual and churchly rights and responsibilities of Christians. While there are widely divergent policies regarding specific issues from persons within the Reformed churches, such divergent practices can actually be rooted within the same theological framework.

In summary, then, Reformed theology arises within and serves the flourishing of Reformed churches. It is confessional, though its testimony takes diverse forms. In fact, Reformed theology celebrates its ever-renewing impulse that is rooted in its affirmation of the living Word of God which brings light, life, and love from the triune God. For more reflection on the way in which God and humans enjoy such communion, read on.

Chapter 1

Word of God

Reformed theology, as theology, is thinking or reasoning about the one true God rather than human religious experience. Thus, this book is an exercise in intellectual work, considering the ways in which Reformed churches and Christians think about God, the world, and themselves. In this chapter, then, issues of theological method will be addressed in theory. Praxis and actual use of revelation, especially of the Bible, will not be addressed as primary concerns, except in so far as actual praxis is mandated or normed by doctrine.

Reformed confessions are distinctive in the primacy they give to the doctrine of the Word of God. For example, the Ten Theses of Berne (1528) state first that "the holy, Christian Church, whose only Head is Christ, is born of the Word of God, abides in the same, and does not listen to the voice of a stranger."[1] The material claims made are linked with polemical and cultural debates, with Roman Catholic dogma on the one hand and burgeoning modern skepticism on the other hand. The Reformed approach to theological method navigates between these two extremes. God can truly be known, *contra* skepticism, yet only in as much as God reveals himself in the divine Word, *contra* the Roman Catholic doctrine of ecclesiastical authority. This Reformed approach to the knowledge of God will be explicated further under three headings. First, I will explain the enduring worry about idolatry and, thus, the Reformed tendency toward iconoclasm. Second, I will examine divine revelation as the prerequisite for human knowledge of God. Third, I will describe various issues regarding the nature and reading of the Bible as the Word of God written.

Idolatry and Iconoclasm

Reinhold Niebuhr famously claimed that God made humanity in his image, and humanity has forever been repaying God the favor. Contemporary culture promotes human inventiveness, ingenuity, and imagination as intrinsic goods: "just do it" is an apt motto not only for athletic endeavors, but indeed for the whole moral and aesthetic compass of humanity left to itself. Human inventiveness extends beyond mere self-fashioning to attempted creation and recreation of the divine. Humans do not merely refashion the image of God. Rather, as John Calvin stated, "man's nature, so to speak, is a perpetual factory of idols . . . Man's mind, full as it is of pride and boldness, dares to imagine a god according to its own capacity; as it sluggishly plods, indeed is overwhelmed with the crassest ignorance, it conceives an unreality and an empty appearance as God" (*ICR*, I.xi.8, vol. 1, p. 108).

Niebuhr and Calvin merely restate biblical depictions of human ingenuity, with the Old Testament narratives from Exodus to Ezra and beyond portraying the sinful creativity employed in the course of human religiosity. The incident recorded in Exod. 32 exemplifies this propensity toward idolatry. The Israelites have grown weary of waiting for Moses to return from atop Mount Sinai: "Up, make us gods who shall go before us. As for this Moses, the man who brought us up out of the land of Egypt, we do not know what has become of him," they say to Aaron (Exod. 32.1). A golden calf is fashioned, to which they confess: "These are your gods, O Israel, who brought you up out of Egypt!" An altar is placed before the calf, a feast to the LORD is summoned, and "the people sat down to eat and drink and rose up to play" (Exod. 32.6). YHWH proves to be unimpressed, even angry, declaring to Moses: "I have seen this people, and behold, it is a stiff-necked people. Now therefore let me alone, that my wrath may burn hot against them and I may consume them, in order that I may make a great nation of you" (Exod. 32.9). Moses intercedes, and God relents from the disastrous exercise of divine wrath. Nonetheless, Moses is sent to purge the Israelites of this idolatry. The calf is destroyed, along with "about three thousand men of the people" (Exod. 32.20, 28). Finally, God sends a plague amongst the people to "visit their sin upon them" (Exod. 32.34).

Reformed theologians, from Zwingli and Calvin onward, have emphasized the importance of this incident for understanding the nature of human idolatry and the enduring justice of God. First, human idolatry can be easily mistaken for deep devotion. The Reformed polemic against Roman Catholic theology and praxis must not be understood as an argument against non-religious practices. Rather, the polemics were so heated precisely because it was between two parties who were both fervent about their religious practice. Furthermore, both parties claimed the name "Christian" for their religious vision. Reformed theologians insisted that right intentions—say, desire to honor God—do not make moral and liturgical acts or theological reasoning appropriate. As evidenced by the episode in Exod. 32, God defines the means as well as the end of religious life. Notice that the idolatry of the Israelites is not directed away from the god who raised them from deathly bondage in Egypt. Aaron declares the calf an instrument for praising and feasting with YHWH (Exod. 32.5). Idolatry often flows from those with good intentions, which are necessary but not sufficient for genuine obedience. As Calvin puts it: "God should be purely worshiped by us according to his nature and not according to our imagination. That is one point. The other is that we should know that it is unnecessary to parade our 'good intentions' as a cover-up for what we have invented, indeed; but on the contrary we should know that the principal service which God requires is obedience."[2]

Idolatry can certainly be heinous and obvious, as witnessed to in the Old Testament as well as the New Testament. For example, Paul speaks of the Gentiles who have received the plain witness to God's character "ever since the creation of the world, in the things that have been made. So that they are without excuse" (Rom. 1.20). The idolatrous ways of these pagans are described as exchanging "the glory of the immortal God for images resembling mortal man and birds and animals and reptiles" when "they exchanged the truth about God for a lie and worshiped and served the creature rather than the Creator" (Rom. 1.23, 25). This pagan idolatry is blatant and easily spotted, prevalent throughout the narratives of Israel's interaction with neighboring peoples. So we must realize that idolatry can be obvious: worship of "Money" or "Nation" or "Security" or "A Rich Harvest" or "Ethnic Status" instead of God.

Paul suggests that we ought not be surprised by abominations flowing forth from those of a "debased mind" (Rom. 1.28).

Yet idolatry can also be more subtle, like a wolf in sheep's clothing. Kristine Culp has described the almost indiscernible presence of idolatry in contemporary global culture:

> In our day any sense of the glory of God is already shaped by the mediation of a market economy (as it would be mediated by any economy) and, almost inevitably, becomes entangled with the market's cultivation of consumption as a dominant way of engaging the world. Any notion of God's truth is already shaped by the global flow of language and images and, almost inevitably, becomes appropriated and spun into byte-sized, quickly assimilable, media-ready information. Any construal of a well-ordered kingdom of Christ is already shaped by the relations and patterns that order our lives and, almost inevitably, becomes distorted by grotesque rifts in wealth and by tenaciously entrenched patterns of power and privilege. ("Always Reforming, Always Resisting," in *FWERD*, p. 153)

Cultural accretions can be so widespread and seemingly inevitable as to be virtually indecipherable. Atheism and triumphalist paganism are not rampant so much as syncretistic paganism and relativistic reductionism. As Walter Brueggemann reminds us, "the issue for God's people is characteristically wrong God, and not no God."[3] Wrong thoughts about the right God may be more threatening than thoughts about the wrong god.

With the Reformed tradition, we might say that the First Commandment is followed by the Second Commandment for this very reason. Whereas the First Commandment demands that worship be directed exclusively to "the LORD your God, who brought you out of the land of Egypt, out of the house of slavery" (Exod. 20.2), the Second Commandment mandates the manner or means by which such worship of YHWH is to proceed. God does not allow images to be employed as representations of the divine persona (see, for example, Ten Theses of Berne [TTB], VIII, in *RCSC*, p. 50). Reformed theologians have insisted that the prohibition against images is one particular example of a broader divine mandate: worship as God commands *and no other way.* T. F. Torrance, a renowned theologian in the Church of Scotland, described the epistemology of this second commandment as such:

> God is not imaginable. All the images we invent are idols of the mind, products of our own imagination, for God ever remains like himself and is not a spectre or phantasm to be transformed according to our desires. It is a fact, however, that the mind of fallen man remains a perpetual factory of idols and false imaginations of God, so that he is always projecting his own inventions or figments upon God. That is to say, he is constantly tempted to corrupt the knowledge of the truth through the creations of his own brain. True knowledge is objectively derived and cuts against the speculations and imaginations of the human mind.[4]

Second, the golden calf episode also manifests the enduring validity of divine justice. God does not change, and divine expectations for fellowship do not change either. God cannot be likened to an auctioneer who will eventually take the best offer, even if below the initial asking price. Divine justice is rooted in the very character of the eternal God and, thus, is itself eternal. What does this have to do with idolatry? God shows a thoroughgoing concern for proper worship, what used to be called "true religion." The Second Commandment is the only one of the Ten Commandments which warrants lengthy expansion regarding God's reasoning: "for I, the LORD your God, am a jealous God, visiting the iniquity of the fathers on the children to the third and fourth generation of those who hate me, but showing steadfast love to thousands of those who love me and keep my commandments" (Exod. 20.5–6). Not only does God provide a basis for his command that is rooted in the divine character (jealousy), God also reminds Moses and the Israelites of the consequences of disobedience. This is not mere posturing, either, as the body count tallied after the episode with the golden calf demonstrates.

Thus, Reformed theology is iconoclastic. This claim must be defined, however, so that it is not understood as a manifestation of the very inventiveness it is meant to oppose. Unless one understands why, when, and how iconoclasm proceeds, one will simply use it as a surrogate for one's own creative interests (often approximating the ideals of broader culture). In this vein, some have usurped the name "Reformed" for any brand of theology that emphasizes the need for continual mortification and vivification of reasoning, ongoing reform and conceptual revolution. While these deconstructive impulses can bear great affinity with some Reformed criticisms of various ideologies, cultural practices, and ecclesial tradition(s), they do not necessarily warrant the title "Reformed." This entirely methodological tie to the Reformed tradition can occur in both more liberal and more conservative circles. Jürgen Moltmann has been known as a Reformed theologian, yet there is little about his project that actually deserves identification with this particular ecclesial tradition.[5] His "theology of hope" certainly promotes an eschatological disruption and ever-reforming development of greater societal and ecological justice; yet his categories and sources are largely foreign to the Reformed tradition. This interpretation of "Reformed theology" as a commitment merely to "prophetic"/ methodological purposes is not only offered by liberals or revisionists; evangelicals have made similar moves. For example, the methodological proposal of Roger Olson, *Reformed and Always Reforming*, emphasizes the ceaseless need for theological reform and, yet, has virtually no claim to "Reformed" identity.[6] Olson affirms that he prefers to write his own confessions rather than sign on to any existing examples (Reformed or otherwise; a position which Chapter 7 here will show to be anything but Reformed), and he has written elsewhere a good defense of Arminian theology (which was expelled from the Reformed tradition).[7]

Brian Gerrish has suggested that Reformed identity is best discerned by talking of certain "habits of mind," not the least of which is criticism of the past. Olson and Moltmann can only be dubbed "Reformed" if such free-floating iconoclasm is its sole arbiter. Yet we do well to listen to Bruce McCormack's assessment:

> "Habits of mind" . . . cannot be divorced from serious
> attention to doctrinal distinctives without a serious
> reduction of his list . . . I would submit that neither
> deference nor criticism is possible where we do not take

seriously what these "fathers" themselves took seriously: viz. church doctrine. The cultivation of "habits of mind" in the absence of a serious catechizing in the faith of the church could, in my judgment, only serve the "narcissism and faddism" about which Gerrish rightly worries.[8]

Iconoclasm is not free-floating, then, but constrained and impelled by the material content of Christian doctrine. Particular convictions about divine holiness and human sinfulness lead to ceaseless concerns that our tradition be critically reforming; hence, Reformed theology can be aptly dubbed "critical traditioning."

Reformed churches and theologians, then, have always confessed themselves to be naturally inclined toward sinful imagination and untoward creativity. Furthermore, they have not hesitated to declare that such arrogance is nothing less than sin, transgression of divine law worthy of death. This human propensity toward idolatry and self-aggrandizement has been suitably characterized by Augustine, Luther, Barth, and others, as *homo incurvatus in se*.[9] This "humanity curved in on itself" manifests itself in varying ways (e.g., sloth, pride), each of which constitutes a turn away from God and toward the inward hopes and aspirations of the individual or the collective human identity. This imagery of "curving inward" is drawn from the prophet Isaiah: "All we like sheep have gone astray; we have turned every one to his own way" (Isa. 53.6). That this prophetic description is of sin, not merely errant decision making, is highlighted by the next phrase: "and the Lord has laid on him the iniquity of us all," which clearly identifies universal human self-indulgence as "iniquity." Because Reformed theology takes sinfulness seriously—even the enduring, indwelling sinfulness of the church and all Christians—it must continually look away from its own witness toward God for continual judgment and growth.

Following the narratives of the Old Testament, Reformed churches have recognized the seriousness with which God takes worship and confession, language and expression. In all these affirmations, Reformed theology has simply enlarged or expanded the catholic belief that divine law oversees human response to God. Having considered those laws regarding thinking of God, we must now examine the gracious provision of divine self-revelation.

Law and the human failure to fulfill it is not the final or primary note of Christian teaching, but is merely anticipatory to the sound of divine grace shown in the works and words of the triune God. In fact, humans only know of their sin because God has told them of it. Thus, we turn to the grace of the "Word of God" revealed to us.

Revelation

The Word of God may basically be identified as the self-communication of the one true God. Reformed theology affirms with the whole catholic tradition that God is communicative, because holy writ witnesses to the centrality of God's speech. God reveals himself to be creative by speaking this order into being (Gen. 1.1; Jn 1.1–3). God shapes fellowship between humanity and God by engaging in conversation. Eventually, the divine Word takes human flesh that he might interpret (*exegato*) the Father to humanity (Jn 1.18); "truth came through Jesus Christ," this Word who was God in the beginning (Jn 1.17). Thus, God is imaged by a Word, for Jesus shows himself to be the very "image of the invisible God" (Col. 1.15). Reflecting on the pivotal place given to divine speech by the biblical writings, Reformed theology (along with that of the magisterial Reformation as a whole) has emphasized the importance of communication and, thus, of words.

"God's speaking is also his deed," says G. C. Berkouwer.[10] What does that mean? God is not known *in se*, in himself, precisely because we do not exist within that internal life of the Trinity. Thus, we know God through the works of God, and only through these works. As Calvin puts it, "we know the most perfect way of seeking God, and the most suitable order, is not for us to attempt with bold curiosity to penetrate to the investigation of his essence, which we ought more to adore than meticulously to search out, but for us to contemplate him in his works whereby he renders himself near and familiar to us" (*Inst*, I.v.9, vol. 1, p. 62). Calvin seeks to honor the biblical warrant for theology, as witnessed to in Deuteronomy: "The secret things belong to the LORD our God, but the things that are revealed belong to us and to our children forever, that we may do all the words of this law" (Deut. 29.29). Knowledge of the triune God belongs to humanity only when revealed. Yet when such knowledge is revealed, it is not ephemeral or passing; rather, it belongs to both the original recipients and their children forever. Revelation is not so existential as to be non-transferable, we might say. A definition which is broad enough to fit a wide swath of Reformed approaches was offered recently by John Webster, for whom "revelation is the self-presentation of the triune God, the free work of sovereign mercy in which God wills, establishes and perfects saving fellowship with himself in which humankind comes to know, love and fear him above all things."[11]

Speculation continues to be denounced within the Reformed tradition. Calvin insists that Reformed reasoning will appear simplistic at times. He comments on the attitude of the wicked toward the righteous in Ps. 1, with "the greater part of mankind being accustomed to deride the conduct of the saints as mere simplicity."[12] Theology must go as far as the biblical witness impels, yet no further. Natural theology bears witness as a confirmation of certain truths about God revealed more clearly in the Bible, not as a supplement to the special revelation of the prophetic and apostolic writings. The Westminster Larger Catechism insists that the first commandment—"You shall have no other gods before me" (Exod. 20.3)—forbids any "bold and curious searchings into his secrets" (Westminster Larger Catechism [WLC], 105, in *BC*, pp. 265–266). This implication is drawn from the second giving of the law: "The secret things belong to the LORD our God, but the revealed things belong to us and to our children forever, to observe all the words of this law" (Deut. 29.29). Speculation is idolatry, the move to equate our knowing with the knowledge enjoyed only by God.

Why is speculation so seductive and at the same time so problematic? A number of doctrinal beliefs sustain this iconoclastic emphasis. First, God is incomprehensible to finite minds. Second, finite minds are fallen minds, living East of Eden. Third, the redemption and sanctification of human reasoning has not been completed yet. Taken together, these three theological affirmations promote a theological method wary of inventiveness and imagination.[13]

Finitum non capax infinitum. This Reformed adage summarizes the epistemological and soteriological effects of divine incomprehensibility. "The finite cannot comprehend the infinite" or, more literally, "the finite is not capable of the infinite." While finite creatures may apprehend divine truth in so far as it is revealed to them, creatures are forever limited by their finite form and, thus, constitutionally incapable of gleaning truths with infinite depth. In fact, Reformed theologians affirm that even the all-surpassing good (*summum bonum*) of glorified knowledge will remain finite and, thus, noncomprehensive. God makes himself known to humans, and eventually perfects this knowledge, but in so doing God never makes them anything other than human and finite.

The incomprehensibility of God cannot be viewed as a mysterious part of the divine character which remains undisclosed and is distinct from those parts which are manifested. Rather, incomprehensibility goes all the way down precisely because God is of a different sort of being. Asked to produce an identifying name, God simply tells Moses: "I AM who I AM" (Exod. 3.14). Strictly speaking, you must speak about God and God alone to identify or explain God; no comparison fits exactly. Various types of terminology express this point: while classical theism would speak of God's transcendence, Karl Barth talks of God as "wholly other." In either case, God is not an item or person in this created order and, thus, cannot be known in the same way that one knows their neighbors or possessions. Again, this is not to say our knowledge is false; it is simply to say that its adequacy should not be confused with comprehensiveness. Reformed theology adopted a modified Thomism in its view of theological language, insisting that words taken from human discourse apply to God neither univocally nor equivocally, but always and only analogically. That is, God's transcendent distinction from the world is a metaphysical reality with linguistic and epistemological implications: God *is* different, thus God is *spoken* of and *known* differently.

Human knowledge is not only limited by finitude but also marred and distorted by the pernicious effects of sin and death. Total depravity (the "T" in the famed TULIP acronym) does not mean that humans are as bad as they might be, but that humans are extensively skewed by sin's effects. Sin affects every nook and cranny of human being and doing, including the mind and its thinking. As the 1559 French Confession of Faith says of the human, "being blinded in mind, and depraved in heart, he has lost all integrity, and there is no good in him. And although he can still discern good and evil, we say, notwithstanding, that the light he has becomes darkness when he seeks for God, so that he can in nowise approach him by his intelligence and reason" (French Confession of Faith [FCF], IX, in *RCSC*, p. 147).

Finally, human rationality is being redeemed, though this sanctifying work is not yet completed. John Webster has compellingly spoken of the drama of reason's sanctification and its consequential limits upon theology.[14] "For now we see in a mirror dimly, but then face to face. Now I know in part; then I shall know fully, even as I have been fully known" (1 Cor. 13.12). The apostle Paul juxtaposes dim knowledge with full sight, further explaining his earlier statement that "we know in part and we prophesy in part, but when the perfect comes, the partial will pass away" (1 Cor. 13.9–10). Speaking to a Christian congregation about the communal life of believers, he removes any pretension about fully realized epistemic hubris. Again, the French Confession of Faith makes the point about sin's continuing effects: "it is a perversity always producing fruits of malice and of rebellion, so that the most holy men, although they resist it, are still stained with many weaknesses and imperfections while they are in this life" (FCF, XI, in *RCSC*, p. 148).

Contrary to the more hackneyed versions of Enlightenment optimism (and well before the so-called linguistic turn of the latter twentieth century), Reformed theologians insisted that human knowledge of God was always perspectival and limited (see, for example, Bavinck, *RD*, vol. 1, pp. 298–300). A scholastic distinction was crafted to highlight this quality of theology: whereas God enjoyed *archetypal* knowledge of God and creation, humans receive only *ectypal* knowledge of these subjects.[15] The principal characteristic of *ectypal* knowledge is its mediated nature, always derivative and limited by context (however narrow or wide). Thus, Reformed theology that remains aware of its historical distinction between *archetypal* and *ectypal* theology need not require the contextualist deconstruction of late modern or postmodern theologies. Having never endorsed modern notions of universal or a-contextual intellectualism, perspectivalism is neither an external ideal nor a threat.

Revelation, thus, does not make the human knower anything other than human. Finitude goes all the way down. Seventeenth-century churchman and theologian John Owen referred to *ectypal* theology as "wayfaring" or "journeying" knowledge of God, pointing to its location within two orbits: (1) a socio-historical context, and (2) the long history of God's redeeming work of the world as well as that individual Christian (*WJO*, vol. 17, pp. 38–39). For all the limits of their knowledge, however, humans really do know God as God makes himself known.

Holy Scripture

The revelation of God takes a number of forms, each traditionally referred to as the divine word. While Karl Barth made famous the phrase "threefold Word of God" only in the last century, the pluriform nature of God's Word was recognized in the era of Protestant orthodoxy. According to Richard Muller, the Reformed dogmatics of this earlier era spoke of a fourfold nature to the Word of God, linking all divine presence with the second person of the Trinity in some manner and, at the same time, really employing persons as auxiliaries or instruments of this divine speech (*PRRD*, vol. 2, p. 194). The deep concern of Barth and the orthodox dogmatics of earlier centuries was to guard the Reformational beliefs *sola gratia* and *solus Christus*. Knowledge of God must always be wholly of grace and, furthermore, owing solely to Christ's mediation.

Barth's emphasis was upon the divine person, the eternal Word, who proceeds from the Father and from whom (with the Father) the Spirit proceeds. Again, his concern is to highlight God's grace shone forth in Jesus, noting the way in which noetic activity (and, by derivation, our theory about such knowing, called epistemology) is rooted in the ministry of Jesus. "As ministers we ought to speak of God. We are human, however, and so cannot speak of God. We ought therefore to recognize both our obligation and our inability and by that very recognition give God the glory."[16] The very mission of the divine Son provides for human speech about and toward God, our creator, sustainer, redeemer, and perfector. In fact, speech from God in Jesus is related to speech for God also in Jesus (for he is our high priest and advocate, praying on our behalf). All this is to say that covenantal relationship or friendly fellowship between the fully alive God and heinously dying humans is only realized in the Messiah from Nazareth. He communicates the truth about God to us, and he offers perfect prayer and praise to the Father for us.

The eternal Word acts both in creation and in redemption. The same Word who creates in the beginning (Jn 1.1–4) is the "Lamb of God who takes away the sin of the world" (Jn 1.29). Thus, Reformed theologians have insisted that there are two basic avenues of divine revelation: (1) creation and providence, and (2) redemption. The 1559 French Confession of Faith says, "God reveals himself to men; firstly, in his works, in the creation, as well as in their preservation and control. Secondly, and more clearly, in his Word, which was in the beginning revealed through oracles, and which was afterward committed to writing, in the books which we call the Holy Scriptures" (FCF, II, in *RCSC*, p. 144). The first type of knowledge is gleaned from the world *writ large*, as the Belgic Confession clarifies that God is known,

> first, by the creation, preservation, and government of the universe; which is before our eyes as a most elegant book, wherein all creatures, great and small, are as so many characters leading us to contemplate *the invisible things of God*, namely, *his eternal power and Godhead*, as the Apostle Paul said (Rom. 1.20). All which things are sufficient to convince men, and leave them without excuse. (Belgic Confession [BC], II, in *RCSC*, pp. 189–190)

However, knowledge of God drawn from creation and providence is merely sufficient to render sinners culpable for their wickedness. It does not point to the nature of sin or the shape of the gospel of Jesus. "For us and our salvation," Christ had to offer forth redemption and to reveal it in a special manner. As the Belgic Confession puts it, "secondly, he makes himself known more clearly and fully known to us by his holy and divine Word; that is to say, as far as is necessary for us to know in this life, to his glory and our salvation" (BC, II, in *RCSC*, p. 190). Thus, "in these last days he has spoken to us by a Son . . . the reflection of God's glory and the exact imprint of God's very being" (Heb. 1.2–3). Jesus Christ and the economy of salvation wrought by him provides for the fullness of knowledge, in as much as he is "full of grace and truth" (Jn 1.14).

What concrete form does the Word of God take? While Jesus Christ is certainly the Word Incarnate, the testimony of the prophets and apostles precedes and follows his incarnation as witness and warning. "Long ago God spoke to our ancestors in many and various ways by the prophets," says that anonymous theologian of the early church who wrote Heb. 1.1. These prophetic witnesses wrote words given by God: "no prophecy of scripture is a matter of one's own interpretation, because no prophecy ever came by human will, but men and women moved by the Holy Spirit spoke from God" (1 Pet. 1.20–21). The apostle Peter's analysis of prophetic ministry clarifies his own action in composing an epistle. He writes of spiritual things, "though you know them already and are established in the truth" (1 Pet. 1.12). His ministry in laying out these exhortations is spurred "since I know that my death will come soon" (1 Pet. 1.14). Why does his looming death spur redundant teaching? This happens "so that after my departure you may be able at any time to recall these things" (1 Pet. 1.15). The apostolic witness is meant to be normative and enduring, precisely because it *is* communication from God.

The Word of God also takes the shape of human proclamation. The self-communicating God has a long history of self-manifestation, all of which is characterized as divine speech or the threefold Word of God. Thus, ministers proclaim the testimony of the prophets and apostles about the very divine life which reaches out to redeem humanity. Well before Karl Barth, this third category was recognized by the Reformed confessions. For example, the Second Helvetic Confession affirms that "when this Word of God is now preached in the church by preachers lawfully called, we believe that the very Word of God is proclaimed, and received by the faithful ... and that now the Word itself which is preached is to be regarded, not the minister that preaches" (Second Helvetic Confession [SHC], I, in *RCSC*, p. 225). God speaks through these very words.

Humility is required to listen to the divine Word expressed through human mediation, whether that of the prophets and apostles or of one's local parish minister. As Calvin so discerningly put it:

> [T]his is the best and most useful exercise in humility, when he accustoms us to obey his Word, even though it is preached through men like us and sometimes even by those of lower worth than we. If he spoke from heaven, it would not be surprising if his sacred oracles were to be reverently received without delay by the ears and minds of all. For . . . who would not be confounded at such boundless splendor? But when a puny man risen from the dust speaks in God's name, at this point we best evidence our piety and obedience toward God if we show ourselves teachable toward his minister, although he excels us in nothing. (*ICR*, IV.iii.1, vol. 2, p. 1054)

Human speech is determined by God to be his Word, not of its own merit but due to his sanctifying gifts. The Bible is the Word of God, then, and may be called *holy* writing (viz. scripture) in as much as it is God's speech through human writers. God has sanctified these texts, setting them apart for particular purposes. Thus, with John Owen, Reformed theology has affirmed God as the ontic ground of theology (its relational source) and Scripture as the noetic ground of theology (its cognitive source).[17] The Bible is critical precisely because God creates it and makes use of it as an instrument for self-manifestation. Thus, the Bible's importance is neither innate in a naturalistic sense nor fleeting; it is graced by God and instilled with enduring importance in as much as God is faithful and constant.

The doctrine of biblical inspiration was fashioned by Reformed theologians to attest the divine roots of this witness. The prophet Amos and the apostle Peter were not religious sages or philosophical titans to be accorded respect because of their intellectual prowess or deep piety. Rather, Christians have confessed that God has spoken through these witnesses, and that their testimony is compelling in and of itself (quite apart from investigation of an educational or vocational dossier). Inspiration links divine and human action. God has willed to communicate from eternity past. And any communication with humanity has to take creaturely form, be it pictorial or audible. But such communication, really to reveal God to humanity, cannot be merely human. Mediating the divine and human, then, is the inspiring work of the Holy Spirit, whereby scribal work becomes "the word of the LORD."

The Holy Bible exemplifies certain attributes which follow from its divine inspiration. Chief among these is authority, in as much as God's own words carry a certain moral and theological force. The way in which the Bible's authority has been construed across the Reformed tradition will be discussed in Chapter 7. Other attributes include the Bible's sufficiency and clarity. First, the Bible is sufficient for the task of knowing God's good news of salvation wrought in Jesus. As the apostle Paul teaches, it is "useful for teaching, for reproof, for correction, and for training in righteousness." Not only is it useful, but it functions "so that everyone who belongs to God may be proficient, equipped for every good work" (2 Tim. 3.16–17). While many types of knowledge must be sought elsewhere (e.g., how to run Microsoft Windows), the path to godliness is fully revealed within this canon. Second, the Bible's basic message is clear enough for the interested layperson to grasp its contours. In contrast to medieval clericalism, where the Bible was kept fenced from common folk, the Reformational movement insisted that God's written Word was given for all and should be made available for all. Thus, schools were founded to aid literacy, and commentaries were written as guides for right interpretation, and a whole literary culture was jumpstarted by this basic Protestant impulse.[18] Of course, the Bible's clarity was not understood to mean that all themes or texts within its pages were clear. Even the apostle Peter found parts of Paul's teaching to be difficult (2 Pet. 3.16), and the Reformed tradition has continually noted that certain beliefs are quite thorny (e.g., predestination and reprobation). The Westminster Confession admits, "All things in Scripture are not alike plain in themselves, nor alike clear unto all" (Westminster Confession of Faith [WCF], I.7, in BC, p. 175). Nevertheless, the "word of the LORD" is "living and active, sharper than any two-edged sword" (Heb. 4.12). The gospel –"those things which are necessary to be known, believed, and observed, for salvation"—is manifest for scholar and drop-out, pastor and neophyte alike to "attain unto a sufficient understanding of them" (WCF, I.7, in *BC*, p. 175).

In recent decades, Reformed confessions have noted the need for critical study of the Bible. Of course, such historically minded study of these writings is nothing new, having begun even before Zwingli and Calvin were preaching and writing. The Reformation and post-Reformation theologians were well aware of the interpretive questions raised by humanist scholarship, with its rallying cry: *Ad fontes* ("back to the sources"). The sources raise questions regarding unity and truthfulness, precisely because parts of the Bible are opaque and complex. The Reformed tradition has always engaged critical study of the Bible, though not always in affirming ways. At times, critical study has been rejected as modern hubris. At other points, it has been embraced hook, line, and sinker, even carelessly. Truth be told, there is no consensus view regarding the place of critical study within the Reformed churches and the nature of the Bible's truthfulness. We do well, then, to note key tendencies and concerns of divergent visions.

The modern ethos within which follows critical study of ancient texts—in this case, the Christian Bible—tends to subvert any claims for metaphysical or moral authority in liberal Protestantism. Thus, we read of Lessing's famed "ditch" between the accidental facts of history (discerned by historical-critical study) and the universal truths of religion, ethics, or philosophy (not capable of historical-critical demonstration). Many modern theologians treat the biblical writings as merely human reflection upon God, thereby ridding them of any universal authority. The ascendancy of the "history-of-religions" school based at the University of Tübingen and spearheaded by F. C. Baur was only the most notable example of this naturalistic study of the Bible as a common ancient text. Combined with the romanticist tendencies of nineteenth-century culture, religion was interpreted in its ancient and modern forms as the patterns taken by moral and spiritual experience (on which see *RD*, vol. 1, pp. 289–290, 292–295). Thus, religion is defined "from below," by inductive investigation of what experiences people undergo. As Ben Quash puts it: "What unites the various strands of the liberal Protestant project . . . is the conviction that access to the divine is in one way or another a natural phenomenon."[19] The Bible, then, has been reduced by many moderns to an ancient attempt to make sense of the religious life of those who followed a supposed Jewish leader. Against this, Reformed theology has insisted that God speaks through the Bible, so that it really is God's Word and not merely human ideas about God.

Critical study of the Bible in the modern context has led to further clarification regarding the truthfulness of the Bible's teaching. While Reformed theologians across the board affirm that the Bible is true, divergence arises regarding the nature of this truthfulness. The serpent's lie in the Garden of Eden is clearly not a truth (Gen. 3.4–5); rather, the book of Genesis truthfully records an event, which itself involves the telling of an untruth. Thus, no one affirms that the Bible's truthfulness results in the immediate truthfulness of every statement or quotation within its pages. Beyond this, however, agreement ends fairly quickly. The major fault line is whether or not the Bible's trustworthiness is limited to its theological and moral teaching or extended to its scientific and historical claims as well. Biblical diversity regarding the chronology of Jesus' life and ministry has fueled this debate, as theologians have differed over the logical possibility of harmonization. Debates on this topic have been most heated and most fully developed within American Presbyterianism, so note should be made of the parties there.

The recent American "Confession of 1967" represented the triumph of Karl Barth's doctrine of Scripture, wherein the Bible functions as witness to revelation.[20] Speaking of appropriate beliefs about the Bible's nature and interpretation, it declares:

> The Scriptures, given under the guidance of the Holy Spirit, are nevertheless the words of men, conditioned by the language, thought forms, and literary fashions of the places and times at which they were written. They reflect views of life, history, and the cosmos which were then current. The church, therefore, has an obligation to approach the Scriptures with literary and historical understanding. (Confession of 1967 [C-67], 1.C.2, in *BC*, p. 325)

Intended by its authors as a rebuke of conservative notions of biblical truthfulness, which were viewed as "docetic" or overly supernatural, this confession endorses the necessity of reading the Bible within an ancient context. The Bible is the "Word of God," according to this confession, though not itself the object of faith. As Edward Dowey, chairman of the drafting committee of this confession, says, "Faith means to believe and trust in Christ. The Bible is an instrument through which faith's encounter with Christ takes place." How does this affect thinking about the Bible's nature? "It is through the Scriptures rather than to them (as the Westminster Confession teaches) that the Spirit bears witness."[21]

The so-called Princeton theology of Charles Hodge, A. A. Hodge, B. B. Warfield, and J. Gresham Machen, presented a different approach to the Bible's trustworthiness. Particularly in the hands of Warfield, the doctrine of biblical inerrancy was clarified at great length and in direct contrast to the skeptical approach of modern historical critics. We should note that the Princeton approach continued the classical teaching of the Reformed churches and put it in new idiom; that is, while Calvin did not speak of the term "inerrancy," he clearly predated the judgments made by Hodge and others by use of this modern term.[22] The "history-of-religions" school of F. C. Baur had suggested that the New Testament was merely the natural evolution of religious thought loosely based on the life and witness of Jesus of Nazareth, a moralistic religion codifying into an "early catholicism" within a couple of generations. Against this, Warfield insisted that the biblical writings were *theopneustos*, "God-breathed" or "inspired" according to 2 Tim. 3.16. Conservative Reformed theologians who followed Warfield and the "Princeton theology" eventually led the way in organizing the International Council on Biblical Inerrancy in the 1970s and 1980s. This pan-evangelical gathering produced a number of documents to define carefully biblical "inerrancy" and locate it both dogmatically and hermeneutically. Most notable was the "Chicago Statement on Biblical Inerrancy."[23] Put simply, inerrancy involves being free of falsehood, error, and untruth. Inerrancy follows from verbal inspiration, in as much as those following Old Princeton believe God inspired the very words of Scripture, not merely its religious ideas. Thus, every letter is divinely intended; however, inerrancy was not meant to fore-shorten historical and literary study of the biblical writings in pursuit of their meaning. Every claim of the Bible is true; thus its readers should expend great energy to interpret each statement and text rightly.

One common criticism of the Westminster Confession of Faith, chapter I on Holy Scripture, was that it spoke only of a supernatural Bible. As Dowey states this concern about Westminster's doctrine of inspiration, "Nothing intervenes between God's revelation and the written text. Accordingly, no human writers, not even apostles and prophets, are mentioned."[24] It is true: there is no reference to human activity in this chapter. Yet absence is not necessarily denial. Furthermore, the "Princeton theology" clearly affirmed the concrete activities of human apostles and prophets in the production of the biblical writings (see, for example, Charles Hodge, ST, vol. 1, pp. 157–158). It would seem obvious then that "inspiration" and "inerrancy" need not imply that God somehow dictated books to otherwise uninvolved writers. It is very odd that critics think "inerrancy" incapable of cohering with complex accounts of human writing and compiling behind the canon of Scripture. That God acted here and guided providentially does not mean humans were not also acting, writing, and editing. The theologically savvy observer gathers the impression that many discussions of inspiration flounder on a drastically problematic understanding of providence.[25]

What should be made of the difference between the "Princeton theology" and the Confession of 1967? We cannot simply say that one favors historical criticism, while the other rejects it. Similarly, we cannot reduce one to viewing the Bible as an instrument of hearing Christ, while the other lauds the Bible as an object of faith in its own right. The Confession of 1967 is not naturalistic, just as the "Princeton theology" was not in favor of bibliolatry. In saying this, I am denying Dowey's claim that only with the newer confession is the Bible finally located as a subordinate revelation to the personal revelation of Jesus Christ (the lone object of faith). When the Westminster Standards speak of believing the Bible, they follow the church's long tradition of trusting mediate authorities like the church ("I believe one, holy, catholic, and apostolic church," confessed in the Nicene-Constantinopolitan Creed) and, yes, the Bible as ways that God is trusted. As Calvin and others clarified, "believing the church" is not the same as "believing in

Father (or Son or Spirit)"; the Bible is not autonomously an object of faith, to be sure. Yet the church and the Bible are means of grace, creaturely auxiliaries of divine revelatory and redemptive work, which must be trusted as such. Thus, any deep contrast between these two traditions must be shirked, for both view the Bible metaphysically as "secondary" to Christ, yet epistemically as "primary" for our knowledge of God. They do diverge, however, in whether they view the Bible in whole or in part as God's Word: whereas Old Princeton took the whole Bible to be true, the newer paradigm at Princeton and evident in the "Confession of 1967" finds parts of the Bible to be errant and actually detached from witness to Christ (and, therefore, no longer a word for the church today).

Differences arise with regard to the proper interpretation of the Bible, the role of churchly confessions, the reality of contextualization, and the nature of ecclesiastical authority (issues to be dealt reengaged in Chapter 7). For present purposes, the chief difference regarding beliefs about the nature of the Scriptures involves the term "plenary" (meaning "fullness"): whereas the "Princeton theology" believed in plenary inspiration such that every word of the Bible is God's Word, the newer approach found in the Confession of 1967 and so-called Neo-Orthodoxy spoke of the whole Bible as witness to God's Word without thereby suggesting that every text within it was a word for the church today. The Confession of 1967 was actually a compromise text, attempting to paste together two different emphases: Jesus as *the* Word, and Scripture as God's Word. Its admission that parts of Scripture may not witness to Jesus rightly and truly can have sizable effects on Christian faith and practice. This is evidenced by the way in which doctrines like the virgin birth have been attacked by some as aberrations found in only two gospel accounts and in which ethical issues like sexuality and gender can be removed almost entirely from biblical reasoning by many, who would suggest that the Bible is hopelessly outmoded in its categories here. In both cases, biblical texts can be eschewed as archaic or unhelpful words reflecting ancient beliefs, but not present day words from God. Obviously, the approach embodied in the "Confession of 1967" allows much greater flexibility in doing constructive theology than does the older approach of Princeton.

More recent debates amongst Reformed theologians have involved the issues of pluralism and contextualization. White males not only wrote the sixteenth- and seventeenth-century confessions, but also the more recent confessions (like the Theological Declaration of Barmen or the aforementioned Confession of 1967). As cultural studies have demonstrated the way in which context shapes content, theologians and churches have begun to question the way in which cultural embeddedness limits and distorts the witness of the church. Feminist, black, womanist, liberation, and *mujerista* theologies were developed, each of which approached the doctrinal task from a particular socio-cultural perspective. For some, relativism is the obvious result of contextualization. For others, as relativism is the obvious result of contextualization, this very contextualization must be denied as an appropriate way of describing human knowing and com-municating. Still others are attempting to navigate the relationship between universal human commonalities and cultured particu-larities, as these apply to hearing the Word of God well.[26] I will return to such issues in Chapter 7.

In the face of modern historical study, it is important to emphasize the way in which Reformed theologians have dis-cerned the divine nature of the Bible. They have not argued in empirical, inductive fashion from observation of human qualities toward divine realities. In so doing, they have refused to allow secular standards of truth to set the parameters for God's speech. Neither have they suggested that the church creates or fashions the Bible. By denying this construal of the Bible's formation, they have denied the Roman Catholic conception of ecclesial authority. Rather, Reformed churches insist that the written Word of God is self-attesting. The divine authenticity of these writings is made manifest by the writings themselves or, better put, by the divine presence in and through these divine writings.[27] As the prophet says, "For as the rain and the snow come down from heaven, and do not return there until they have watered the earth, making it bring forth and sprout, giving seed to the sower and bread to the eater, so shall my word be that goes out from my mouth; it shall not return to me empty, but it shall accomplish that which I purpose" (Isa. 55.10–11). God makes the Word effective and known. In so doing, God makes himself known and acknowledged.

Another auxiliary should be considered as well, in as much as Reformed theology affirms *sola Scriptura* as the sole *norma normans* ("norming norm"), but not *nuda Scriptura* apart from any other *norma normata* ("normed norms"). Church traditions are represented in liturgies, prayers, aesthetic practices, canonical law, and especially in the history of biblical interpretation (itself represented in diverse genre: explicit biblical commentary, dogmatic theology, sermons, etc.). While Holy Scripture is unique in its authoritative role, Reformed confessions have insisted that tradition (exemplified by these very confessions) aids the churchly practice of reading the Bible well.

Church traditions, however, are binding only when they agree with the words of Holy Scripture. The Ten Theses of Berne (1528) state that "all human traditions, which are called ecclesiastical commandments, are binding upon us only in so far as they are based on and commanded by God's Word" (TTB, II, in *RCSC*, p. 49). The Westminster Confessions also affirms that "all decrees of councils, opinions of ancient writers, doctrines of men, and private spirits, are to be examined" by the "Holy Spirit speaking in the Scripture" (WCF, I.10, in *BC*, p. 176). That traditions and dogmas are being examined presupposes their potential fallibility; they are not perfect, nor are they expected to be. Rather, critical traditioning is the self-awareness of the Reformed confessions themselves. More attention will be given to this relativization of church traditions in Chapter 7.

Having considered the doctrine of the Word of God, ultimately the belief that God speaks, we do well to ask how Reformed theology makes sense of this divine self-revelation. This is not simply a move from formal matters to material issues, in as much as the very methodology discussed formally in this chapter is derived from and shaped by the material of Christian doctrine itself. That is, prolegomena are themselves theological and, thus, not scientifically neutral. Accordingly, we will move from consideration of revelation to the relationship born of this self-revelation; in the next chapter, the doctrine of the covenant will be shown to function as the organizing principle for Reformed biblical theology.

Chapter 2
Covenant

Perhaps more than any other major theological tradition, Reformed theology has insisted that the ways and works of God must be interpreted without losing their storied form. In other words, history or sequence matters. This is worth pointing out, because many might assume Reformed theology to be "predestinarian" and, thus, overly focused on matters of eternal divine decision, which somehow empty history of its meaning and absolve creaturely agents and events of real responsibility and content. Sure enough, Reformed theology strongly affirms that history follows from eternity, as the determination for life by the one eternal God, named Father, Son, and Spirit. Yet Reformed theology has majored on conceptual expansion of the story of God's life with creatures.

The way in which Reformed confessions and dogmatics have described God's life with creatures follows from the very categories found in Holy Scripture. The doctrine of covenant permeates the Bible, appearing in various books and across the testaments, and has been employed by Reformed thinkers to describe the form of God's fellowship with humanity. From the Hebrew *berith* to the Greek *diatheke* to the Latin *pactum*, covenantal terminology has loomed large in biblical and theological scholarship.

While a certain brand of Reformed theology has oftentimes been called "covenant theology," all Reformed theology involves attending to the nature of God's covenantal life with humanity. Thus, so-called covenant theology will be called "federal theology" throughout my exposition, for two reasons. First, simply to note that virtually all Reformed churches and thinkers have talked about covenant. By "federal theology," I will refer to that stream of Reformed theology which developed especially in the last few decades of the sixteenth century and was codified in the seventeenth century. Until in the late-nineteenth-century dispensationalism developed as a competing system for viewing the story of the Bible, the term "covenant theology" was not widely used. Thus, second, "covenant theology" is not the most widely used term deep within the tradition and may be set aside without much loss. For some decades and across a couple of centuries, "federal theology" was the dominant form of Reformed theology, such that John Hesselink could say (not entirely inaccurately) of the tradition: "Reformed theology is covenant theology," or what we shall call "federal theology."[1] To this day, many conservative Reformed churches continue to affirm it as the most biblical approach to the story in Scripture. However, a number of challenges have been raised to the "federal theology," especially by Karl Barth and his followers in Europe and North America, which we must note in so far as they have gained wide purchase in mainline denominations and in much recent theology. Thus, as with the previous chapter, we will move through common affirmations about God's covenanting activity toward more recent disagreements regarding the precise shape this takes in contemporary Reformed circles. Along the way, I will point to ways in which certain differences might be negotiated, though without thereby acting as an imperialist in restating varying viewpoints in commonalities embraced by neither. Even so, certain emphases are shared by virtually all Reformed churches, confessions, and theologians, and we do well to consider these before attending to in-house differences.

The One Covenant

The Reformed churches in the sixteenth century primarily avoided two extremes, which were viewed as theological dangers: Roman Catholicism and the Anabaptist "radical Reformation." We do well to describe these two alternatives in terms of their approach to the story found within the Bible. A methodological concession can be offered at this point: it is likely that proponents of both church traditions would describe their own projects in very different terms, so the following should be read as the common way in which Reformed theologians of the sixteenth century characterized their opponents.

First, the Roman Catholic system of religion maintains that the Old Covenant and New Covenant are continuous. Not only is Jesus Christ the lamb of God for both Israelites and catholic believers, but the style of piety, liturgy, and polity to be followed now is basically similar to that which was practiced then. In Reformation era debates, then, the Roman church pointed to the trappings of the Old Covenant temple worship as precedent for her own elaborate Mass. The Roman Mass was not merely pomp and circumstance devised according to high cultural standards within the late medieval period; rather, it was intended to convey the aesthetic complexity of temple and tabernacle worship in contemporary format. A belief in the continuity of God's people—Israel and then the Roman church—led to an affirmation of similar vestiges in ethos and culture. This emphasis on continuity also affected issues of polity, authority, etc. Such doctrinal implications will be considered at length in Chapter 7.

Second, the Anabaptist churches presented the opposite temptation. In place of Rome's emphasis on continuity, the radical Reformation accentuated all discontinuities between Israel and the churches. These reformers pointed to Paul's contrast between letter and spirit as illustrative of this broader historical difference: "we act with great boldness, not like Moses, who put a veil over his face to keep the people of Israel from gazing at the end of the glory that was being set aside" (2 Cor. 3.12–13). This new boldness arises from the fully redeemed composition of the church, over against the mixed multitude of ethnic Israel in the Old Covenant: "their minds were hardened. Indeed, to this very day, when they hear the reading of the old covenant, that same veil is still there, since only in Christ is it set aside . . . when one turns to the LORD, the veil is removed" (2 Cor. 3.14–15). The Anabaptist churches birthed communities, in fact, for they secluded themselves from broader society in an effort to remain pure and unmixed. Whereas Israel was plagued by syncretism, idolatry, unfaithfulness, the churches were now—in Jesus Christ—capable of true devotion and steadfastness. This new self-identity of the Christian community, of course, played itself out in broader reforms, leaving behind all antique forms of church life as external, physical, inferior, and Jewish. Against these mere trappings, the Christian life was spiritual, pure, regenerate, and immediate.[2]

The Reformed churches—along with confessional Lutheran and (at times) Anglican churches—attempted to steer a middle course between these two extremes. Thus, Reformed theology can be viewed as attempting to negotiate the tensions of mediation, tradition, and structure, as reformed by the ever-new disruptions brought by the proclamation of the Word of God. In other words, Reformed theology affirms continuity in discontinuity, and discontinuity in continuity. This was not a minor issue either, as can be witnessed by looking to the language employed in confessional writings on the topic. For example, consider the way the issue was put in the confession used by the English exiles gathered at Geneva in the year 1556:

> And as Moses, Hezekiah, Josiah, and other godly
> rulers purged the Church of God of superstition and
> idolatry, so the defence of Christ's Church against
> all idolaters and heretics, as Papists, Anabaptists and
> such rascals or antichrist pertains to the Christian
> magistrates, to root out all doctrine of devils and men.
> (IV, in *RCSC*, p. 135)

Clearly, the two grave dangers are following the Papists and the Anabaptists, that is, the Roman Catholic Church with its emphasis on continuity and the radical Reformation with its concern for discontinuity. Against these false alternatives, the Reformed churches focused on the precise nature of the unity of God's covenant.

The key texts regarding the unity of the covenant were Jer. 31, Rom. 9, and the Epistle to the Hebrews. In each case, the Old and the New Covenant are being related. In Jeremiah the New Covenant is being prophesied and differentiated from the Old Covenant. In Rom. 9 Paul shows concern that the people of God in the Old Covenant seem to be outside the New Covenant: has Israel's failure to believe proven God's promises false? In Hebrews, the ministry of Jesus is related to that of prophet, priest, and king; just as God spoke in many ways in various times and places in the past, now God speaks in his Son (Heb. 1.3–4). In each case, God's new work in Jesus is continuous with yet fulfilling the earlier promises of God.

Why is there such continuity? It follows from the fidelity and constancy of the triune God. As John Calvin describes this singular way of living with creatures:

> God works in his elect in two ways: within, through his
> Spirit; without, through his Word. By his Spirit, illuminating
> their minds and forming their hearts to the love and
> cultivation of righteousness, he makes them a new creation.
> By his Word, he arouses them to desire, to seek after, and to
> attain that same renewal. (*ICR*, II.v.5, vol. 1, p. 322)

The gospel, then, is found throughout the writings of Holy Scripture, according to Calvin and the Heidelberg Catechism, which says "God himself revealed [the gospel] in the beginning in the Garden of Eden, afterward proclaimed through the holy patriarchs and prophets and foreshadowed through the sacrifices and other rites of the Old Covenant, and finally fulfilled through his own well-beloved Son" (Heidelberg Catechism [HC], Q.19, in *BC*, p. 61).

The structures of the Old Covenant are not simply useless now that they have been fulfilled. Ulrich Zwingli, the first generation Reformed leader of Zurich, saw 1 Cor. 10.11 as the key biblical witness to this: "These things happened to them to serve as an example, and they were written down to instruct us, on whom the ends of the ages have come." That is, the experiences of Israel in the wilderness are applicable to the church in Corinth in the era after Christ's resurrection and ascension. Christ's Incarnation brings discontinuity, to be sure, but does not thereby do away with all commonality. As the French Confession of Faith, written in 1559, stated:

> We believe that the ordinances of the law came to an end
> at the advent of Jesus Christ; but, although the ceremonies
> are no more in use, yet their substance and truth remain
> in the person of him in whom they are fulfilled. And,
> moreover, we must seek aid from the law and the prophets
> for the ruling of our lives, as well as for our confirmation
> in the promises of the gospel. (XXIII, in *RCSC*, p. 152)

Notice the multiplicity of ways in which the law, the whole Old Testament, shows itself to be of use to the Christian: substance and truth remaining in Jesus, with the writings providing rule and assurance as aids. These uses of the law and Old Testament writings are noted in other confessions (e.g., Belgic Confession of Faith [BCF], XXV, in *RCSC*, p. 206), and we will consider these details in later chapters. For now, simply note that the Reformed churches insist that God has one people throughout history.

This affirmation of the one covenant can be summarized by looking to the Scots Confession of 1560, where two claims are tied together. First, we read that the promise "was embraced with joy, and most constantly received by all the faithful from Adam to Noah, from Noah to Abraham, from Abraham to David, and so onwards to the incarnation of Christ Jesus" (IV, in *RCSC*, p. 167). There is only one promise. Second, therefore, "we most surely believe that God preserved, instructed, multiplied, honoured, adorned, and called from death to life His Kirk in all ages since Adam until the coming of Christ Jesus in the flesh" (V, in *RCSC*, p. 167). Even in the days of the patriarchs, God was gathering "His Kirk," that is, the church of the ages. Again, this is rooted in God's constancy, rather than that of God's people. Indeed, "as we believe in one God, Father, Son, and Holy Ghost, so we firmly believe that from the beginning there has been, now is, and to the end of the world shall be, one Kirk, that is to say, one company and multitude of men" (XVI, in *RCSC*, p. 175; see also BCF, XXVII, in *RCSC*, p. 208).

There is only one people of God.

Federal Theology

Later in the sixteenth century, the doctrine of the covenant was viewed not only as an organizing principle for uniting Old and New Covenant, but also as an anthropological principle to relate creation, sin, and redemption. Heinrich Bullinger's "A Brief Exposition of the One and Eternal Testament or Covenant of God," finished in 1533, organized the whole of theology under the banner of covenant. Indeed, "the entire sum of piety consists in these very brief main points of the covenant," says Bullinger, so that the teachings of the whole Bible "have been summed up in these few words: 'You, however, shall keep my covenant, you shall walk before me, and you shall be complete or upright'."[3] As the concept of covenant came to have great purchase, it was necessary to distinguish between various forms of covenant life. In due course, the "federal theology" typically (though not unanimously) acknowledged the presence of three covenants within Holy Scripture.

The first covenant, the so-called *pactum salutis* or "covenant of redemption," occurs between the Father and Son in eternity past. In this agreement between Father and Son, the salvation yet to unfold in time and space is planned. Thus, "salvation belongs to the LORD" (Ps. 3.8), because the triune God freely determines to live with creatures and do all necessary things to ensure such fellowship. More specifically, the Son agrees to fulfill the vocation of true humanity in obedience to the Father's express will. The Son's obedience will be met by divine approval and vindication as is due a victor. Thus, the Father will give the elect to the Son as his spoils. In some later forms, the "covenant of redemption" involves the Holy Spirit as well; nevertheless, the brunt of the tradition focuses solely on the relation between Father and Son (in as much as only their agreement is sketched by John's Gospel).

The "covenant of redemption" is the most disputed of the three covenants for, indeed, some adherents of the federal system do not acknowledge its reality. This hesitancy arises precisely because the Bible nowhere mentions the word "covenant" in relation to intratrinitarian relationships or determinations. However, such differences typically involve no more than terminological and methodological disagreement—a desire not to extend the word "covenant" beyond where the Bible mandates. Even so, detractors continue to affirm the doctrines of the immanent Trinity and pretemporal election. It is hard to see how the combination of those two doctrines does not necessarily lead to something quite like the "covenant of redemption." That is, all Reformed theologians are agreed that the triune God has predetermined to bring about redemption in Jesus, for "he was foreknown before the foundations of the world but was made manifest in the last times for your sake" (1 Pet. 1.20). Especially in John's Gospel, furthermore, the Son speaks effusively of the plan of the Father to which he has agreed and submitted (e.g., Jn 12.28; 17.2, 4; 19.30). As the roots of this salvific work are both free and eternal, there is little logical reason to protest the content of the "covenant of redemption."

The second covenant was instituted by the Father upon creating Adam and Eve, at which point God declared the terms of this "covenant of works." This first covenant made with humanity has been termed the "covenant of works," "covenant of creation," "covenant of nature," "covenant of life," and the "Adamic Administration." Note that these terms do not imply substantially different understandings, a point made evident by the Westminster Standards' use of two terms for this arrangement. In the Westminster Confession, this relationship is termed the "covenant of works" (VII.2, in *BC*, p. 180), whereas the Westminster Shorter and Larger Catechisms refer to it as the "covenant of life" (Westminster Shorter Catechisms [WSC], Q. 12, in *BC*, p. 230; Westminster Larger Catechisms [WLC], Q. 30, in *BC*, p. 253). While John Murray refused to apply the term "covenant" to this arrangement, preferring the term "Adamic Administration," he otherwise approved of the traditional federal understanding of its content. Murray's terminological hesitancy stemmed from the reticence of Genesis to term this arrangement a "covenant." However, most Reformed interpreters have read Hos 6.7 as teaching that "like Adam they [Israel] transgressed the covenant." Thus, we should note that the Genesis account of God's original dealings with humanity is read through the broader canonical witness (see also Rom. 5.12–21, an influential text in this regard).[4]

What distinguishes this "covenant of works," then, in "federal theology?" God relates to humanity akin to the way that an ancient near-Eastern lord (suzerain) deals with their servant-dependents (vassals).[5] A number of components can be noted. First, God provides beneficently for humanity; in Genesis, God has given life and a beautiful, blessed context for creaturely life. Second, God sets the terms by which fellowship can continue; in Genesis, God commands humanity's participation in the task of ruling and filling the earth and prohibits eating of a specific tree. Third, God points out the ensuing curses which follow disobedience; in Genesis, God reveals that failure to obey leads to death.

Assumedly, most interpreters have suggested, Genesis implicitly affirms that continued life would follow from a life of obedience; some construe this promise of blessing to involve immortality, though most Reformed interpreters speak of it as confirmed, unending life as finite humans in God's presence. With all these components in mind, we see that the "covenant of works" speaks of past, present, and future in as much as it (1) declares what God has done, (2) demands perfect obedience for continued life with God, and (3) delineates the blessings or curses which follow (dis)obedience.

The "covenant of works" was rendered useless by Adam's folly. That is, a single sin breaks the demands of this first administration. "Dying you shall die" is the most accurate translation of the predicted curse revealed in Gen. 2.17. Such gruesome punishment follows "in the day that you eat of it," the forbidden fruit. And God does not hesitate, for curses immediately follow the first sin (Gen. 3.14–19). The entrance of death at this point is highlighted by the expulsion of Adam and Eve from the Garden of Eden, "lest he reach out his hand, and take also of the tree of life and eat, and live forever" (Gen. 3.22). The death brought upon Adam and Eve was not theirs alone, in as much as it spread to the whole of their progeny. As the apostle Paul says, "sin came into the world through one man, and death came through sin, and so death spread to all because all have sinned" (Rom. 5.12). In brief, Adam's sin is that of his descendents who are, somehow, "in Adam." Details of how sin can be passed from one person to another will be discussed in Chapter 5. Here we simply note that the "federal theology" insists that sin dissolves fellowship with God: "the Fall brought upon mankind the loss of communion with God, his displeasure and curse; so as we are by nature children of wrath, bondslaves to Satan, and justly liable to all punishments in this world and that which is to come" (WLC, Q. 27, in BC, p. 252).

In response to sin and in keeping with the eternal inclination of God's gracious will, the Father then put forward the "covenant of grace." In fact, the account in Gen. 3 is drenched in unexpected acts of grace and mercy offered by God toward those who have just disobeyed the divine law. God provides garments for Adam and Eve, dealing with their naked shamefulness (Gen. 3.21). God keeps them away from the divine presence, so that they are not further harmed (Gen. 3.24). Most importantly, however, God offers a promise in the midst of curse and misery. Just as God is declaring the curses befalling upon the sinful serpent, woman, and man, God also offers words of hope: "he shall bruise your head, and you shall bruise his heel" (Gen. 3.15). The so-called *protoeuangelium* declares that the seed of the woman will, in due time, defeat the offspring of the tempter.

Here and throughout the biblical writings, sin is met by the divine faithfulness which refuses to give death the final word. God's character is merciful; thus "salvation belongs to the LORD" (Ps. 3.8). Or, as recorded in Jeremiah, "I have loved you with an everlasting love; therefore I have continued my faithfulness to you" (Jer. 31.3).

The "covenant of grace" took many forms throughout the history of redemption, especially visible in comparing the Old Covenant with the New Covenant. Nevertheless, each manifestation is a variation of this one grand relational framework for the renewal of friendship between the holy God and sinful creatures. In this administration, the "covenant of works" is fulfilled on behalf of God's people by the seed of the woman (Gen. 3.15) and garners their salvation on the condition of faith. Thus, God promises to save the ungodly provided that they trustingly embrace God's good news as their lifeline. Strictly speaking, the "covenant of grace" is bilateral, requiring faith from the people of God. While faith is neither meritorious nor the ground of one's acceptance before God, faith is a real condition. Unlike the "covenant of works," however, salvation is not limited to those who can muster perfect obedience and fortitude in the midst of all temptations.

Most disputed in this area was the Mosaic or Sinai Covenant, that administration begun with the giving of the Ten Commandments and witnessed in the Book of Exodus. Some theologians understood the Mosaic administration to be a republishing of the "covenant of works," while most interpret it as one manifestation of the one "covenant of grace." This disagreement shadows that wider debate amongst Protestant theologians: whether the Sinai administration is "Law" or "Gospel." Here we see that "federal theology" follows the Lutheran and, yes, Reformed approach of dividing divine-human relations into two sorts. "Law" is any schema whereby divine favor is curried by human obedience and merit. By contrast, "Gospel" involves promise and blessing apart from perfect performance of faithfulness, instead standing upon the accomplished work of the divinely sent mediator.[6] How to locate the Mosaic administration in this binary typology remains difficult, considering the varied witness of the New Testament to the "law" or *torah*. Some approaches within the "federal theology" treat the Mosaic Covenant as some form of social covenant based on the "covenant of grace" yet extending beyond its spiritual purview to include issues of national obedience and enjoyment of the promised land.[7]

In this system, the feature with greatest systematic importance was the dual nature of God's life with creatures, that is, the existence of two ways in which humans relate coventantally to their LORD. Humans are born into the "covenant of works" and are brought into the "covenant of grace." Thus, the "federal theology" can be aptly termed "bicovenantal," in as much as two covenants directly shape the fellowship of God and humanity.[8] The seventeenth-century divines, especially Johannes Cocceius, Franz Burman, and Herman Witsius, gave codified form to this "bicovenantal" approach and modeled its use in a multitude of literary genres: ecclesial confessions, sermons, biblical commentaries, polemical tracts, and dogmatic systems. That said, it must be noted that such institutionalization, especially the systemic or "scholastic" development of dogmatics in the "bicovenantal" and "federal" vein, is a methodological procedure very much in keeping with the wider Western culture (from the twelfth century onward) and even the impulses of the earlier Reformed thinkers (e.g., Calvin's *Institutes*). "Scholastic theology" developed as a teaching tool meant to serve the biblical witness, rather than an apologetic procedure based on some supposedly neutral reason. As many theologians consider "scholastic" and "orthodox" theology of the post-Reformation era to be arid, dry, rationalistic, and the like, they have viewed it as a degeneration from the biblical, fluid, dynamic teaching of Calvin and the early Reformers. Delightful as such a picture may be, it simply does not fit the facts. As Richard Muller has said, "the methodological vehicle of scholasticism carried Calvinist thought forward into the seventeenth century different in form but virtually the same in basic content as the thought of Calvin and his contemporaries." Furthermore, "a Reformed or Calvinist thinker who used scholastic method in the classroom of a university would not use it in preaching or in catechizing the young."[9] Thus, the "federal theology" was an approach to view systematically the relationships between God and humanity as revealed across the whole swatch of the apostolic and prophetic witnesses of Scripture. While it was oftentimes taught via more academic or analytic forms, it actually gave great weight to the dynamics of the long history of redemption. It was used to structure lessons from the lectern as well as pastoral exhortation from the pulpit.

Some historians of doctrine have suggested that the "federal theology" was developed as a way to mellow the otherwise one-sided predestinarianism of Reformed teaching.[10] That is, this interpretation takes the Reformed doctrine of predestination to be unilateral and to exclude human action from any sphere of meaning or ultimacy. Thus, the bilateral covenants allowed a certain level of responsibility to humans, thereby alleviating the decidedly antinomian tilt of the Reformed view of predestination. Sadly, however, this interpretation gets neither predestination nor covenant right and, thus, fails to get at their historical and logical relationship accurately. As will be seen in Chapter 4, predestination is not meant to reduce human responsibility in any way; there is, indeed, a bilateral element in divinely decreed human activity. The elect are "predestined to be conformed to the image of his Son" (Rom. 8.29); thus conformity and ethical service are incumbent upon those chosen. While God's grace is not conditional or based upon such action, such action does truly follow from this grace. Similarly, the covenants are unilaterally bestowed by God, who did not ask Adam or Israel's permission to sketch such a frame for fellowship. Yet such covenants involve bilateral conditions with real human obligations, so that their maintenance is dependent upon creaturely action. Contrary to some descriptions, then, covenant and predestination are parallel and compatible concepts (see, for example, *WJO*, vol. 11, pp. 207–218).

The "federal theology" was upheld by numerous theologians and undergirded several confessional symbols. It came to its most rigorous formulation, perhaps, in the Savoy Declaration in the late seventeenth century. In this text, John Owen and others deepened the testimony of the Westminster Standards regarding the "federal theology." The Savoy Declaration affirmed the "covenant of works" and "covenant of grace," following Westminster, and went one step further, also mentioning the "covenant of redemption": "It pleased God, in his eternal purpose, to chuse and ordain the Lord Jesus his onely begotten Son, according to a Covenant made between them both, to be the Mediator between God and Man."[11] The famed American theologian, Jonathan Edwards, also upheld the "federal theology" and planned a masterwork, which would address the whole of divinity under the organizational categories of the economy of salvation. While he never lived to write this tome, Edwards' miscellanies suggest his devotion to the "federal" model. Thus, the "federal theology" was affirmed by the greatest Reformed theologians of the seventeenth (Owen) and the eighteenth centuries (Edwards).

A number of conservative denominations continue to affirm either the Westminster Standards or the Three Forms of Unity as their sole subordinate standards. Thus, the "federal theology" of these confessional texts still exercises great sway within a plethora of Reformed churches. For example, the Presbyterian Church in America and the Christian Reformed Church both affirm this "federal" approach as the most fitting way of viewing the story found in the Bible. A number of seminaries continue to teach this theology as well, for example, Westminster Seminary, Reformed Theological Seminary, and Calvin Theological Seminary in the United States, and Free Church College and Highland Theological College in Scotland. In a four volume dogmatic project, Michael Horton has shown how "federal theology" can be reaffirmed and put to brilliant systemic usage in the realm of contemporary dogmatic theology.[12] Thus, "federal theology" is alive and kicking in the twenty-first century, especially in the Scottish churches and their American descendents across the Atlantic.

Karl Barth: Gospel and Law

While Reformed theology may have traditionally been "federal theology" through and through, this is no longer unanimously so. If one searches for a reason for this, the influence of Karl Barth must be mentioned as a major factor. The European continent in the early twentieth century was not exactly a fortress of Reformed theology, exemplified by the confession-less life of the Reformed churches in the wake of the Prussian Union of the previous century. During that time, the government forced the merger of the Reformed and Lutheran churches, with the larger Lutheran body swallowing the cultural identity of the Reformed congregations. When Barth was called as Honorary Professor of Reformed Theology at Göttingen in 1921, there was no ecclesial theology to which he could turn as a guide. By the time he retired in 1962, he had led his contemporaries to reengage the Reformation and its program for a more traditionally engaging modern theology. While Barth will be mentioned in relation to virtually every doctrine in this book, the influence of his theology is especially linked to the way in which he construed the life of "God with us," otherwise known as the doctrine of the covenant.

Barth wrote of the precedence of Gospel before Law, Christ before Adam, Grace before Nature. Thus, his theology has oftentimes been characterized as "christocentric" or even "christomonist," the latter employed in a pejorative sense. What leads to such terminology? Barth insists that Christian theology begin with the Word of God, the very person of Jesus. Thus, the true, the good, the beautiful, must all be determined only by looking to the revelation of true God and true humanity as found in the union of divine and human, this particular Nazarene. No secular truth may precede thinking long and hard about the person of the eternal and very human Son, for to do so would be the equivalent of serving God and one's own rationality or culture or political cause. Barth's concern in this regard was based on his interpretation of the "first commandment as an axiom of theology."[13] That is, "that He is the one Word of God means further that His truth and prophecy cannot be combined with any other, nor can He be enclosed with other words in a system superior to both Him and them" (CD, IV/3.1, p. 101).

Barth's approach to Gospel and Law comprises three moves: (1) distinguishing them, (2) uniting them, and (3) putting them in proper order. First, the Gospel is a "once-for-all" event, whereas the Law's command never ceases. The Gospel is about that which has been done by Jesus, and the Law clarifies the ongoing work of the human (CD, IV/2, pp. 50, 115–116). Second, the Gospel propels the Law, giving it momentum or legs on which to move. That is, the good news of the risen Jesus leads his people to follow gratefully the God who has chosen to be with them in Christ (*CD*, IV/2, pp. 62–64). Third, then, the Gospel must come before the Law, so that Barth agrees with the Heidelberg Catechism in describing the Christian life under the banner of gratitude (*CD*, I/2, pp. 136, 168; IV/2, pp. 45–54). God comes to humanity well before the human does anything good or laudatory; Barth took this emphasis from the apostle Paul: "for while we were still weak, at the right time Christ died for the ungodly . . . God proves his love for us in that while we still were sinners Christ died for us" (Rom. 5.6, 8). For Barth, then, Law and Gospel each exist, relate to each other, and always move from the latter to the former.

Barth insisted that two major doctrines of the "federal theology" were simply untenable: the "covenant of redemption" and the "covenant of works." Barth viewed the "covenant of grace" as the only administration directly shaping fellowship between God and humanity; thus, he can be called "monocovenantal." In so doing, Barth wished to testify to God's constancy and faithfulness, as well as the fact that we can really know God. Thus, Barth argued against anything he suspected of dividing God or implying a "hidden God" somewhere behind what is revealed in Jesus. There is no arm behind God's back; rather, the hands of Son and Spirit are placed before humanity in exactly the same, determinate way for all times. How does this relate to "federal theology?" First, Barth interpreted the "covenant of works" as an alternative arrangement with no connection to Jesus and, thus, as implying a "hidden God" who wishes his own pound of flesh prior to showing grace or mercy. The bi-covenantalism of "federal theology" actually described a "theology of biblical histories" (*CD*, IV/1, p. 58). As to be expected, then, Barth vehemently objected to this seemingly natural theology, which augmented the work and reign of Jesus with that of the natural, secular order. In its place, Barth insisted that God has always related to humans by means of the "covenant of grace," one arrangement whereby grace precedes command and in which Jesus is always mediator and focal point. Second, Barth denied the propriety of the "covenant of redemption" which seems to imply a hesitancy or division within the Godhead, whereby one member of the Trinity had to broker the other into the Incarnation. Barth suspected that this led to tri-theism and downright mythological views of God, neither a happy result. Thus, he affirmed that the God who elected to be with humanity in Jesus Christ could not have engaged in such a "covenant of redemption."

Karl Barth denied two central tenets of "federal theology," then, and advanced a strong polemic against anything which smacked of natural theology. Barth's context must be understood, however, if one is to understand his reformulation and its intent. He wrote in the early twentieth century, during the era of liberal Protestantism and amidst the dashed hopes of the humanistic intelligentsia after the First World War. Thus, the concept of nature was not unproblematic in Barth's eyes. His context becomes even more crucial for right interpretation when one takes into account the Theological Declaration of Barmen, which he substantially wrote by himself (except for nineteen words added to his initial draft).[14] The Declaration begins: "Jesus Christ, as he is attested for us in Holy Scripture, is the one Word of God which he have to hear and which we have to trust and obey in life and in death." The polemical concern is made clear in the next phrase, the denial which follows from that Christological affirmation: "We reject the false doctrine, as though the Church could and would have to acknowledge as a source of its proclamation, apart from and besides this one Word of God, still other events and powers, figures and truths, as God's revelation" (II.1, in *BC*, p. 311). In this situation, the totalitarianism employed by National Socialism was a "false doctrine," a claim to represent God's speech through nature, which must be rejected. The singular authority of Jesus revealed in the Bible undercut the claims of the Nazis.

We should note that Barth did not deny the usefulness of the "federal theology" in every respect. In fact, he highlighted four exemplary moves to be found in their thought (*CD*, IV/1, pp. 55–61). First, they rightly understood that the God of the Bible was a *living* God. Second, they originally (though not always) confessed the universal nature of the covenant, that is, how God relates to all the inhabitants of the world. Third, their covenantal theology emphasized that every relationship between God and humanity depends upon divine accommodation or condescension, what we term "grace." Fourth, their emphasis upon history and dynamism did not undermine the concept of "eternity," but flowed from it as the outgrowth of God's eternal character. Thus, Barth was not entirely dissatisfied with the "federal theology" even as he showed some serious misgivings about certain tenets in the system.

What can we say of Barth's criticisms of the "federal theology?"[15] Ryan Glomsrud has suggested that the historical study of the Reformed tradition available to Barth in his day was, sadly, misleading at best.[16] While Barth shows familiarity with the best historiography of his day, one gets the sense that the "federal theology" has not really been understood on its own terms. For example, in those genuine terms the "covenant of works" is not somehow dislocated from Christ but fulfilled by Jesus. Further-more, Barth's revolutionary doctrine of election is eerily similar to the "covenant of redemption" put forward by the "federal theology." In both cases, the concern is to affirm heartily that God's works really manifest the divine character from eternity past. With regard to the "covenant of redemption," Barth worries about mythology and tri-theism, to be sure, but this timidity must be contextualized. His real worry was that the God of the covenant might be identified apart from the gospel or, better put, might be identified by rationalizing, secular thought about what such a god should be. He worried about human-based and human-judged concepts of divinity somehow shaping what a divine act in eternity past might be. But, as two recent defenders of the "covenant of redemption" say: "the claim that the *pactum salutis* is eternal is not so much a claim about 'eternity past' as about eternal *persons*, persons whose fellowship remains unbroken throughout the course of redemption and thus guarantees that redemption."[17] Perhaps a way forward in Reformed theology will be found by combining Barth's knack for lovingly describing the epistemic priority of God's self-revelation, with the variegated narrative described in the "federal theology."

Such a proposal, however, goes against the grain of much "Barthian" theological work done in mainline Reformed denom-inations in these past few decades. With the "Confession of 1967," the theology of Barmen was exported across the Atlantic and gained wide influence across the spectrum of Reformed churches. As this theology has been delineated, "christocentrism" has become something of a catch phrase, which excludes natural theology rooted in any biblical bi-covenantalism (*a la* "federal theology") yet tends to load a great deal of contemporary cultural baggage into the name "Christ." Many followers of Barth have vehemently insisted that theology must begin, organizationally as well as materially, with the person of Jesus. Doing so, many traditional doctrines have fallen by the wayside or been radically reconfigured (e.g., divine eternity, impassibility, aseity) in as much as the Old Testament witness to the self-revelation of YHWH has been minimized or delayed until later in theology. This tendency will be discussed in the next chapter. Furthermore, an account of human salvation which begins with the person and work of Christ and his once-for-all action (*historia salutis*) and, then, moves to describe the outworking of this event in the lives of his people (*ordo salutis*) has been foreshortened by many who wish to avoid any talk of conditionality in the "covenant of grace." Thus, many go well beyond Barth in the direction of universalism. This tendency will be discussed in Chapter 5.

Biblical Theology

Attention to the covenantal framework within which God lives with creatures has been a mainstay in the Reformed tradition. Historically, this has led to an insistence that the dynamic nature of the history of redemption be taken at face value. God truly involves Godself in the exigencies of human history precisely because God wills to be with humans. Many Reformed theologians, therefore, sketched theologies of various epochs in redemptive history. Herman Witsius's *The Economy of the Covenants between God and Man* is the most notable, but John Owen, Jonathan Edwards, and others, attempted such feats as well. While such works go back as far as Irenaeus, theologians in the Reformed churches have demonstrated an unusually strong interest in this particular direction.

Most notably, Geerhardus Vos exemplified the discipline of modern "biblical theology" during his long teaching career at Princeton Theological Seminary and especially in his *Biblical Theology: Old and New Testaments*. Extending the "federal theology" into the realm of modern biblical studies, Vos and his followers attempted to articulate the unfolding and progressive nature of revelation. So-called biblical theology had been differentiated from "dogmatic theology" a century before by J. P. Gabler, so that an attempt to reflect carefully on the complexities and intricacies of discrete literary sections of the Bible (e.g., the Pauline writings, the Pentateuch) was not new. For Gabler's modern children, however, "biblical theology" would undermine the claims of authoritarian dogma taught by the church (e.g., F. C. Baur). To the contrary, Vos demonstrates that "biblical theology" can be done as a servant and purveyor of a dogmatic tradition.

As noted in Chapter 1, Reformed churches have taken different views regarding the usefulness of historical criticism in the modern era. Accompanying this diversity has been disagreement regarding the degree to which biblical scholars view the Bible to manifest unity. For many, "biblical theology" quickly became an attempt to demonstrate the presence of multiple biblical theologies, the religious thought of Paul, John, etc. Indeed, apart from an operative doctrine of divine inspiration, such pluriformity seems a likely result of merely historical or archaeological study. For others, the inspiration of the Bible provides fallible writers with true and consistent witness to God's works amidst Israel, in Jesus, and through the church, so that the Bible actually is unified in teaching. Hence two traditions of "biblical theology" arose in the twentieth century, each representing congregations and denominations either more or less inclined to work within the parameters of historical criticism. The now-defunct book series "Studies in Biblical Theology" (Westminster Press) and now the academic journal *Interpretation* have fueled this movement, which has claimed biblical scholars such as G. Ernest Wright, and others. In the mainline churches, the so-called biblical theology movement attempted to describe the living God by means of focusing on the history of God's works, witnessed to by the biblical writings though not tethered to their literary forms. In the more conservative Reformed churches, the followers of Vos continued to describe redemptive history as the progressive unfolding of God's covenantal plans, culminating in Jesus and codified in a unified, inerrant Bible. The more recent book series *New Studies in Biblical Theology* (InterVarsity Press) has become a primary avenue for this work, with contributors from inside and outside the Reformed world following the example of earlier practitioners of evangelical "biblical theology," like John Murray, Herman Ridderbos, and Richard Gaffin. Both the so-called biblical theology movement and evangelical approaches to "biblical theology" have been fueled by the Reformed emphasis on God's works in history.

The unity and diversity of the biblical witnesses are related to the nature of the God attested by these texts. In fact, the doctrine of revelation is best considered amidst the doctrine of covenant, in as much as God's testimony to himself is a part of life with God and, thus, called "covenant." So we do well to turn in the next chapter from the formal principle of Reformed theology (the Scripture principle) and a leading material principle (covenant) to the central feature of any veritable Christian theology: the doctrine of God, revealed as the Father, the Son, and the Holy Spirit, one God now and forever.

Chapter 3
God and Christ

This chapter focuses on two related topics, even as they have gained vastly different prestige within the Reformed tradition. In one sense, there has never been widespread appreciation for an unique Reformed doctrine of God in its broader contours. In another sense, the distinctiveness of the Reformed churches from their Lutheran counterparts in the mid-sixteenth century owed largely to a developed and polemically focused Christology. Thus, the doctrine of God and that of Christ appear at first glance to be quite different, one an afterthought, the other a major topic for identifying Reformed theology. As will be shown, however, the Reformed approach to the person and work of Christ follows from a particular doctrine of God. The two are connected in ways not often made explicit.

The Reformed confessions consistently speak about the character of the triune God, though largely assuming the consensus of the medieval tradition on these (and many other) issues. When one looks at the writings of noted individuals in the early Reformed churches, like John Calvin, they seem to spend few pages exploring the so-called divine attributes in any detail. As Richard Muller has shown, however, theologians who came in succeeding generations, whose thought can be termed "Reformed orthodoxy," offered lengthy biblical and philosophical ruminations on the nature of God (see *PRRD*, vol. 3).

Though much else could be said, if commonalities with other traditions were to be noted *in extenso*, here then we must limit ourselves to ways in which this Reformed ecclesial tradition breaks new ground or reappropriates traditional concerns for new purposes. Five topics will thus be highlighted, ever so briefly: the nature of divine perfection, the tri-unity of God, the divine Son as *autotheos*, the humanity of Jesus, and the threefold office (*munus triplex*) of the Christ.

Divine Perfection

When considering the Reformed doctrine of God, we most immediately turn to the idea of divine sovereignty and the divine decrees of election and reprobation. To be sure, election is an essential component of the Reformed approach to God's identity. However, care must be taken to avoid a fixation on one subject simply because it has proven controversial. Election will be discussed in Chapter 4. Two comments can be hazarded now, however, for the sake of clarification. First, the Reformed doctrine of election remarkably lacks novelty; in reality, it simply reaffirms that which Luther and, before him, Thomas Aquinas taught. Second, the doctrine of election is neither the focus of Reformed thought about God, nor a central principle from which all other doctrines follow. If we are to concern ourselves briefly with the main focus of Reformed reflection on God's character, we must turn elsewhere and consider the "divine perfections."

The Scots Confession offers a relatively early confessional witness to the doctrine of God: "We confess and acknowledge one God alone . . . who is eternal, infinite, immeasurable, incomprehensible, omnipotent, invisible" (Scots Confession of 1560 [SC], 1, in *BC*, p. 33). Similar statements are found in the Second Helvetic Confessions (SHC, 3, in *BC*, p. 96). A slightly later statement that has proven more widely acknowledged, the Westminster Shorter Catechism offers a relatively brief depiction of the triune God: "What is God? God is a spirit, eternal, infinite, and unchangeable, in his being, wisdom, power, holiness, justice, goodness, and truth" (WSC, Q. 4, in *BC*, p. 229). Notice the three primary adjectives employed to describe God: eternal, infinite, and unchangeable. These three terms characterize the way all other descriptions fit this identity, for example, God is truthful in an eternal, infinite, and unchangeable way. We can consider the importance of only one term to show the influence these three carry; Auguste Lecerfe calls "the doctrine of the infinity of God the foundation of Calvinism."[1] Infinity in Reformed dogmatics does not simply mean non-finitude (though that is a subsidiary claim)[2]; rather, infinitude points to God's fullness or plenitude as the overflowing fountain of all life and being. Thus interpreted as "fullness," God's infinity depicts all God's characteristics as those of this one, the limitless and boundless maker of heaven and earth.

The Westminster Confession of Faith points to the wider witness of the classical doctrine of God in its lengthier description:

> There is but one only living and true God, who is infinite in being and perfection, a most pure spirit, invisible, without body, parts, or passions, immutable, immense, eternal, incomprehensible, almighty; most wise, most holy, most free, most absolute, working all things according to the counsel of his own immutable and most righteous will, for his own glory; most loving, gracious, merciful, long-suffering, abundant in goodness and truth, forgiving iniquity, transgression, and sin; the rewarder of them that diligently seek him; and withal most just and terrible in his judgments; hating all sin, and who will by no means clear the guilty. (WCF, II.1, in *BC*, p. 176)

Thus far, the first of three paragraphs "Of God, and of the Holy Trinity" in the Westminster Confessions of Faith. While the third paragraph describes the triune nature of God, the first two paragraphs speak of the divine perfections, the characteristics that mark the divine life. Thomas Tracy has aptly referred to the "divine attributes," what I prefer to call "divine perfections," as "character trait predicates," terms that characterize a person sufficiently to identify them.[3]

Shirley Guthrie, a mainline Presbyterian theologian writing in the last quarter of the twentieth century, gave the famed Warfield Lectures at Princeton Theological Seminary in 1995. As *per* his title *Always Being Reformed*, Guthrie articulated a new way of thinking about God's life, which would make greater sense when placed alongside modern philosophy and provide better traction for contemporary ethical reflection. Guthrie's proposals neither were novel nor have proven very influential, yet they cogently and simply summarize some basic concerns prevalent in the Reformed churches in recent decades. Here, as well as in later chapters, Guthrie will be used as a figure who represents very widespread movements toward revisionary thinking about God, salvation, and humanity. Guthrie's book focuses on the three persons of the

Trinity, culminating in chapters on each one; however, the way he relates some of those Trinitarian comments to other issues will be best treated in later chapters.

Guthrie notes that the classical doctrine of God majors on the inner divine life and employs terms of ancient philosophy to do so. The "infinity" and "eternality" of God settle in alongside the "simplicity" of the divine "being"; all this sounds awfully similar to the way pagan philosophers talk about the "perfect being."[4] In this regard, he stands with many who find use of "substance" terminology to be theologically problematic, in as much as it requires a belief in static essences and, thus, denies the dynamism (or even evolution) of all species and types of being. Not only that, but contextualization has shown twentieth-century persons that all things are shaped by their situation and, as situations shift, so will they. "Substances," be they divine or creaturely, simply cannot exist in this changing world, at least not after Martin Heidegger performed his philosophical duties a few decades ago.

Not only is the language of the older Reformed tradition considered outmoded, but also its social implications are deemed dangerous. Indeed, Guthrie follows various liberation and feminist theologians in tracing forms of abuse to roots in the classical doctrine of God. The belief that God is absolutely determinative of reality, sovereign in every respect, leads to a "patriarchal" stance of superiority and an ethic of violence against minorities. He elaborates on the evil implications of this classical thinking: "extreme individualism, competitive struggle to achieve and maintain a position of superiority (especially male superiority) over other people, freedom understood as freedom from anyone or anything that limits one's self-sufficient autonomy, and the exploitation of the natural world that is understood to be there to be used or misused as we see fit" (*ABR*, p. 34).

Guthrie does not merely point to problems, however, in as much as he also suggests ways in which more recent Reformed confessions speak of God with us. Most importantly, "in contrast with early Reformed confessions, the doctrine of God in contemporary confessions is not grounded in metaphysical speculation about the nature and attributes of God"; rather, "it is grounded in the word and work of God in the history of Israel and above all in Jesus Christ" (*ABR*, p. 37). Guthrie can then point to the new idea that God's freedom is "not freedom and power to do anything God pleases, to dominate and control," but "to be with and for us, setting us on our feet and empowering us to be God's faithful covenant partners" (*ABR*, p. 41). One wonders who this "us" is, precisely because many would seem not to be so empowered. Furthermore, the denial of God's freedom to do things other than live with humanity seems to deny the standard notion of "freedom"; perhaps that is valid, but why call it "freedom" rather than "determination" or "bias" to live with humans? Guthrie seems to have gone well beyond Karl Barth in limiting divine freedom to certain actions culled from the gospel accounts.[5]

Might Reformed theology hold on to its classical heritage and, yet, avoid the dangers that Guthrie and others have so stridently flagged? John Webster has deliberately begun a project of reconstructing language of God's "aseity," "immensity," and "holiness," to name but a few perfections that he has tackled. Webster basically affirms the classical doctrine of God, showing how it is rooted in biblical exegesis attuned to the divine self-revelation in the life of Israel, climactically in the person and work of Jesus of Nazareth, and in the testimony of the church. More than anything, Webster has pointed to the continuing importance of talk about God's "inner life." As he puts it, "the movement of God's triune life has its perfection in and of itself and is utterly sufficient to itself, but this perfect movement is not self-enclosed or self-revolving."[6] God is with us, to be sure, but in so doing God is still the perfect one, the "holy one in your midst" (Hos 11.9).

The dogmatics of post-Reformation Reformed churches— say, the late sixteenth and seventeenth centuries—employed a distinction between the "communicable attributes" and the "incommunicable attributes" of God. That such a distinction can be made, of course, follows from this qualitative holiness ascribed to God. God is of a different sort; thus, the divine perfections or attributes will not all be shared with creatures. As Richard Muller says, "the term incommunicable is reserved as a term for those attributes proper to God which have neither a similitude or analogy nor an image or vestige in God's creatures, but represent the difference or 'opposition' between God and the creature" (*PRRD*, vol. 3, p. 225). Typically, infinity, aseity, omnipresence, omniscience, etc., were listed as "incommunicable," whereas others, like goodness, mercy, life, etc., were considered "communicable." Even those character traits that could be shared by God and humanity, however, were not held in exactly the same ways on either side of the Creator-creature distinction. God is alive in ways which are not entirely the same with living creatures: for example, God is self-existent and eternally and fully alive, whereas creatures are by definition formed at a particular point and mortal. To use a linguistic term, we could say that the "communicable attributes" are shared analogously, whereas the "incommunicable attributes" are not shared at all (*PRRD*, vol. 3, p. 224). That God shares some attributes points to a "life with us," whereas the insistence that some character traits are God's alone sustains the idea of holiness as differentiation or qualitative perfection.

Thus, the second paragraph offered by the Westminster divines in their consideration "Of God, and of the Holy Trinity" may yet prove important:

> God hath all life, glory, goodness, blessedness, in and of himself; and is alone in and unto himself all-sufficient, not standing in need of any creatures which he hath made, nor deriving any glory from them, but only manifesting his own glory in, by, unto, and upon them: he is the alone fountain of all being, of whom, through whom, and to whom, are all things; and hath most sovereign dominion over them, to do by them, for them, or upon them, whatsoever himself pleaseth . . . (WCF, II.2, in *BC*, p. 176)

The God who has all life in himself will also have life for others, precisely because this one needs nothing (and derives nothing) from them. God's freedom to be for us, graciously and totally, derives directly from God's own life of self-fulfillment and aseity. Only the God who is full can pour into others. And the God revealed in the Gospel is the kind of being who would do so, because this one has determined to do so in actuality. Thus, we can attest that God is both able and willing to share the divine life with humans. As Webster puts it, "in its perfection, it is also a movement of self-gift in which the complete love of Father, Son, and Spirit communicates itself *ad extra*, creating and sustaining a further object of love."[7]

From a different angle than Webster, feminist theologian Cynthia Rigby merges concern for social justice with a desire to further faithfully orthodox and classical Reformed theology, thinking it biblical. She notes the way in which knowledge of God can quickly be turned into a tool for mastery and abuse: "with Peter, we expect our right confession that Jesus is 'the Christ, the Son of the living God' to mean that we will have the upper hand, not that we will enter with him into the way of the cross"("Scandalous Presence: Incarnation and Trinity," in *FWERD*, p. 66). Rigby does not lay all the ills of Christian abuse at the doorstep of the classical doctrine of God; rather, she insists that "it is a far different thing to say *what God likes* than it is to say *what God is like* on the basis of the divine self-disclosure" ("Scandalous Presence," in *FWERD*, p. 70). Knowledge of God is not a genie's bottle by which one may claim an elitist prestige, and knowledge of a sovereign God is certainly not itself *carte blanche* for one's own attempts at earthly rule. Here, Rigby turns to the task of reinvigorating a classical program for contemporary churches: "it is necessary to 'reinterpret' classical ideas in ways that both take theological and philosophical developments into account and make sense to our contemporary faith journeys" ("Scandalous Presence," in *FWERD*, p. 70). Rigby, then, suggests a middle way between sheer contemporization and blasé repetition of classical statements. Most importantly for my purposes, her feminist project shows that classical resources might not be to blame for the social ills of human history (in as much as human ingenuity for sin seems to make use of all manner of theological grids).[8]

Both the revisionist approach of Guthrie and the classical approach of Webster lay claim to roots in the work of twentieth-century giant Karl Barth. Indeed, current Reformed debates regarding theology proper (the doctrine of God) are oftentimes exercises in exegesis of Barth. The Swiss theologian, of course, formulated his doctrine of God by offering vast exegesis of biblical material while engaging historical and philosophical resources in an almost endless fashion. He spoke of God as the "one who loves in freedom" (*CD*, II/1, §27), implying that divine perfection and divine presence stand in a dialectical relationship. Maintaining balance between these two terms is the question of the day, with Guthrie, Webster, and others like Bruce McCormack, providing various readings of both Barth and the biblical testimony.[9] Obviously, there is overlap here between the divine perfections and the covenant life of God with creatures; the debate circles around this link: how does fellowship with humanity relate to God's own character? Karl Barth insisted that God's determination to be with us says as much about God as it does about us; how does that relate to the classical attributes?

Trinity

As with the divine perfections, the Reformed confessions about God's triunity follow a deep catholic tradition that spans the entire medieval era and, indeed, goes all the way back to the reflection of the early councils (Nicaea, Constantinople, Chalcedon). God is "one substance" in "three persons," using terminology taken from Tertullian.

Guthrie suggests that here as well, moral ills and social injustices have flowed from Trinitarian misconceptions in the classical heritage of the Western churches. The earlier Reformed confessions could leave one with the idea that there is "God the Father first of all as a solitary number-one, 'top' God, with a begotten Son and proceeding Spirit who are somehow inferior to 'him'" (*ABR*, p. 41). Just as sovereignty and omnipotence are perfections that can be used to justify abusive policy, so divine patriarchy might be the grounds for misogynist behavior.

In place of the static and arid classical approach to God's being, Guthrie and others propose a view of the Trinity culled from the Eastern Orthodox tradition.[10] Most importantly, "contemporary confessions speak in a purely functional way of what the Three Persons *do* and are typically silent about who they *are* in their interrelationship" (*ABR*, p. 38). Guthrie notes a danger: simply listing things that the triune God does in the economy risks implying that there are three persons, each divine in their own separate way. Enter the "social trinity" and the idea that the oneness of God "is the unity of a *community* of Persons" (*ABR*, p. 40). The three persons just are persons-in-relationship, each existing only in their life together. Guthrie here echoes language employed by many other famed contemporary theologians, such as John Zizioulas, Robert Jenson, and Stanley Grenz. The political payoff comes when one sees how human relationships mirror those of the egalitarian trinity: "if in the divine community there is no above and below, superior and inferior, but only the society of equals who are different from one another but live together in mutual respect and self-giving love, so it is also in a truly human society of people who are sexually, racially, socially, politically, and religiously different from one another" (*ABR*, p. 41). Power and unity are not practiced as homogenizing forces, but as the lifestyle of diverse yet equal persons. As Miroslav Volf has put it, "the Trinity is our social program" in this new "Eastern" model.[11]

Unfortunately, for such accounts, historical scholars have shown the way in which the Western tradition of Trinitarian theology (both pre- and post-Reformation) has been misunderstood. Lewis Ayres and others have largely demolished the supposed distinction between "Eastern" and "Western" models of the Trinity: in actuality, Augustine and the Cappadocians made use of both "substance" language and "social" metaphors to describe the divine tri-unity.[12] Not only that, but the claim that the classical doctrine of God was simply cribbed from pagan philosophy and overly concerned with the "inner life" of God has also been challenged. First, classical doctrine (including traditional Reformed theology) drew on philosophical resources to express cogently what was found within the biblical witness. Second, reflections on the "inner life," the relations between the divine persons throughout eternity, are implications of what is revealed within history and not mere speculation. As the persons interact in the biblical narratives (e.g., Father sending Son, Son obeying Father, etc.), these same persons must relate in their own life eternally. Why? Because Reformed theologians believe we really encounter God, and truly so, in these prophetic and apostolic witnesses. The way God acts in the gospel history must be right, so there must be talk of the "inner life" of God to some degree.

Where do we go from here? Perhaps a recovery of Trinitarian theology within the Reformed churches would best be stimulated by looking to the roots of early Reformed Trinitarian thinking. Two sources should be consulted in this regard. First, certain biblical texts fueled development of this doctrine (e.g., Jn 17), so

Reformed pastors and theologians might focus exegetical and homiletical energies on such passages.[13] Second, the first Reformed theologians relied on a rich tradition of Dominican dogmatics as grist for their own doctrinal mill. In our own day, some of the finest reflection on Trinitarian thought comes from Dominican faculties of theology (e.g., Gilles Emery).[14] Reformed theologians would do well to learn from Roman Catholic meditations on biblical and dogmatic issues in this realm. Reformed theology must see its way to being a catholic theology, never taking its Trinitarian basis for granted.

Autotheos

The Reformed tradition has affirmed the decrees of the major ecumenical councils, especially the Nicene-Constantinopolitan Creed (AD 381) and the Definition of Chalcedon (AD 451). As noted above, the Reformed doctrine of God fits within a deep catholic tradition, with roots much deeper than Zwingli and Calvin or, even, Luther. But the Reformers did not simply accept the ecumenical creeds as such; they reformed even as they affirmed the creedal tradition. In fact, John Calvin provided a grid through which the creeds needed to be interpreted. Very briefly, then, we shall consider Calvin's worry about some Nicene terminology as such before viewing his proposed addendum.

Calvin worried about subordinationism, the idea that the Son is actually less divine than the Father. The important Nicene phrase, "God of God, light of light, very God of very God," was matched by the traditional teaching on the "eternal generation" of the Son. While this worry could extend further to the Holy Spirit, Calvin's own concern related primarily to the Son. The idea of generation, of course, implies beginning and, by further implication, prior nonexistence. Calvin is concerned that the divinity of the Son is impugned if one takes the term "begotten" in its ordinary sense and as far as its logical implications could go.

In the face of this danger, however, Calvin never proposed jettisoning these classic phrases. As Douglas Kelly states, "Calvin clarifies the Trinitarian teaching of the Christian tradition, but he does not innovate."[15] Just as he maintains the creedal claims, so he follows Augustine in showing how they are to be understood rightly. He supplements it with a clarifying statement: just as God the Father is *autotheos* (God of Godself), so God the Son is *autotheos*. He manages this by distinguishing between the Son's divinity and the Son's distinct personality as second person of the Trinity: "therefore we say that deity in an absolute sense exists of itself; whence likewise we confess that the Son, since he is God, exists of himself, but not in respect of his Person; indeed, since he is the Son, we say that he exists from the Father. Thus his essence is without beginning; while the beginning of his person is God himself" (*ICR*, I.xiii.25). The Son can be considered as of the one and as of the three: as the one true God, the Son is eternal and *autotheos*; as the second person of the Trinity, the Son is eternally begotten of the Father. To be highlighted here is the adverb "eternally," which clarifies that this personal relation cannot be construed as a development to an already existent yet amorphous divine essence. Rather, threeness and oneness both go all the way back.

Many interpreters have misunderstood Calvin's negotiation of this issue, juxtaposing Reformed Christology against Chalcedonian or even Nicene Christology. Some suggest that a "Reformed Christology" can be contrasted with "Nicene Christology," with the former denying the latter's doctrine of "eternal generation." However, this is less than plausible for a number of reasons. First, Calvin continued affirming the Nicene Creed, which continued to have influence in Genevan church polity. Second, Calvin clearly makes a distinction which would not be necessary unless one maintained the tenet of "eternal generation." This distinction is clear in his writing: "it is clear from our writings that we do not separate the persons from the essence, but we distinguish among them while they remain within it" (*ICR*, I.xiii.25). Thus, the Son is "very God," *autotheos* with all that is involved in divine being; yet the Son is "very God of very God," having personal distinction only by derivation from the Father (*ICR*, I.xiii.4, 5, 29). Third, Robert Bellarmine was a major opponent of Calvin and Reformed theology more broadly, precisely because he was a Roman Catholic theologian of Calvin's era. In spite of the polemical edge to be gained by claiming that Calvin here denied Nicaea, Bellarmine refrained from doing so: "when

I examine the matter and carefully scrutinize Calvin's thoughts I am not so bold to pronounce him to be in error since he teaches the Son to be of himself in respect of essence, not of person, and he is seen to speak well that the person is begotten of the Father, and the essence not begotten."[16] As Calvin's Roman Catholic interlocutor demurred from what would have been a polemically expedient judgment of heresy and rather noted Calvin's continuity with Nicaea, we ought to do likewise. For these reasons, then, we suggest that John Calvin affirmed the Nicene theology of Christ's "eternal generation" from the Father, qualified by this new emphasis on the Son as *autotheos*. Here a Reformed theologian accepts creedal language regarding the Son's relation to the Father, nuanced by the novel claim that the Son's deity is on par with that of his Father.

Humanity of Jesus

One of the most famous claims of the Reformed churches has been *finitum non capax infiniti* ("the finite cannot comprehend the infinite"). Many might take this to be a denigration of the finite and creaturely, specifically, of the human. They see this as a statement of God's disinterest or distance from the world—divine aloofness. However, the Reformed tradition has resolutely maintained this claim for exactly the opposite reason: the human and creaturely and finite order has its own integrity. The creaturely is not infinite and divine, yet it is still worthy of care and respect. In this regard, a second claim makes this apparent: *infiniti capax finitum* ("the infinite can comprehend the finite"). Humans were created for fellowship with God, precisely as someone other than this God.

Controversy between the Reformed and Lutheran churches served as the presenting issue for this claim to be developed. The Lutherans believed that the Eucharist involves the physical presence of the human Jesus in, with, and under the elements of bread and wine; that is, by prayer and the Spirit the embodied Son comes in alongside the elements of communion. Believers really eat Jesus physically, according to the Lutheran view, which has been termed "consubstantiation." The Reformed churches protested this analysis, in as much as it requires belief that Christ's human body can be in multiple places at one time. While not requiring physical omnipresence *per se*, because Jesus only needs to be located in so many Eucharistic elements across the cosmos and not in every nook and cranny of the universe, the Lutheran view does require a belief in multiple local presences. How can the human Jesus manage that? The Lutherans posited the doctrine of ubiquity, wherein the divine nature of Christ shares attributes with the human nature (*communicatio idiomatum*). Thus, in the case of the Eucharist, the divine Son shares the ability to transcend time and space with the human nature of Jesus.

According to Reformed theologians, this whole argument would make the Son something other than a human. As Stephen Edmondson puts it, "for Calvin, this Lutheran notion of an exchange of attributes (*communicatio idiomata*) contradicted a proper doctrine of the distinction of Christ's natures because it threatened the reality of his human nature. Again, a ubiquitous human nature is not human nature at all."[17] Indeed, this interpretation of holy communion is not the only doctrine based on a faulty view of Christ's humanity; Reformed theologians have also been leery of viewing salvation as deification or divinization, precisely because that often tends toward viewing human perfection as becoming something other than human. Whichever resurrected life is in view, be it that of Christ in his presence to his body or that of the risen saints in glory, it must never be considered anything other than human and creaturely. As Karl Barth describes the giving of grace to nature,

> It is the secret of grace that God does this, and the creature experiences it. But it is also the secret of grace that even when he does it he alone is God, that he alone has and retains the divine essence, that the essence of the creature is not affected or altered. By his unconditioned and irresistible lordship he does not subtract anything from the creature or add anything to it, but he allows it to be just what it is in its creaturely essence . . . There is still a genuine encounter, and therefore a genuine meeting, of two beings which are quite different in type and order. (*CD*, III/3, pp. 136–137)

Along with belief that the Son remains human throughout eternity to come, Reformed churches have also insisted that Jesus took on full humanity such that every aspect of human existence characterizes the life of the incarnate Son. The only exception to this claim would be sin (which is not essential to humanity anyway); for Jesus did not succumb to temptations as all other humans do, and his own character was not marred by depravity. Reformed theologians have debated whether or not the one who came "in the likeness of sinful flesh" (Rom. 8.3) assumed a fallen or unfallen human nature; however this question is decided, the tradition has been consistent in affirming that the Messiah did not sin and was not personally responsible for any guilt.[18] His service as a sacrifice and substitutionary mediator depends on his own innocence. Even so, "the owning of the alliance unto us cost him, as it were all he was worth; for being rich, 'for our sakes he became poor'. He came into the prison and into the furnace to own us" (*WJO*, 19, p. 422). Truly he became a "man of sorrows," enduring the trials and troubles of this miserable world.

This misery and alienation assumed by the Son culminates, of course, in that God made "him who knew no sin to be sin for us" (2 Cor. 5.20). The cross and its message of judgment upon evil marks the full measure of pain and wrath experienced by Jesus. Reformed theologians showed a willingness to reconceive a traditional doctrine, even a creedal doctrine, so as to affirm the depths of this abandonment to punishment. Whereas the Apostles' Creed was traditionally interpreted to speak of a "descent into hell" (*descendus ad inferna*) between the death and the resurrection of Jesus, thereby referring to something like a subterranean journey through the underworld, Calvin and other Reformed theologians understood this phrase as describing the humiliation of Jesus' life. To clarify, the traditional interpretation would read the Creed chronologically: first death, then descent, until resurrection. The Reformed approach is to take the descent as a conceptual gloss on the crucifixion and death, witnessing to the spiritual realities behind what might appear to be just another political execution. Karl Barth lengthily engaged this reality in his discussion of "the judge judged in our place," itself an extension of his earlier topic, "the way of the Son of God into the far country" (*CD*, IV/1, §59).[19] Jesus, the Word made flesh, experiences not only shame and death, but that which is bound to the truthful judgment of God upon sin. This is meant to give troubled Christians an abiding assurance, knowing "that in my deepest tribulations I may be assured that Christ my Lord has redeemed me from hellish anxieties and torment by the unspeakable anguish, pains, and terrors which he suffered in his soul both on the cross and before" (HC, 44, in *BC*, p. 65). We will circle back round to this topic when discussing justification in Chapter 4.

Another key aspect of human existence, which must also be ascribed to Jesus, is growth in maturity. Calvin notes that "it seems strange that anything should have been lacking in the perfection of God's Son," who is full of truth and grace (Jn 1.14). Yet, Calvin says, "we may readily answer that if it takes nothing from His glory that He was utterly 'emptied out' (*exinanitus*), then it was not alien for Him to wish, for our sakes, to grow in body and also in spirit."[20] Calvin is representative here of the Reformed tradition as a whole, which affirms incrementalism in the life of the mediator. This is not adoptionism with an incrementalist view of his deity; rather, the eternal Son assumes a humanity which grows. This maturation serves as part of human salvation, as well, for "from the time when he took the form of a servant, he began to pay the price of liberation in order to redeem us" (*ICR*, II.xxvi.5). Jesus, the second Adam, obeys and develops perfectly, whereas the first Adam disobeyed and went awry. Not only the passion and death, but also the life and faithful service of the Son functions as part of his mediation.

Along with the claim that the incarnate Son enjoys full human integrity, Reformed theologians have also been among the first to insist on the fully active humanity of Jesus. For example, Thomas Aquinas serves as a representative example of broader medieval theology and its tendency to affirm that the incarnate Son perpetually enjoyed the "beatific vision" of God's essence from the moment of his conception in Mary's womb. Having that *visio Dei*, Christ knew all things and did not need to exercise faith. Against this relatively static scheme, Reformed theologians have affirmed that the Son exercised faith and fidelity precisely by depending on God the Father and God the Holy Spirit. The Son was truly faithful, even in the midst of misery and pain. He met his sufferings with prayer and fortitude, just as he had endured the wilderness temptations in the power of the Holy Spirit.

If Jesus is dependent as any human is, then Jesus required divine aid to meet the many challenges of life. To account for his perfect obedience as a needy human, Reformed theologians have led the way in speaking of a "Spirit-Christology."[21] Indeed, John Owen emphasized the role of the Spirit in inspiring the humane life of the incarnate Son more than anyone else. As ever-deepening difficulties impinged upon him from all sides, "in new trials and temptations he experimentally learned the new exercise of grace" (*WJO*, vol. 3, p. 170). The divinity of the Son needed no such inspiration, yet the humanity of the Christ was sanctified and empowered by the Holy Spirit to be the "Anointed One" (*Messiah* or *Christos*).

Jesus, the incarnate Son of God, was fully God and fully human. Both natures exist and maintain integrity. George Hunsinger, a contemporary Presbyterian theologian, has spoken of a "Chalcedonian pattern" that characterizes Reformed Christology. First, both natures maintain their own integrity. Second, the natures exist in the greatest intimacy imaginable—personal union. Third, the natures relate asymmetrically, with the divine nature having preceded and now exceeded the bounds of the human nature.[22] How do actions occur in this life? As John Owen says,

> each nature operates in him according unto its essential properties. The divine nature knows all things, upholds all things, rules all things, acts by its presence everywhere; the human nature was born, yielded obedience, died, and rose again. But it is the same person, the same Christ, that acts all these things—the one nature being his no less than the other. (*WJO*, vol. 1, p. 234)

There is no mixture of the natures, even as they really mark the one person known as the incarnate Word. They do not turn on and off, with Jesus sometimes knowing all things, and sometimes lacking awareness. Rather, they both mark this person's life at all points.[23] To be sure, there is asymmetry here: the divine person of the Word preceded the assumption of a human nature; there was an eternal Word who, only at a certain point in time, became flesh (Jn 1.14). Owen is insistent, however, that the lived existence of this person involves full humanity just as well as full divinity; any seemingly supernatural works accomplished humanly flow, then, from the miraculous work of the Spirit (*WJO*, vol. 3, p. 160).

Again, the Reformed view of the two natures is intimately tied to a strong "Spirit-Christology" as well as an emphasis upon the saving worth of not only Jesus' death, but also his life and faith.

While Reformed Christology has emphasized the full humanity of Jesus and the ministry of the Holy Spirit on the Son, these churches have further placed great weight upon the *munus triplex* ("threefold office") of the mediator. Jesus is not only a real human, but he fulfills offices outlined in the Old Testament and prefigured in the very human ministry of particular Israelites. In concluding this chapter, then, we will consider what it means to say that the incarnate Son is prophet, priest, and king.

Prophet, Priest, and King

As part of its emphasis upon the unity of the "covenant of grace," Reformed theology has looked to the Old Testament for categories with which it may interpret the significance of Jesus' life, ministry, death, and resurrection (see esp. *ICR*, II.xv). Noting that Jesus is "the Christ," anointed offices in the Old Testament have been emphasized as particularly illuminating for making sense of what this person came to do.[24] G. C. Berkouwer has noted that the term "office" is used here to signal that one is doing a work for which one has been commissioned by God, that is, not simply of one's own initiation.[25] In the Old Covenant, these three ministries were established by YHWH and enacted by the ceremony of anointing with oil. The Westminster Confession makes a point of saying that Jesus did not take the mediatorial office(s) upon himself, "but was thereunto called by his Father" (WCF, VIII.3, in *BC*, p. 182). By focusing on these similarities with predecessors, we are not reducing Jesus to just another minister or mediator of the covenant; rather, he is seen as the fulfillment and perfection of all ministries, being "God with us" himself. We should not be surprised that Reformed churches look to these offices as categories for understanding the work of Christ, precisely because the threefold office flows forth from the ministries of the Old Covenant.[26] Indeed, the emphasis on the unity of the covenant of grace results in a very Israelite set of concepts for thinking about Jesus. As it always tries to do, Reformed theology allows the covenantal parameters for fellowship found in the Old Testament to prepare one to rightly interpret the Gospels and later New Testament witnesses to what happened in the life of Jesus.

The Messiah is the king of the nations, the one who sits at the right hand of the Father and to whom the nations are but a footstool (Ps. 110.1). The Westminster Larger Catechism offers a much lengthier description of this office than the other two, worth quoting in full:

> **Q. 45. How doth Christ execute the office of a king?**
> A. Christ executeth the office of a king, in calling out of
> the world a people to himself; and giving them officers,
> laws, and censures, by which he visibly governs them; in
> bestowing saving grace upon his elect, rewarding their
> obedience; and correcting them for their sins, preserving
> and supporting them under all their temptations and
> sufferings; restraining and overcoming all their enemies,
> and powerfully ordering all things for his own glory, and
> their good; and also in taking vengeance on the rest,
> who know not God, and obey not the gospel. (WLC, 45,
> in *BC*, p. 255)

The kingly work of the Messiah takes the form of salvation and calling a people to himself. It culminates in the judgment yet to come, when he will reward the faithful and take vengeance upon "the rest, who know not God, and obey not the gospel." The king, then, serves to mediate God's justice in the world and to administer wisely the life of the kingdom. As Handel's "Hallelujah Chorus" affirms, "the kingdoms of this world have become the kingdom of our Lord and of his Christ, and he shall reign forever and ever, King of kings and Lord of lords." The human Messiah reigns as God's intermediary, fulfilling the original blessing of dominion by those created in God's image (Gen. 1.26–30).

The Anointed One is not only king, but also priest of the covenant. Indeed, the Old Covenant witnesses to the need for sacrifice as a result of sin. God's forgiveness seems cheap if it is not satisfied by a worthy offering on the mercy seat; Paul notes this need in his reflection on the atoning work of Christ (Rom. 3.25–26). Jesus is the sacrificial offering brought before the Father, wounded and bruised for the sins of others. The martyr's death of a perfectly innocent human satisfied the demands of justice in ways which all the animal and agricultural offerings of the Old Covenant could not. Reformed churches have been insistent, against the Roman church, that the sacramental work of Jesus Christ is not extended into the ministry of an ongoing earthly priesthood. Ministers merely testify to the finished work of Christ, whose blood was shed "once for all" (*ep hapax*, a recurring phrase in Heb. 7.27; 9.12; 9.26). In the modern era, the notions of sacrifice, wrath and retribution have been criticized as beneath God. God ought to forgive and, in fact, condemn any claim to wrath or violent retribution. Many root this claim in a reading of Jesus as primarily coming to teach and model an ethic of nonviolence. By and large, however, most Reformed Christians continue to speak of Christ as the sacrifice.[27] Christ dies for sin (Rom. 3.25–26). In addition, the priestly ministry of the incarnate Son is teased out in terms of the intercessory prayer that flows forth from the ascended Messiah to his (and our) Father. As the great hymn "Before the Throne of God Above" says, "before the throne of God above I have a strong and perfect plea, a great high priest whose name is love, who ever lives and pleads for me." The Westminster Larger Catechism exemplifies developed Reformed thinking on the matter when it links reconciliation provided by Christ's death with his now "making continual intercession for them" (WLC, 44, in *BC*, p. 255). Jesus was and is the one true sacrifice, and Jesus continues to minister this grace to those for whom he prays.

The Son of God speaks the wisdom of the Lord as the true prophet. Speech from God was promised to Israel in the wilderness: "I will raise up for them a prophet like you from among their own people; I will put my words in the mouth of the prophet, who shall speak to them everything that I command" (Deut. 18.18). On the far side of Jesus' ministry, another reflection is offered: "Long ago God spoke to our ancestors in many and various ways by the prophets, but in these last days he has spoken to us by a Son" (Heb. 1.1–2). The anonymous writer to the Hebrews, of course, speaks of Jesus, who had been identified as a prophet and, yes, more than a prophet by John the Baptist (Mt. 11.9). Like the prophets before him, Jesus lived within a religious milieu and simultaneously critiqued that very context with the word of God. Indeed, Jesus' prophetic message is heightened by the apocalyptic nature of his teaching; while he rarely speaks in this genre, his teaching itself is shown to separate the currently fading age from the age to come. Indeed, his prophetic witness ushers in the kingdom of God or the kingdom of heaven. He has revealed God's "mystery" (1 Cor. 2.7). He is the herald of good news as well as the content of that gospel. "Behold, I make all things new"—only the one who is prophet and the very message himself can claim this.

That he fulfills these ministries was important enough to merit mention in the Heidelberg Catechism:

Q. 31. Why is he called CHRIST, that is, the ANOINTED ONE?

A. Because he is ordained by God the Father and anointed with the Holy Spirit to be *our chief Prophet* and *Teacher*, fully revealing to us the secret purpose and will of God concerning our redemption; to be *our only High Priest*, having redeemed us by the one sacrifice of his body and ever interceding for us with the Father; and to be *our eternal King*, governing us by his Word and Spirit, and defending and sustaining us in the redemption he has won for us. (HC, 31, in *BC*, p. 63)

More recent confessions and theological writings highlight the ways in which ordinary believers also play important roles in the economy of the Old Covenant and that of the New, eschewing any clericalism or authoritarianism which might follow from an emphasis on these offices (see C-67, I.2.B, in *BC*, p.324). There is a worry that speech about Jesus as "king" will enfranchise the aspirations and arrogance of the powers that be, or that confessing Jesus as priest will imply a closer intimacy with those in ordained ministry. Of course, such errors follow from misunderstanding about the singularity and finality of Jesus' work in each of these offices: he is the king over all kings, the priest offering the final sacrifice, and the final Word from the heavens. While there are potentially harmful applications of this doctrine in the social and political spheres, several of the most profitable works on the person and work of Christ being currently written from the Reformed churches continue to focus on the *munus triplex*.[28]

In this chapter, we have considered the way that Reformed theologians witness to the character of the triune God and to the nature of the incarnation. In so doing, we have pointed to logical relations with other doctrinal topics—for example, Eucharistic presence, atonement—so we can expect the doctrines of God and Christ to arise elsewhere as we consider salvation, the life of the church, and the sacraments. More immediately, we should introduce the Reformed approach to Christian salvation by focusing on the work of Jesus in justifying and sanctifying those who are "in Christ."

Chapter 4
Faith and Salvation

Protestant theology, of which Reformed theology is a major tributary, has always been the religion of "faith alone" (*sola fide*). Having considered the way in which Reformed churches reflect on the character of God and the person of the incarnate Son, this doctrinal survey necessarily moves to the work of Christ. Indeed, a great challenge that largely shapes the breadth of any theology is how the human activity of faith relates to Jesus and his life; in Reformational terms, how *sola fide* and *solus Christus* ("Christ alone") are intertwined. This chapter will sketch that link by focusing on four major ideas: faith as the only instrument of salvation, justification based on the life and death of Christ, sanctification, and the danger of over-inflating the work that faith is meant to do in Christian salvation. Before beginning, a few introductory comments should be offered regarding Jesus and salvation in him.

The so-called *historia salutis* ("history of salvation") traces the actual life story of the incarnate Son: conception, birth, ministry, passion, resurrection, ascension, intercession, return in judgment, reign in glory. Reformed theologians have typically agreed with broader catholic thinking about the shape of Christ's life; such issues are not, by and large, divisive along denominational lines. To be sure, within various denominations (including the Reformed churches) there have been those who deny certain tenets of the *historia salutis*. However, the various Christian churches have affirmed these articles of faith as reflected in the Apostles' Creed and Nicene Creed. When some liberal Reformed theologians and churches have denied or revised certain articles—say, the virginal nature of Christ's conception—there has been sharp blowback. As manifest by the earliest ecumenical creeds and the most recent American Presbyterian statement, "A Brief Statement of Faith" (in *BC*, pp. 341–342), the classic narrative of Christ's life is still affirmed by the Reformed churches.

As Calvin insisted, however, the mighty works of Christ do not benefit those who have nothing whatever to do with Jesus Christ (*ICR*, III.i.1, vol. 2, p. 537). Thus, theologians have matched the *historia salutis* with an *ordo salutis* ("order of salvation"), whereby the accomplished work of Christ is applied to particular persons in their own life stories. The order of salvation basically sketches the contours of the Christian life, describing the activities of God for and within the believer and then locating the believer's actions in this theological context. As Reformed churches have sought to organize their faith and practice according to the Word of God, they have seen fit to fashion a fairly distinctive order of salvation. Indeed, the way in which the Christian life unfolds marks a key difference between the Reformed churches and the Roman Catholic Church, from which they emerged in the sixteenth century. G. C. Berkouwer taught that the importance of the *ordo* was its aid in ensuring that we think of all salvation as in Christ.[1] Differences regarding the Gospel and the Christian life circled around two human actions (faith and works) and two divine actions (justification and sanctification). John Murray summarized the Reformed order of salvation: calling, regeneration, faith and repentance, justification, adoption, sanctification, perseverance, and glorification.[2]

In this chapter, the Reformed approach to faith and justification will be considered in some depth, and a broader perspective on the whole Reformed order of salvation will be sketched in brief.

In thinking about this order of salvation, the Christian life must be construed in such a way that "Christ alone" (*solus Christus*) saves. As the First Helvetic Confession affirms, "in all evangelical teaching the most sublime and the principal article and the one which should be expressly set forth in every sermon and impressed upon the hearts of men should be that we are preserved and saved solely by the one mercy of God and by the merit of Christ" (First Helvetic Confession [FHC], XI, in *RCSC*, p. 104). The lived experience of the believer must be viewed "in Christ" and as part of his company, so that the ebbs and flows of everyday life do not gain too great a purchase on one's ultimate worth. This sixteenth-century confession is simply trying to expand conceptually on the Apostle Paul's statement, "I have been crucified with Christ; and it is no longer I who live, but it is Christ who lives in me. And the life I now live in the flesh I live by faith in the Son of God, who loved me and gave himself for me" (Gal. 2.19–20).[3]

Sola Fide

The Protestant movement gathered around God's Word, focusing on five key tenets known as the "five *solas*": *sola Scriptura, solus Christus, sola fide, sola gratia,* and *soli Deo Gloria.* Each focuses on an aspect, not a part, of the Christian life and, in doing so, distinguishes the Protestant approach from the mainstream Roman Catholic style. With regard to *sola fide*, a contrast is being made with Rome's doctrine that faith must be formed by love (*fides formata*). The Reformed and Lutheran churches said that Rome essentially required faith and works for justification. Martin Luther famously opposed this compound view of the Christian life after his discovery of Rom. 1.17—"the righteous-ness of God is revealed through faith for faith; as it is written, 'The one who is righteous will live by faith'". Here Luther found a promise that God's righteousness is not the divine inclination to curse those who fall short, but rather provides life for those who believe. Luther's protest was matched by the teaching and preaching of Zwingli, Bullinger, Bucer, and Calvin, each affirming that justification was by faith alone.

What is faith? "By this faith, a Christian believeth to be true whatsoever is revealed in the Word, for the authority of God Himself speaking therein; and acteth differently upon that which each particular passage thereof containeth; yielding obedience to the commands, trembling at the threatenings, and embracing the promises of God for this life, and that which is to come. But the principal acts of saving faith are accepting, receiving, and resting upon Christ alone for justification, sanctification, and eternal life, by virtue of the covenant of grace" (WCF, XVI.2, in *BC*, p. 189). Reformed theologians have insisted on following biblical definition: faith is "the assurance of things hoped for, the conviction of things not seen" (Heb. 11.1). The key, of course, is to see faith as radical trust in the hope that is not yet fully manifest or, put otherwise, that is still but a promise from God. Faith involves the intellect, for one must know and apprehend the promise, that it is good and befitting hope. Faith also incorporates the emotions, which delight and savor in that which is not yet seen. Faith is the full-throated confession that one's life is grounded on God's promise.

How does faith differ from works? This is a crucial question, for if faith alone matters greatly, then distinguishing between faith and other human actions is a necessity. As the Westminster Standards say, the Reformed tradition has spoken of faith as "accepting, receiving, and resting." Faith is not only knowledge of God's works for you, but also joyous and confident trust that they have been effective on your behalf. In all these ways, faith points away from the self toward the divine benefactor who, in Christ Jesus and through the testimony of the Holy Spirit, meets all one's needs. By contrast, works are any attempts by humans to define their own existence and character, to meet their own needs, to point toward themselves as sovereign of their identity. Good things may become "works," then, if they are done for the wrong, self-interested purposes of one who wishes to make one's own way, quite apart from God's guidance and gifts. Indeed, many religious activities (commanded by God and rightly practiced by humans) can become the occasion for works, provided one does them in an attempt to shore up or enhance one's own persona. This is most evident in the apostle Paul's worry that even observance of the God-given law from Sinai may become a "work." While it is the height of piety, it simply cannot be used as a means to appear righteous before God.

The exegetical basis for *sola fide* is, by and large, found in Pauline texts. Especially in the letters to the churches at Rome and Galatia, Paul contrasts faith with works (or "works of the law"). There is a presenting issue in these texts, usually the dilemma of what should be required of Gentile converts for participation in the church of the risen Jewish Messiah. Following the Jerusalem Council (Acts 15.23–29), the apostle Paul emphasizes that Gentiles may remain Gentile in their practice. They do not need to be circumcised, to follow dietary laws, or to follow the entirety of the Jewish *torah*. This reversal of Old Covenant teaching flows from Paul's doctrine of justification by faith alone.[4] Because Jesus saves those who believe, human distinction in the form of moral heroism or (as here) Jewish ethnic identity and religious praxis is simply not essential. Now one can be saved by faith, not by such "works of the law." In Gal. 2, Paul recounts his rebuke of the apostle Peter for failing to act "in line with the truth of the gospel" (Gal. 2.14). Peter, or Cephas, did this by refraining from sharing food with Gentile Christians, separating himself from them because they were not circumcised. Paul is very clear that "a person is not justified by observing the law" (exemplified by becoming and being a *torah*-practicing Jew) "but by faith in Jesus Christ" (Gal. 2.16).

Why does *sola fide* matter? That holiness is by faith alone demonstrates that human identity is not made (by works) but given (received by faith). Faith merely indicates, points to its object. Thus, faith is not an immanent religious phenomenon with its own substance or value. Rather, faith testifies to human definition from without—and, therefore, to God's gracious gift of human being and activity.[5]

In the contemporary context, many have suggested that faith alone justifies because God desires an universal body of believers. Thus, justification by faith alone is a radical teaching, in as much as it defangs a formerly potent Jewish ethnocentrism. These forms of a so-called new perspective on Paul have gained much ground in scholarly circles as well as in some quarters of the Reformed churches. Indeed, this vision is partially correct, accurate enough to be compelling. Justification by faith alone is almost always connected to Jew-Gentile relations in Paul's letters; this need for ethnic inclusivity in the church is a key component of New Testament teaching and exhortation. Yet such perspectives too often fail to see that the banner of Jewish identity represents one potent example of a deeper human problem: the tendency to restrict justification to those who meet some human qualification. The qualification may be moral (good), ethnic (Jewish), gendered (male), economic (poor), and so on. In any case, the Galatian Judaizers believed that faith alone was not enough, but that such faith had to be matched with *torah* observance for one to be saved. In so doing, they exemplified the standard hubris of humans, thinking that something in them is part of the reason that God loves them. In fact, they were the best of all possible human attempts to do this, because their addendum to faith had itself once been demanded by God. Yet even law-observance fails to stand upright before the Lord. As noted above, however, faith points entirely away from itself. Thus, it is absurd to speak of faith and anything else as saving together.

Justification

What then does it mean to be "justified" in biblical and theological terminology? Principally, it means to be in the right with regard to some standard or rule. This basic definition fits the variety of ways in which the Bible and Christian tradition have employed this language. For example, someone may be justified in a legal proceeding, having proven their innocence and, indeed, uprightness. Quite differently, someone may be justified in relation to God their Creator on account of what they have received from the saving work of Jesus. Are these uses so very different? Well, they both fit the basic definition (uprightness and conformity to a rule or standard), though the context of each affects the nature of the norms, the party to which they relate, etc. Most frequently in the Bible, God is the judge to whom human creatures owe sole allegiance and, when they render this, receive justification by declaration of this judge. Given this biblical emphasis on divine-human relations with regard to the terms "just," "justified," and "justification," the theological doctrine of justification is affixed to this heavenly courtroom, where conformity to the divine law is measured.[6]

Reformed theologians, along with their Lutheran counterparts, considered justification to be a pivotal article of the faith. Whereas it was within the Lutheran tradition that one spoke of this as "the article upon which the church stands or falls," John Calvin did not refrain from calling this "the hinge on which swings true religion" (*ICR*, III.xi.1). Whatever metaphor is employed to depict its conceptual and spiritual centrality, the Reformational churches were at one in emphasizing its importance. James Buchanan surveyed the Protestant teaching of the first and second generations of the Reformation, arguing that there was an incredibly deep consensus.[7] Only in recent decades has a considerable challenge arisen to this primacy, largely for reasons of pursuing theological and social unity with Roman Catholics.

In assessing this we do well to offer a confessional synopsis of the Reformed doctrine of justification, looking to the Westminster Standards:

> Christ, by his obedience and death, did fully discharge the debt of all those that are thus justified, and did make a proper, real, and full satisfaction to his Father's justice in their behalf. Yet, inasmuch as he was given by the Father for them; and his obedience and satisfaction accepted in their stead; and both, freely, not for anything in them; their justification is only of free grace; that both the exact justice and rich grace of God might be glorified in the justification of sinners. (WCF, 13.3, in *BC*, pp. 187–188)

As the Belgic Confession noted in 1561, Christ alone is just or righteous. All others who long to live with God and to be declared righteous must find their own righteousness wholly in Jesus, so that

> those who possess Jesus Christ through faith have complete salvation in Him. Therefore, for any to assert that Christ is not sufficient, but that something more is required besides Him, would be too gross a blasphemy; for hence it would follow that Christ was but half a Saviour. Therefore we justly say with Paul, *that we are justified by faith alone*, or *by faith without works*. (BC, XII, in *RCSC*, p. 204)

Again, justification is *solus Christus*. "You are in Christ Jesus, who has become for us wisdom from God—that is, our righteousness, holiness, and redemption" (1 Cor. 1.30).

When one is declared righteous or just, two things have occurred according to the teachings of the Reformed faith (represented here by the Heidelberg Catechism):

Q. 60. How are you righteous before God?
A. Only by true faith in Jesus Christ. In spite of the fact that my conscience accuses me that I have grievously sinned against all the commandments of God, and have not

kept any one of them, and that I am still ever prone to all that is evil, nevertheless, God, without any merit of my own, out of pure grace, grants me the benefits of the perfect expiation of Christ, imputing to me his righteousness and holiness as if I had never committed a single sin or had ever been sinful, having fulfilled myself all the obedience which Christ has carried out for me, if only I accept such favor with a trusting heart. (HC, 60, in *BC*, pp. 67–68)

First, one is forgiven because of the "perfect expiation of Christ," whereby one's sins have been transferred and dealt with in his passion. Second, one is considered righteous owing to his "imputing to me his righteousness and holiness." Seen in Christ, it is as though "I had never committed a single sin or had ever been sinful" and as if I had "fulfilled myself all the obedience which Christ has carried out for me." Taken together, the Reformed doctrine of justification includes a twofold imputation. Traditionally, these two aspects were tied explicitly to the components of the covenant of works, whereby restraint from sin is mandated, to be sure, but so is perfect obedience. Thus, removal of sin is not enough to be made right with God; one must also possess perfect obedience or righteousness before God's law.[8] Christ fulfills both needs for those within the covenant of grace. In his death, Christ really died and bore our curse (Gal. 3.10–12). Earlier in his life, Christ obeyed in our place.

Why does God go to such lengths? Why not simply forgive and be done with it? According to the Westminster divines, "both the exact justice and rich grace of God might be glorified in the justification of sinners" (WCF, 13.3, in *BC*, pp. 187–188). God is not like an auctioneer willing to take the highest bid of human loyalty available, even if less than perfect. Rather, God is holy and perfect; similarly, God's law is perfect, demanding complete and absolute submission. As God does not change like the shadows, God's justice will not bend for the sake of God's mercy. Yet this does not set justice and mercy against each other, like two battling compulsions tugging at the ear of the Lord. God's mercy works through and in concert with God's justice. Rom. 3 highlights this compatibility, when it reflects on a theological problem. In the Old Covenant era, God forgave sinners who faithfully brought animal sacrifices to him. But animal sacrifice does not really atone for human sin against God, so God appears to be less than an honest broker here. Do animals really right the way of humans? In the Pentateuch, in fact, God is the only one not really getting rightful restitution for mistreatment; yet YHWH was always forgiving the people of God. With this concern in mind, Paul says: "God put forward a sacrifice of atonement . . . He did this to show his righteousness, because in his divine forebearance he has passed over the sins previously committed; it was to prove at the present time that he himself is righteous and that he justifies" (Rom. 3.25–26). Justification proves that God is righteous, not straying from his own standards, even while vindicating his creatures.

Another question arises: what is imputation? To impute means to credit something. The importance of imputation is to clarify the way in which one is in "union with Christ." In union with Christ, his righteousness becomes ours, even as our sin and misery became his. However, Reformed and Lutheran theologians realized that this could easily be understood in an existential direction, whereby one actually moves beyond personal sin and into lived perfection. The danger was an introspective psychologizing of what was really an extrinsic reality. Though one continues to sin at times, one is really righteous in Christ. If this seems unbelievable, one should compare it to its counterpart: just as Christ seemed to be perfect, he was really laden with our sin and misery. Imputation, a term rooted in legal conceptuality, preserves the extrinsic and judicial nature of our union with Christ and all his benefits.

The Reformed tradition spoke of the twofold nature of Christ's obedience as footing the bill, to put it crassly, for the double aspect of justification. Calvin led the way in viewing obedience as a comprehensive category: "Now someone asks, How has Christ abolished sin, banished the separation between us and God, and acquired righteousness to render God favorable and kindly disposed toward us? To this we can in general reply that he has achieved this for us by the whole course of his obedience" (ICR, II.xvi.5). The "whole course of his obedience," that is, the lifelong submission of the Son to the Father's will, fulfills the covenantal demands of the Messiah: suffering and dying for sin and living righteously for acceptance. Later scholastic theology observed a distinction, then, between the "active obedience" of Jesus and his "passive obedience." While one could not divide his life story moment by moment between activity and passivity (a common misunderstanding of the distinction), there was a need to note that Jesus suffered for our sin and acted for our righteousness. The "whole course of his obedience" managed both.[9] Every aspect of the justification of the ungodly is provided for by the one truly human Son: *solus Christus*. As the modern hymn "In Christ Alone" states, "In Christ alone my hope is found, he is my light, my strength, my song."

Sanctification

Karl Barth entered the academy by studying frantically the classical texts of the Reformation, especially of the Reformed churches, in preparation to give lectures for which he felt grossly unprepared. In his preparation, and as evident in his famed lectures, he discovered a marked difference between the Lutheran and Reformed wings of the Protestant movement. The Reformed churches were not satisfied to speak of the vertical relationship of the human being to God, but pressed on to speak of ethical relations, horizontal issues which flow from that vertical encounter. Such horizontal relations were dealt with under the banner of sanctification, the teaching that salvation in Christ involves one's being made holy. While sanctification involves one's renewed love for God, it also includes one's right relations with other creatures.

Barth was certainly not the first to note this emphasis. Before him, Max Weber could speak of a "Protestant work ethic," by which he really meant a Reformed work ethic. Barth and Weber represent a common tendency to see a sharp affinity for gradual transformation of the self and society by the gospel.[10] In other words, the Reformed churches speak not only of the justification of the ungodly, but also of the sanctification of those made godly. There are such things as "good works," and Christians are transformed such that they perform them. More recently, H. Richard Niebuhr hinted at the Reformed approach to culture being transformative, rather than dismissive, paradoxical, etc.[11] Throughout the centuries, Reformed churches have insisted upon the life-giving work of the gospel for real human life.

Of course, sanctification is "in Christ Jesus" (1 Cor. 1.30). The Reformed churches are no more intending to attribute sanctification to innate human ability or to human works, than they are to consider justification a triumph of anthropological exercise. The Scots Confession emphasizes this, "to put this even more plainly: as we willingly disclaim any honor or glory for our own creation and redemption, so do we willingly also for our regeneration and sanctification; for by ourselves we are not capable of thinking one good thought, but he who has begun the work in us alone continues us in it, to the praise and glory of his undeserved grace" (SC, 12, in *BC*, p. 38). In reality, sanctification is living out what one already has become in Christ. J. I. Packer, an influential Reformed Anglican theologian, puts it this way in his classic book *Knowing God*: sanctification is "simply a consistent living out of our filial relationship with God, into which the gospel brings us. It is just a matter of the child of God being true to type, true to his Father, to his Saviour, and to himself. It is the expressing of one's adoption in one's life. It is a matter of being a good son, as distinct from a prodigal or black sheep in the royal family."[12]

Sanctification is also by faith, then, as it flows from the Christian's dependence upon the promise and the work of the triune God. John Webster says that "evangelical freedom"—that is, freedom according to the gospel—"comes from not being finally responsible for my own being." When this happens, "I am so bound to God's grace and God's call that I am liberated from all other bonds and set free to live in the truth."[13] Justification actually fuels sanctification, for the knowledge that one is redeemed fully in Christ allows one the liberty to turn attention to meeting the needs of others. Rom. 6.6–7 makes this link clear, in as much as it says that "we know that our old self was crucified with him in order that the body of sin might be brought to nothing, so that we would no longer be enslaved to sin. For one who has died has been justified from sin" (my translation). Many find the phrase "justified from sin" to be strange, translating it as "set free from sin" instead. That translation, then, suggests to some that the Roman Catholic doctrine of justification is right, in as much as the Greek term for "justify" (*dikaioō*) can speak of transformation, as well as judicial declaration. However, all of this is unnecessary. The text does speak of freedom from enslavement to sin (v. 6); yet the odd phrase "justified from sin" does not merely repeat this claim, but offers an explanation. Note the introduction to v. 7 with the word "for," suggesting that being "justified from sin" explains why one is now free from captivity to sin. When we consider that the Evil One is most frequently called "the accuser," we see that our being justified in Christ Jesus should free us from the debilitating accusations of sin and allow us room to live righteously. Thus, knowledge of justification grounds our sanctification.

The chief way in which the Reformed confessions and catechisms speak of "good works" is by way of gratitude and expressing thankfulness to God for divine grace.

Q. 86. Since we are redeemed from our sin and its wretched consequences by grace through Christ without any merit of our own, why must we do good works?

A. Because just as Christ has redeemed us with his blood he also renews us through his Holy Spirit according to his own image, so that with our whole life we may show ourselves grateful to God for his goodness and that he may be glorified through us; and further, so that we ourselves may be assured of our faith by its fruits and by our reverent behavior may win our neighbors to Christ. (HC, 86, in *BC*, p. 73)

Sancification, or "good works," flow from the Christian as a witness to their gratitude for God's goodness. While warnings and prohibitions as well as the promise of rewards also spark human energies for obeying God's law, delight in the goodness of God's grace sustains "good works" more than anything else.

Still, sanctification remains a work in progress until the moment the believer is finally perfected at the last day, that is, the resurrection of the body and the glorification of the saints. Until then, faithfulness and "good works" come in fits and starts, imperfect yet persevering. This is taught in the confessions, where one reads that "even the holiest of them make only a small beginning in obedience in this life. Nevertheless, they begin with serious purpose to conform not only to some, but to all the commandments of God" (HC, 114, in *BC*, p. 78). Even Christians groan with the rest of creation in this age, awaiting the full redemption of the heavens and earth (Rom. 8.23–25). Many Reformed theologians, along with other believers, have found the teaching of Rom. 7 to testify to the continuing inroads of sin in the life of believers. Today, however, many question this interpretation as failing to account for both broad and narrow textual hints, reading it as speaking of (1) Paul's pre-Christian days, or (2) the unbelieving people of Israel personified. Irrespective of such debates about this one text, the idea that even those "in Christ" continue to falter in their obedience is a hallmark of Reformation theology. Indeed, our works, even those aided by the Spirit, are "filthy as rags" (Isa. 64.6).

Assurance of salvation has been a concern of the Reformed ministry, beginning with the presenting issues involved in the break from the Roman Catholic Church. Puritan pastor-theologian Thomas Manton emphasized that this was owing to varying gifts of freedom from the Spirit, that some grasp and savor their salvation more than others.[14] On the other hand, Calvin goes so far as to define faith as assurance (see, for example, *ICR*, III.ii.14). Some interpreters (notably R. T. Kendall) have suggested that although Calvin thought assurance was based wholly on looking to Christ, later Reformed thinkers also based assurance on one's own sanctification. The "practical syllogism" teaches that one can be assured of one's salvation inasmuch as one not only believes in Christ but also discerns transformation of one's moral character (sanctification). Kendall here opts for Calvin's supposedly "christo-centric" view of assurance over the Puritan and Westminsterian approach, with its emphasis on the *syllogismus practicus* ("practical syllogism"). In so doing, Kendall follows Karl Barth, who thought the "practical syllogism" and the Puritan emphasis on the application of redemption to the individual threatened "to make Reformed theology into anthropology."[15] Suffice it to say that Kendall clearly misreads Calvin, for the Genevan Reformer was sober-minded in his analysis of assurance. He did not equate faith with a steady psychological grasp of assurance, even though he did believe assurance belonged to biblical faith. Even in his *Institutes*, he manifested a realistic and pastorally sensitive approach to the ebbs and flows of Christian faith and doubt (see, for example, *ICR*, III.ii.18, 21).

The Reformed tradition actually shows consistency here, contrary to the claims of Kendall and a host of other skeptics regarding Reformed orthodoxy.[16] The Reformers and their successors rooted assurance in Christ's work, witnessed to by what they called a "reflex act" of self-investigation. In reality, this is an argument from the lesser to the greater. By noting their own growth in hatred for sin and love for God, they infer that Christ has indeed justified them and freed them from bondage to the power of sin. The "practical syllogism" does not mean one is saved by one's works, even though "good works" point to the fact that one has been saved in Christ.[17]

What of non-Christians and the possibility of "good works?" The Westminster Confession puts it bluntly:

> Works done by unregenerate men, although for the matter of them they may be things which God commands; and of good use both to themselves and others: yet, because they proceed not from an heart purified by faith; nor are done in a right manner, according to the Word; nor to a right end, the glory of God, they are therefore sinful, and cannot please God, or make a man meet to receive grace from God: and yet, their neglect of them is more sinful and displeasing unto God. (WCF, 18.7, in *BC*, p. 191)

Works done by the unregenerate, non-Christians, "cannot please God, or make a man meet to receive grace from God." The reason for this restriction is that motives matter, specifically, theocentric motives matter. Works not only may, but even must be done in faithful gratitude to God. As the Epistle to the Hebrews states, "without faith it is impossible to please God, for whoever would approach him must believe that he exists and that he rewards those who seek him" (11.6; see also Rom. 14.23). Lacking Christian faith, nonbelievers cannot manifest the sanctifying work of Christ Jesus and his Spirit.[18]

Faith and Religious Experience

Finally, the so-called great awakenings of the seventeenth and eighteenth centuries were the triumph of religion by and for common folk. No longer held hostage by religious authorities or tied solely to the cloisters and cathedrals of the church, services were now held out in the open air and led by itinerants. John Wesley's claim for the whole world as his parish represented the fluid nature of these "Methodist" and revivalist movements. Authority, hierarchy, and tradition were *passé* and oppressive, what with so many unreached peoples yet to receive the good news. As the establishment proved inadequate for gaining and sustaining a feverish and faithful piety, "new measures" were sought to stoke the fires, though eventually they would leave districts simply "burned-over" in England and America.

Historically, we must note that the First Great Awakening (1730–1755) and the Second Great Awakening (1790–1840) are distinct, though not totally unrelated, phenomena. The movement beyond the bounds of churchly piety heralded by Wesley, George Whitefield, Jonathan Edwards, and others opened the door for the more problematic practices and beliefs of Charles Finney and others.[19] For example, Edwards offered lengthy treatises that assessed and critiqued emotional fanaticism (most famously his *Religious Affections*). But he did encourage an emphasis upon introspection in piety, taking "experiential Calvinism" from the Puritans and putting it into a more modern format. When adopted by lesser minds and by those with less devotion to the classical tradition, the revivalism of Edwards and his ministerial colleagues moved in a more radical, "revivalistic" direction. It is of this "revivalistic" tendency, really found in the Second Great Awakening, of which I am now speaking. Further, we should note that though this revivalistic development was largely occurring in America, the location of the Second Great Awakening, the United States has exported this style of religion throughout the world in more recent decades.

Chief among these "new measures" was itinerant preaching in evangelistic crusades. In such gatherings, either in open air or later in large tents, a traveling preacher offered a lengthy and passionate exhortation for those wallowing in sin and dissatisfaction to come to Christ. Indeed, they were literally to come to the front, where they could sit in the "anxious bench." A famed method of Charles Finney, the most influential nineteenth-century evangelist, the "anxious bench" offered a time for considering one's sins in a heightened atmosphere of intense pressure and fervent intimidation.

The "invitation" following an evangelistic sermon became a staple of revivalist services. Though such practices are more frequently identified these days with Baptist, nondenominational, or charismatic churches, we must remember that Charles Finney worked within the Reformed orbit.

One marked result of revivalism has been the equation of faith and certain forms of religious experience as psychologically apparent to the individual. Many would follow Finney in asserting that such experience can be naturally guaranteed by the proper use of means, though most would refrain from such blatant Pelagianism. Quite apart from the theological details, all revivalists emphasize the role of emotions and activism as ends in themselves (distinct from doctrinal parameters). Indeed, Finney wrote a systematic theology largely based on lessons learned in his revivalist work, what Herman Bavinck and others would call a "psychological perspective" on the Christian faith. The rise of the "history of religions" approach to theological studies simply took this further intellectually; Adolf von Harnack and others interpreted Christian teaching as the experience of one human religious community, that is, phenomenologically. To grasp the shift between a theology of revelation by the intrusive grace of God and a study of human religious experience, the correspondence between Harnack and Karl Barth proves illuminating and indicative.[20] Not only were they battling over two different religions, they were debating the merits of *religion* itself.

Darryl G. Hart distinguishes between the confessional Reformed and the revivalist Reformed in his jeremiad *The Lost Soul of American Protestantism*.[21] He is merely the latest in a long line of "Old Side" or "Old School" Reformed thinkers standing in opposition to the "New Side" or "New School" progressives.[22] What the theologians of Princeton Seminary in the nineteenth century (especially its chief exponent Charles Hodge) and Hart today realize is that revivalism is a thoroughly pragmatist movement. Following cultural critics like Louis Menand and Cornel West, we could say that pragmatism is the only authentically American philosophy. Of course, in emphasizing the importance of the right means and methods one can quickly lose focus of the goal and the framework; technique can easily replace *telos*. American and Western European Reformed churches have struggled with the tendency to minimize the importance of church doctrine for pragmatic reasons, to draw in new converts more easily or to partner with other denominational bodies in social action. Certain methods, be they ecumenical partnership or seeker-sensitive services, overwhelm any distinctive church identity derived from dogma and theology.

Revivalism has fared well with recent turns in linguistic philosophy, especially those identified with postmodernism. By definition, revivalist methods minimize the extent and importance of truth-claims, focusing instead on particular practices meant to heighten and shape one's emotional experience. Religious practice is simply another example of sociological activities, capable of description in the same terms as numerous other cultural events. Indeed, my wife recently commented that a rock concert we attended was eerily like an evangelical gathering for worship: the same outstretched arms in the crowd, similar repetition of choruses up to a final crescendo, the standard emulation of an iconic figure up front. And, of course, evangelical or revivalist Reformed churches are not the only ones who pattern themselves after secular counterparts; many more liberal churches and theologians sound like baptized spokespersons for certain varieties of social activism. Politics, rather than personal piety, dwarfs any distinctive doctrinal identity. Of course, there are examples of both pietists and progressives who manage to employ such emphases without reducing Reformed distinctives; nevertheless, we must honestly note that they are the exception.[23]

In this regard, both evangelicals and progressives have integrated revivalist-emotive concerns with more traditional Reformed thinking. Feeling and experience have become major guiding principles as well as sources of knowledge, and at times occasions for self-delusion or authoritarian manipulation. Self-manipulation becomes possible in as much as the *ordo salutis* is identified directly with psychological experience. No thinker has been more acute in his analysis of revivalism and subjectivism than that great dogmatic theologian from the Netherlands, Herman Bavinck. Indeed, one might say that his deep roots within the Dutch and broader European traditions of Reformed doctrinal writing helped him be particularly sensitive to an entirely different religious ethos. Bavinck surveys Schleiermacher, Methodism and its effects on other (yes, even Reformed) church traditions, and the rise of thoroughgoing subjectivism in both pietistic and political forms. According to Bavinck, psychologizing the faith harms the doctrine of salvation (taking the focus away from the sole sufficiency of Christ's work for us; see *RD*, vol. 3, pp. 538–540) as well as the entire method of theology more broadly (turning one's gaze from the Spirit's speech through Scripture to more tangential or even twisted revelations; see, for example, *RD*, vol. 1, p. 594). Psychologizing narrows one's gaze inward, away from Christ even if (at best) looking for some of the blessings given by him.[24]

How might confessional Reformed thought respond to revivalism? Surely, the emotive and affective dimensions of faith and salvation cannot be ignored, though they cannot be simply adopted according to a particular cultural form (e.g., raised hands somehow always signaling true devotion). Bavinck is quite clear that knowledge comes subjectively from without and is, by faith, internalized and treasured; affection is not a vice (see, for example *RD*, vol. 1, p. 566). The Spirit is given to bring this life to us, within us, precisely by guiding us deeper into the inspired truths of the biblical testimony which we believe and cherish. Theological work proceeds in prayer, then, and seeks to be sustained by an increase in grace from the Son's advocacy. Faith comes in varying degrees and forms, as even the Westminster Confession affirms: "This faith is different in degrees, weak or strong; may be often and many ways assailed, and weakened, but gets the victory: growing up in many to the attainment of a full assurance, through Christ, who is both the author and finisher of our faith" (WCF, XVI.3, in *BC*, p. 189).

In this regard, we see how Friedrich Schleiermacher stands outside the Reformed movement doctrinally, even though he served as a Reformed pastor. Schleiermacher, certainly the most famous theologian of the nineteenth century and the so-called father of modern theology and of "liberal theology," denied the doctrine of *solus Christus* as he overemphasized the function of faith. Consider what he says of Christ:

[I]f we are to express ourselves with any accuracy we cannot say, either, that Christ fulfilled the divine will *in our place* or *for our advantage*. That is to say, He cannot have

done so *in our place* in the sense that we are thereby relieved
from the necessity of fulfilling it. No Christian mind could
possibly desire this, nor has sound doctrine ever asserted it.
Indeed, Christ's highest achievement consists in this,
that He so animates us that we ourselves are led to an
ever more perfect fulfillment of the divine will ... Neither
can He have fulfilled the divine will in any way *for our
advantage*, as if by the obedience of Christ, considered in
and for itself, anything were achieved for us or changed in
relation to us.[25]

For Schleiermacher, salvation involves the imitation of Christ's
own God-consciousness, his favorite term for what might be
called faith or openness to God. Indeed, the works of Jesus as
suffering Messiah and Risen Lord have little bearing on human
salvation.[26] As the great problem of humanity is not sin, but
"Godlessness" understood as "God-forgetfulness," Jesus meets this
need by showing what life fully attuned to God looks like.[27] In
Schleiermacher's view, the deep issue is a wrongly ordered psyche
or mindset; there is no deeper ontological or covenantal issue
related to lawbreaking and disobedience before a holy God.

Ironically, perhaps, liberal and revivalist notions of Christian
salvation are quite similar. They certainly appear different, in as
much as liberal-revisionist approaches tend to line up the Christian
life with rather progressive social ideals while revivalist theology
often comes hand in hand with fundamentalist or legalist mores.
In reality, however, both are revisionary and progressive in form,
differing mainly in application. Furthermore, both assume that
human faith is the main act in Christian salvation. Religious
experience—be it God-consciousness, social activism, or pietist
conversion under the big top—is the defining human act and
itself perfects the creature. Jesus Christ largely, if not entirely,
functions to exemplify this morality. The death of Jesus may serve
to atone or pay for any failings in the believer's devotion (especially prior to conversion); however, there is no positive account
of what Christ brings. Specifically, the idea of imputing Christ's
righteousness to the believer is denied and replaced with an
affirmation of the worth of the believer's own imperfect, yet persevering faithfulness. In this regard, *sola fide* wrongly understood

may displace or eclipse *solus Christus* by forcing faith into fulfilling functions it was never meant to.

Ultimately, however, religious experience and the intensity of faith are not the chief concern of the Reformed tradition. The Heidelberg Catechism clarifies:

Q. 61. Why do you say that you are righteous by faith alone?

A. Not because I please God by virtue of the worthiness of my faith, but because the satisfaction, righteousness, and holiness of Christ alone are my righteousness before God, and because I can accept it and make it mine in no other way than by faith alone. (HC, 61, in *BC*, p. 68)

The "worthiness of my faith" is not the ground of confidence or assurance, nor is it the basis for salvation. Rather, the singular work of Jesus the Christ saves his brothers and sisters, the children of the covenant of grace. Justification is by faith alone, precisely because faith points away from the recipient of justification. In other words, justification is by faith alone, precisely because faith alone honors the deeper fact that justification is by Christ alone. In the words of Buchanan, "we are justified by faith, and faith is counted, or imputed to us, for righteousness; but faith is not itself the righteousness on account of which we are justified."[28] This is why various prepositional phrases relate justification to faith in the New Testament: "of faith," "to faith," "by faith," "through faith"; not, however, "on account of faith." Faith is the instrument and so necessary, to be sure, but not in and of itself sufficient to save; only Christ, the object of faith, suffices.

Having considered the person and work of Jesus, we must now turn to consider the human creature, who is justified by this savior. While we do not have space to sketch a Reformed approach to anthropology (the doctrine of humanity) broadly, we must examine at least the topics of sin and grace. In so doing, we will draw near to the famed "five points of Calvinism," showing the way in which the elect are enabled to respond rightly to the God of love. We will consider how Reformed theologians have under-stood sinful humans to be made fit and willing for the life of faith according to that other Reformational cry, *sola gratia*.

Chapter 5

Sin and Grace

How is it that humans can enjoy fellowship with God this side of Eden? Note that this is not a question of how they *may* do so, for we have already seen that God's delight is in such restoration and fellowship, doing far more than merely permitting such communion. No, we must ask: how humans are capable of such communion given that they have been cast away from the tree of life, the very sign of God's presence? In answering this question, we engage the doctrines of sin and grace.

This chapter engages what has been the most notable feature of Reformed theology, its doctrine of predestination. Made famous by the "TULIP" acronym, many even identify "Reformed" or "Calvinist" theology with anyone who holds to a predestinarian doctrine. As noted in the Introduction, we are taking a wider view of what is involved in being Reformed, yet we must confess the predestining work of God in Christ if we are to follow in the footsteps of the Reformed tradition. We must also view this salvific work of God in eternity as related to the problem of human sin, thereby prefacing our comments on predestination with reflection on the doctrine of "original sin."

Sin

The Reformed churches have consistently affirmed the doctrine of original sin, that is, that each and every human is tainted with sin from the very inception of their life. While often referred to as "total depravity," the Reformed perspective on sin is not as negative as possible. Indeed, humans do not sin totally or as much as they might. Thanks to God's "common grace" or restraint of even pagans from sin, no one sins at every point in the worst way possible. Even the war criminal might have slaughtered one more innocent or bludgeoned one more subordinate. God really does restrain human evil, gracing us with a more tolerable planet and human society. We call this "common grace" because it is shared with all inhabitants of this earth ("common") and is yet an undeserved gift ("grace"). Even so, Reformed Christians do confess that all humans are radically and extensively depraved. That is, sin has corrupted every nook and cranny of human existence. Every square inch of the earth has been thrown off balance by the intrusive deviation we call sin. Common grace is only necessary because sin has so permeated human life and thwarted the divine design for fellowship.

Different theories have been proposed for exactly how this tainting sin enters the newborn. Some believed that sexual activity marred the offspring based on a disapproving view of such erotic behavior, while St. Augustine believed instead that procreation involved the differentiation of individuals from a human mass which had begun with Adam (and, thus, all humans were seminally in Adam). Biblical reflection and developments in our understanding of anatomy have since sunk these models. Most Reformed theologians have preferred to speak of the "imputation" of Adam's sin. As noted in the last chapter, "imputation" is a term drawn from the world of bookkeeping and refers to the crediting of something into another's account. More recently, many theologians have proposed that original sin is passed along by means of social mediation or what we might call character deformation.[1]

More important than the issue of transmission are debates regarding the essence of original sin. The Bible speaks of sin as power and problem, principality and persuasion. Sin brings death and destruction, darkness and distance. Sin is multifaceted and chaotic.

The majority of Reformed theologians throughout the centuries (and likely even today) affirm that original sin involves both the power of sin and the guilt of sin. This has been the position of most confessions. For example, the Westminster Confession of Faith says of Adam and Eve's sin, "they being the root of all mankind, the guilt of this sin was imputed, and the same death in sin and corrupted nature conveyed to all their posterity, descending from them by ordinary generation" (WCF, VI.3, in

BC, p. 180). Emphasis is laid on the representative role of Adam, who was a "federal head" or "covenant head." Much as a government leader or ambassador might act on behalf of a nation with consequences rightly passing from head to members, so Adam served in a representative capacity.

The key exegetical basis for this argument is the apostle Paul's discussion of Adam's sin in the fifth chapter of his Epistle to the Romans: "Therefore, just as sin came into the world through one man, and death came through sin, and so death spread to all because all have sinned" (5.12).[2] The entrance of sin into the world is linked to "one man" (Adam), death follows sin into the world, and this death spreads to everybody inasmuch as everybody has sinned. The final clause is typically interpreted by Reformed theologians as an inclusive statement about Adam's first sin, namely, "all have sinned" *in Adam's sin*. The force of this argument flows largely from its rhetorical symmetry with the following comments about Christ as a "second Adam," another representative figure: "if the many died through the one man's trespass, much more surely have the grace of God and the free gift in the grace of the one man, Jesus Christ, abounded for the many" (5.15). This comparison is restated four times, with Adam bringing sin and death as opposed to Jesus making righteous (5.16–19).

Yet many Reformed luminaries have insisted on differentiating between the inclination to sin and the guilt of sin. In fact, John Calvin himself argued that while Adam's descendants received their sinful tendencies from him, they by no means were held liable for his guilt *per se*. In other words, depravity is passed along while guilt is not.[3] Thus, while Adam's sin has a causal effect on all subsequent human life, Adam's sin cannot be collapsed into other human lives as though they were simply identified with him. What is passed along? "This is the inherited corruption, which the church fathers termed 'original sin,' meaning by the word 'sin' the depravation of a nature previously good and pure," says Calvin (*ICR*, II.i.5). Even more bluntly, Calvin defines original sin as follows:

> Adam, by sinning, not only took upon himself misfortune
> and ruin but also plunged our nature into like destruction.
> This was not due to the guilt of himself alone, which

would not pertain to us all, but was because he infected all his posterity with that corruption into which he had fallen. (*ICR*, II.i.6)

This mediated notion of inherited sin reads Rom. 5 differently. Looking to the key verse, it notes that a preposition has been translated wrongly and should be corrected: "Therefore, just as sin came into the world through one man, and death came through sin, and so death spread to all with the result that all have sinned" (5.12).[4] Here sin brings death, death passes to all, and each person's sin follows as a necessary result of their receiving death from Adam. In other words, Adam passes along a sinful nature or tendency to his posterity. They then sin in their own ways. It is for this sin that they are held liable and guilty. This exegetical approach suggests that the parallel between Adam and Christ is not entirely symmetrical; rather, Christ directly wins righteousness and vindication for his people, whereas Adam merely passes along the incapacity to do good (which then leads each and every individual to err and incur guilt on their own). Christ brings justification, while Adam makes sin necessary but only mediately so. Hence, the parallels constantly refer to Christ's mediation as "much more" than that of Adam (5.15, 17). Proponents of this interpretation point to wider canonical support for the notion that individuals are held guilty only for their own wrongdoings, even though they may suffer many curses or misfortunes for the sins of their ancestors (2 Kgs 14.6; Jer. 31.29–30; Ezek. 18.20).[5]

However original sin flows from parent to child, and whatever it involves, Reformed theologians are united in opposing the Pelagian error, that is, the belief that individual sins are only related to Adam's first sin by way of imitation. Humans sin because humans are sinners. Original sin does not relate to mere imitation, whereby Adam is a type of all human wrongdoing.[6] The "statement that 'by nature all are children of wrath' [Eph. 2.3] could not stand, unless they had already been cursed in the womb itself" (*ICR*, II.6). Human nature has been tarnished and distorted, turned inward and thus away from God, the fount of life and goodness. As this has occurred, humans have been incapacitated (see the extensive biblical witness: Gen. 6.5; 8.21; Job 14.4; 15.14–16; Ps. 14.1–3; Rom. 3.10–18; 8.7–8; Eph. 2.1). Ian McFarland summarizes the Augustinian tradition (of which the Reformed doctrine is a part) as such: "it is a corollary of the Augustinian doctrine of original sin that human identity is rooted in a reality that is prior to human willing."[7] Indeed, original sin is a corollary of the basic belief that humans are shaped by contexts, for we are finite and related. This basic claim has been highlighted by many recent developments in (post)modern studies in the natural and social sciences (e.g., communitarianism), and it has been fine-tuned by looking to the communal shape of divine-human relations in the Bible (e.g., the primacy of Israel). Original sin—and the passing on of corruption from one generation to another—takes this one step further: humans continue to carry on a sinful existence, reaping the whirlwind of Adam's misdeed. As Serene Jones puts it, "the notion of sin as 'original' grasps well the reality that we are shaped by oppressive dynamics that predate us and that we do not choose to be determined by."[8]

Polemic with Remonstrants

The doctrines of sin and grace within the Reformed church of the Netherlands were questioned in the late sixteenth and early seventeenth centuries by Jacob Arminius (1560–1609) and his followers (the so-called Arminians or Remonstrants). They offered five disagreements for consideration by the church. The Synod of Dordt convened to address these charges and responded with five points of its own (referred to as the "five points of Calvinism" by many). We will now survey these perspectives on grace.

First, humans are radically or extensively depraved. This corruption makes humans entirely incapable of turning toward God in faith. As the Westminster Confession of Faith describes it, "from this original corruption, whereby we are utterly indisposed, disabled, and made opposite to all good, and wholly inclined to all evil, do proceed all actual transgressions" (WCF, VI.4, in *BC*, p. 180). As this definition makes plain, the common term "total depravity" would be better rendered "utter depravity," for humans are marred throughout and altogether incapable of good on their own; nonetheless, they are not thereby doomed to commit every possible evil (thanks to the giving of common grace).

Furthermore, Charles Matthewes is right when he says that "sin is a one way street," that is, "an agent, once gone wrong, cannot reintegrate herself; for the only instrument she would have for such reintegration is sullied by the disintegration."[9] Once humans have gone the way of sin and destruction, they cannot just turn the ship around on their own. God warned Adam and Eve that sin would have death-dealing consequences (Gen. 2.17), visible now in all the nefarious and painful contexts and characters we find ourselves to be. The crucial point made at Dordt was that sinners cannot turn to God in faith, precisely because their sinfulness inhibits their will from desiring and pursuing God. This follows the words of Jesus: "No one can come to me unless drawn by the Father who sent me" (Jn. 6.44). Whereas the Remonstrants believed that God gave prevenient grace that freed everyone from the debilitating effects of original sin, at least enough that they could exercise faith, the Reformed churches found no such grace promised in the Bible.[10]

So humans this side of Eden must do what they cannot do. They must turn to God in faith and repentance, yet they are constitutionally incapable of doing anything good. "Is not God unjust in requiring of man in his Law what he cannot do?" asks the Heidelberg Catechism. The answer: "No, for God so created man that he could do it. But man, upon the instigation of the devil, by deliberate disobedience, has cheated himself and all his descendants out of these gifts" (HC, 9, in *BC*, p. 60). God remains just insofar as human sin has always been willful sin. Humans continue to have free will, that is, they are free to do what they will. Yet they are not free to will whatever they wish, inasmuch as their capacities have been hindered by their history (see SHC, IX, in *BC*, pp. 104–105). Humans have been formed by their context east of Eden.

Second, God unconditionally elects or chooses certain persons to save. Here the Reformed tradition has looked to two biblical sources: the Old Testament accounts of Israel's election and the Pauline Epistles that focus on the doctrine of salvation. First, texts like Deuteronomy make plain that Israel was God's chosen people "not because you were more numerous than any other people" (Deut. 7.7). Rather, God declares that "I will be gracious to whom I will be gracious, and will show mercy on whom I will show mercy" (Exod. 33.19). Paul draws an inference from this, noting the negative side of things as well: "so then he has mercy on whomever he chooses, and he hardens the heart of whomever he chooses" (Rom. 9.18).

Indeed, it is in the ninth chapter of his Epistle to the Romans that the apostle Paul makes this unconditionality most explicit. First, he points out that God's grace is not bound to fleshly descent, for only Isaac's children, and not those of Ishmael, are his "true descendants" (Rom. 9.7–8). Second, he then observes that God's grace was devoted in a special way to Jacob and not to Esau, and that this determination was rendered "before they had been born or had done anything good or bad." In fact, Paul offers an explanatory comment here: "so that God's purpose of election might continue, not by works but by his call" (Rom. 9.11–12). Here the Remonstrant proposal seems to falter, inasmuch as they claim that God foresees those who will respond to the good news in faith and predestines them on that basis. Apart from the stranger problem that this removes any real activity from the active verb "predestine" or "elect" (essentially making it only a synonym for divine foreknowledge of faith), this also runs aground of Paul's insistence in vv. 11–12 that God did this before either Jacob or Esau had done anything good or bad. Reformed theologians have taken from Paul's exegetical reflections on Israel's election in this chapter that God determines some for blessing and others for cursing, and that all this is done apart from any conditions but wholly in God's own way. As the Westminster Confession says, "although God knows whatsoever may or can come to pass, upon all supposed conditions; yet hath he not decreed anything because he foresaw it as future, or as that which would come to pass upon such condition" (WCF, III.2, in *BC*, p. 177). Indeed, the objections Paul then notes seem to confirm that this strong view of election has been affirmed. First, Paul asks if there is "injustice on God's part?" (Rom. 9.14). Second, Paul asks "why then does he still find fault? For who can resist his will?" (Rom. 9.19). More important than any of Paul's responses to these two objections is the very fact that the objections occur; these objections only arise if Paul has already affirmed a strong view of divine predestination or unconditional election to salvation.

This is why salvation is not at all by works. Augustine defended this principle against Pelagius, offering what his interpreter R. A. Markus called "a defense of Christian mediocrity."[11] Just like Israel before them, Christians make no claim to have earned God's favor. Rather, God shows mercy in electing some from the realm of sinfulness and death. "For by grace you have been saved through faith, and this is not your own doing; it is the gift of God—not the result of works, so that no one may boast" (Eph. 2.8–9). Importantly, "this is not your own doing" cannot refer to grace or to faith alone, because the gender of the term "this" does not match the gender of the Greek terms for "grace" or "faith." It must be this entire process of salvation by grace through faith that is, ultimately, not of our own doing. The root of Christian salvation lies in the will of the God before whom "we are what he has made us, created in Christ Jesus for good works, which God prepared beforehand to be our way of life" (Eph. 2.10).

Third, Christ died for these persons and purchased their redemption with his blood. In the controversy with the Arminians, this was often termed a "limited atonement" that sufficed to save a restricted group of persons, but not each and every person. Indeed, Reformed confessions have spoken of the limits of the atonement; not every person ultimately benefits from the salvific work of Christ. There will be a hell, as is evident in many biblical passages that relate the reality of two destinies (e.g., Mt. 25.31–46).[12] Reformed exegesis has taken the various passages in the New Testament that seem to construe Christ's work for "all" as referring to each and every people-group. Thus, these passages speak of salvation for Gentiles as well as Jews, females as well as males, slaves as well as free-persons. They do not refer to reconciliation for each and every individual.

A better term would surely be "definite atonement," for the Reformed approach to the atonement not only limits it in certain ways, but also bolsters its efficacy. The Arminians had suggested that Christ died for every single person, though this is only made effective for those who come to faith. The danger, of course, lies in suggesting that Christ's work is insufficient and requires a human complement: faith. The Synod of Dordt responded by confessing that Christ's death is all sufficient, definitive in its salvific intent. In other words, the Son redeemed those whom the

Father had given him: "this is the will of him who sent me, that I should lose nothing of all that he has given me, but raise it up on the last day" (Jn 6.39). Who are those "given" to Jesus by his Father? The next verse specifies "that all who see the Son and believe in him" will be raised "up on the last day" (6.40). Jesus loses none given to him, but raises them all up. Who is raised up? Those who believe in Jesus. Thus, we see that only those who will believe were given to Jesus.

The key text with regard to this issue of the extent of the atonement is surely John Owen's *The Death of Death in the Death of Christ*.[13] Interestingly, Owen later recanted some of his teaching here in the wake of the Socinian controversy. Whereas in *The Death of Death*, he affirmed that God could save people by mere *fiat*, he later argued that God's justice required atonement and, thus, a mediator in his *Dissertation on Divine Justice*.[14] Owen does emphasize that the atoning death of Christ must be considered a "federal" or covenantal action, whereby those in the "covenant of grace" are willed by God to benefit from the work of Christ. Here Owen links atonement and election.[15]

Fourth, God effectively brings about the calling and conversion of these certain persons through the ministry of the gospel. Some term this tenet "irresistible grace," meaning that the Spirit moves in an unstoppable fashion to work faith within the elect. Yet Lutheran theologian Robert Jenson has noted a problem with this terminology:

> [G]race is neither resistible nor irresistible, since we are never in a position to resist or want to resist, successfully or unsuccessfully. The one who pours out on us the liberating Spirit, does so from his heavenly throne hidden within us. The Spirit indeed opens the gate of our hearts, to the Father and to one another—from inside.[16]

Jenson raises an important point: since God graces us by actually changing us—desires, will, passions, mind, and all—"from inside," there is nothing left with which we can resist. Better to term this "effective grace" than "irresistible grace," then, for the main point is surely that God's election is really made concrete in the here and now. God does not just choose to bless in the recess of eternity. God brings that decision to bear on everyday life by working faith in the elect.

So faith is a gift, not a capacity of sinful humans apart from God's enlivening work. This is evident in reflections on various conversions within the New Testament. For example, consider the report of Acts regarding the testimony of Peter to the believers in Judea, that is, Jewish followers of Jesus, about the conversion of the Gentiles: "When they heard this, they were silenced. And they praised God, saying: 'Then God has given even the Gentiles the repentance that leads to life'" (Acts 11.18). When they see faith and repentance, they infer God's gracious hand. Paul makes this explicit when writing to the Philippians of their sufferings: "he has graciously granted you the privilege not only of believing in Christ, but of suffering for him as well" (Phil. 1.29). Paul's point, of course, is that suffering for the gospel is actually a gift of God. Yet he makes this point by comparing this gift to another one: the "privilege" of believing. Notice the repetition used to describe God's action here: not just "granting" this "privilege," but doing so "graciously." The Lord has given life where there was none before.

Does the giving of faith by the Lord relate to the practices of humans, that is, is it mediated in any way? The Heidelberg Catechism puts the question somewhat differently, but no less helpfully:

Q. 65. Since, then, faith alone makes us share in Christ and all his benefits, where does such faith originate?
A. The Holy Spirit creates it in our hearts by the preaching of the holy gospel, and confirms it by the use of the holy Sacraments. (HC, 65, in *BC*, p. 68)

The Spirit works through the normal "means of grace": the proclamation of the gospel and the practice of the sacraments. Yet it is the Spirit who gives life; these human actions do not have power in themselves or magically convey grace in an automatic fashion. They are effective as determined by God. In other words, God ordains the means as well as the ends. To be sure, God can work outside the box, just as lightning can strike anywhere. But God typically works through these particular practices wherein he has promised to be present (see Rom. 10.14–17).

Some have thought that this renders the task of witness and evangelism moot: "if God wills it, it will be so." This concern takes the doctrine of predestination presented here to be equivalent to determinism or even fatalism. J. I. Packer has responded:

> While we must always remember that it is our responsibility to proclaim salvation, we must never forget that it is God who saves. It is God who brings men and women under the sound of the gospel, and it is God who brings them to faith in Christ. Our evangelistic work is the instrument that He uses for this purpose, but the power that saves is not in the instrument: it is in the hand of the One who uses the instrument. We must not at any stage forget that. For if we forget that it is God's prerogative to give results when the gospel is preached, we shall start to think that it is our responsibility to secure them. And if we forget that only God can give faith, we shall start to think that the making of converts depends, in the last analysis, not on God, but on us, and that the decisive factor is the way in which we evangelize.[17]

Packer is responding to the error of "hyper-Calvinism," on the one hand, and to the Arminian tendency, on the other hand. Against the Arminians, he insists that *God brings people to faith* through the ministry of proclaiming the gospel. Against the "hyper-Calvinists," however, he insists that God brings people to faith *through the ministry of proclaiming the gospel*. Again, God plans and commands and even ensures the right means just as God predestines the ends.

Fifth, God effectively preserves these persons in faithfulness throughout their days until they are raised anew and glorified. The apostle Paul boasted of this expectation: "I am confident of this, that the one who began a good work among you will bring it to completion by the day of Jesus Christ" (Phil. 1.6). He parses this promise out more fully in Rom. 8: "those whom he foreknew he also predestined to be conformed to the image of his Son ... those whom he predestined he also called; and those whom he called he also justified; and those whom he justified he also glorified" (Rom. 8.29–30). The key exegetical issue is that the very same ones who are predestined are guaranteed not only justification but also glory.[18] God loses none along the way.

According to the "TULIP" acronym, this final point is commonly referred to as the "perseverance of the saints." It should not surprise the reader to find that this is slightly misleading, though not incorrect *per se*. The deeper truth is that God promises to preserve the elect from any trouble or trials that would draw them away from the faith irrevocably. This divine pledge, then, results in the ongoing faithfulness of the elect, what is rightly called their "perseverance." This preservation sustains the practice of Christian prayer, inasmuch as it portrays a God who is not only able and willing but also committed to do his children good. The Heidelberg Catechism makes this plain in reflecting on the sixth petition of the Lord's Prayer:

> "And lead us not into temptation, but deliver us from evil."
> That is: since we are so weak that we cannot stand by
> ourselves for one moment, and besides, since our sworn
> enemies, the devil, the world, and our own sin, ceaselessly
> assail us, be pleased to preserve and strengthen us through the
> power of the Holy Spirit so that we may stand firm against
> them, and not be defeated in this spiritual warfare, until at last
> we obtain complete victory. (HC, 127, in *BC*, p. 80)

God's promised preservation of the saints sustains, rather than negates the practice of prayer. Reformed believers affirm that "he who did not withhold his own Son, but gave him up for all of us, will he not with him also give us everything else?" (Rom. 8.32)

The doctrine of Christian assurance is related to this final point, not surprisingly since this text in Rom. 8 is a part of Paul's argument for assurance in the face of ongoing sin. Though the world, and even the moral character and faith of Christians, are imperfect, believers may be assured that "all things work together for good for those who love God" (8.28), because nothing "will separate us from the love of Christ" (8.35–39). Christians are to be assured of salvation. Indeed, this may be the thorniest of issues involved in the Reformed doctrine of predestination. All confessions and dogmatics within the tradition have emphasized the importance of assurance for the Christian life, and they have consistently suggested that grasping the truths of grace aids the pursuit of this assurance (see WCF, III.8, in *BC*, p. 178). There is a somewhat obvious point here: knowing that God saves should free humans from anxiety and fear. Some take this to mean that Reformed believers can have assurance, whereas Arminians and others simply cannot. Of course, things are slightly more complex since the Bible teaches that God saves the elect.[19] The many promises of preservation regarding the elect are only useful to the individual inasmuch as they can self-identify with the elect. Thus, one must "be all the more eager to confirm your call and election" (2 Pet. 1.10). Assurance is no static experience, but involves constant turning toward Christ. Whether Reformed, Arminian, or otherwise, one must pursue and confirm election.

Reformed theologians have differed regarding the various ways in which assurance is pursued, with some emphasizing the sole basis of assurance in looking to Christ's work and others seeing a secondary basis in the evidence of good works in one's life (the so-called practical syllogism).[20] In other words, one's good conscience confirms one faith and good standing in Christ.[21] Some suggest that the "practical syllogism," that is, looking for evidence of faith in one's moral character as a sign of one's election, points away from Jesus as the sole ground of salvation.[22] While this may be a danger, it need not follow from adoption of the "practical syllogism." If God promises to bless the faithful with all other blessings (e.g., good works), then it is not inappropriate to look for such accompaniments as signs of faith and salvation. This merely takes God at his word. Of course, there is always the danger of overblown introspection (to which some Puritans and many revivalists seem to have succumbed), but this is not intrinsic to the Reformed doctrine of assurance.[23]

Thus, salvation is by grace alone (*sola gratia*), because God has provided everything. Not only has God put forward the Son for our redemption, but God has also enabled us to believe in the Son.

Divine and Human Action

The Reformed doctrine of predestination, along with all Augustinian accounts, has been the subject of much derision.

Many believe that it affirms determinism or fatalism and gives too little place to human action and responsibility. David Fergusson suggests that the tradition is "unable to make sufficient distinction between those events that God wills and those that are opposed to the divine intention" and that "its account of human freedom is inadequate."[24] These two objections are really one, for the first is simply an example of the second. Human freedom is undervalued inasmuch as bad uses of it can no longer be termed evil and against God's will. So Fergusson presents the main charge: providence and predestination as construed in the Reformed and Augustinian traditions undersell human action.

The grace of predestination really does awaken human *faith*, however. Creaturely integrity and the workings of nature are actually perfected, not destroyed by grace. A signal text for this is found in Phil. 2: "my beloved, just as you have always obeyed me, not only in my presence, but much more now in my absence, work out your own salvation with fear and trembling; for it is God who is at work in you, enabling you both to will and to work for his good pleasure" (2.12–13). Verse 12 commands human action (obedience, working out salvation), to be pursued "with fear and trembling" that imply real moral gravity. Verse 13 provides a basis for this human doing: God "is at work in you, enabling you." Indeed, this text shows that God's grace empowers human action, rather than replaces it.[25] Predestination or election is purposive, as highlighted by the apostle Paul's statement that "those whom he foreknew he predestined to be conformed to the image of his Son" (Rom. 8.29). Recent Presbyterian confessions have emphasized the vocation given in election, seen most explicitly in the confession that "the Spirit gives us courage to pray without ceasing, to witness among all peoples to Christ as Lord and Savior, to unmask idolatries in Church and culture, to hear the voices of peoples long silenced, and to work with others for justice, freedom, and peace" (A Brief Statement of Faith [BSF], 4, in *BC*, p. 342). The Spirit is really life-giving, enabling not just existence but activity of all sorts.

Kathryn Tanner has shown that theologians as diverse as Aquinas and Barth depict the relationship between divine and human action in a "noncompetitive" or "noncontrastive" manner. In short, "a non-competitive relation between creatures and God means that the creature does not decrease so that God may increase. The glorification of God does not come at the expense of creatures. The more full the creature is with gifts the more the creature should look in gratitude to the fullness of the gift-giver."[26] Whereas many moderns construe God and creation competitively, such a viewpoint necessarily leads to a truncated view of divine grace or human action. Either God does something or humans do, but there is only one doing the action. The Reformed doctrine of God, following Aquinas, instead posits a qualitative doctrine of divine transcendence, wherein God is of a different kind than humans. God is not of our genus, but is God's own genus, to use the language of biology. Thus, God moves in the world unlike any other agent, and God's action cannot be simply contrasted with that of other agents. Furthermore, "what makes God different from creatures is also what enables God to be with what is not God rather than shut up in self-enclosed isolation." Indeed, "immanence and transcendance, closeness and difference, are simply not at odds in God's relationship with us. What makes God different from us enables closeness with us."[27]

With these beliefs about divine transcendence and immanence in place, Karl Barth suggested that God's "omnicausality" is not equivalent to "monocausality." Barth affirms that God causes everything that comes to pass, yet this does not negate the causality of other agents (e.g., humans, cosmic factors).[28] In this vein, a theocentric doctrine of predestination (held by the Reformed and all Augustinians) has gone hand in hand with compatibilist or *concursus* theories of divine and human agency. That is, God's causation of an event is entirely compatible with human causality of that same event; in other words, divine providence and predestination undergird rather than negate human freedom and agency.[29] Only in this light does Barth's praise of the ethical emphasis within Reformed theology (*vis-à-vis* Lutheran theology) make much sense.[30] This is very notable given that Barth revised the Reformed doctrine of election in a way many contemporary theologians have since adopted. That is, Barth found the Westminsterian and Dordtian doctrine of predestination to imply that God delights in punishing humans just as much as loving them in Christ. Thus, to honor the fact that Christ truly revealed God, Barth believed that Christ was the elected human just as he was the electing God; in other words, hell was taken by him. Many have followed Barth's rejection of the classical Reformed tradition, because they agree that it reflects poorly on the divine character.[31] More work remains to be done within the exegetical and dogmatic realms in showing how Jesus talks of judgment and love, and the Reformed tradition needs a new defense of the doctrine of hell and judgment, indeed, of God's justice.[32] More important for my purposes here is to note that Barth maintained the core of the traditional doctrine of predestination in his doctrine of providence (see *CD*, III/3: 58–288).[33]

George Hunsinger has rightly discerned three emphases in Barth's doctrine of providence, regarding divine and human agency: their (1) integrity, (2) intimacy, and (3) asymmetry.[34] First, both divine and human agents have real integrity: just as God really predestines and prevenes, so humans really do act. Our experience is not illusory. Second, divine and human action plays out with the greatest intimacy. That is, God and humans can be causes of the very same chain of events. For example, there is a lengthy narrative teased out across Gen. 37–50, involving betrayals, temptations, conversations, imprisonments, etc. All this is humane and lively, a truly dramatic story. Yet Joseph says to his brothers, "Even though you intended to harm to me, God intended it for good" (Gen. 50.20). The very same verb ("intend") is used to highlight that this narrative and all the events within it are being predicated of two very different agents: the pitifully jealous brothers of Joseph and the beneficent God of Israel. Third, divine action asymmetrically relates to human action. God's providence and predestination make the way for human freedom and responsibility. Because God gives, humans can participate. Though he revised the doctrine of election (and tilted toward an incipient universalism), Barth maintained a theocentric doctrine of providence that does much of the work the confessional doctrine of predestination did (e.g., answering why some have faith and others do not). Behind all creaturely action lies the supervening will of God.

Modern and Postmodern Contexts

George Weigel tells the tale of his return to Paris in 1997, 33 years after his last visit.[35] He visited the relatively new *Arche de la Défense*, commonly known as the *Grande Arche*, a massive structure 40 stories tall covered in glass and marble. The *Grande Arche* was built to commemorate the 200th anniversary of the French Revolution. The tour guides point out that the entire cathedral of Notre Dame can fit within the *Grande Arche*. The medieval sanctuary can be swallowed by the modern trappings of the Enlightenment celebration. This got Weigel to thinking, which culture better upholds the great longings of the "Declaration on the Rights of Man and of the Citizen," the 1789 document that lauded "liberty, property, security, and resistance to oppression" as natural rights of all citizens? Weigel's book *The Cube and the Cathedral* suggests that (post)modern Europe has lost any moral footing on which to promote such visions, in as much as natural rights require a theory of nature. That is, he believes the "discontents of Europe" are theologically based.

We might go further than Weigel in using the *Grande Arche* as the symbolic point whereby we see modernity's desire to swallow Christian theology (marked by the Cathedral of Notre Dame). Modern thinking has attempted to show forth greater explanatory power than that of biblical reasoning. Autonomy has been the cry of the modern subject, king over one's own person.[36] Scientific method and philosophical rationality have attempted to fashion a world, indeed a paradise, devoid of the wisdom of God and the work of providence. Morality has been construed apart from authority, for cultural theorists like Michel Foucault have suggested that "conformity to external norms does not secure moral authenticity. It is much more that being an ethical subject is a matter of self-formation."[37] Each person has been called to determine their own existence. The limits of predestination are seen as altogether violent and abusive inasmuch as they inhibit defining oneself. Yet Cynthia Rigby surmises that "our very quest for autonomy has precipitated a deep yearning for belonging."[38]

John Webster has reiterated a central concern of the Reformed tradition: "if *sola fide* is the bass note of Christian holiness, then the explication of that holiness requires an ontology of the human person, and consequently a psychology and an ethics, in which the being of the Christian is not made but given."[39] The modern fear of grace has caused dreadful problems here, according to Webster, for "this collapse of morality into self-stylization . . . not only entails the most severe contraction of moral ontology; it also makes acutely difficult any conception of moral obligation, for behind style lies *will*, unattached, and, without ends, unchallenged."[40] Of course, the modern desire for autonomy is in reality a hatred of being creaturely, having one's existence as a gift. This is merely to recapitulate the first sin: wanting to determine one's own way apart from God's prevening goodness and love. Reformed churches must show how this doctrine of predestination clashes head-on with the anthropology of the Enlightenment.

In so doing, we must not lose sight of values rightly treasured by those of us living on this side of the Enlightenment. Feminist and other liberationist concerns have been voiced regarding the traditional Augustinian doctrine of predestination and its potential complicity in certain social ills and abuses. Margit Ernst-Habib lists four major concerns:

1. the focus on individuals and their "private" salvation;
2. the tendency to concentrate on the "afterlife" while omitting our life here and now;
3. the limited character of human agency with respect to salvation; and, finally,
4. the implicit or explicit danger of an exclusive and hierarchical understanding of the chosen ones.[41]

The fourth concern deserves mention here, inasmuch as this has been a major fear of modern critics of predestination by grace. Surely the elect will gain a sense of hubris, which will likely turn in violent indignation toward violence against those on the outside. Indeed, the chosen few will identify themselves over against the "other" and do great harm to the "other," culturally and possibly physically. Here predestination fits alongside monotheism as a potential harbinger of cultural and political violence, what Regina Schwarz has called "the curse of Cain."[42] If there is one God, there must be one human ambassador for God. Further, there must be one people of God. And these people, perhaps led by their god-like leader(s), will mete out God's justice on earth. Such an ideology obviously uses monotheism as the basis or justification for tyrannical actions. Is this involved when Reformed folk claim that the faithful are "God's elect?"

Again, focusing on the election of Israel is instructive, even normative. Amy Plantinga Pauw accents this relation: "when Reformed theologians have identified the church with Old Testament Israel, they have opened a way for honest acknowledgment of ecclesial shortcomings."[43] All the more so with regard to the doctrine of predestination, for the biblical teaching on election highlights the undeserved nature of such grace: Israel was no larger or more intimidating than other nations, and Christians are no wiser or more illustrious than other persons. God has even chosen the younger brother (Jacob) in the face of a culture that honors the older (Esau), showing that the values of this world are clearly not the same as the Lord's. Nor is membership in God's family to be a justification for violence against those on the outside (Rom. 12.19) or judgment against those struggling on the inside (Mt. 13.24–30). One cannot know that someone else is (not) elect, and one should not behave differently toward them even if one could know that.

Predestination accentuates grace. Its purpose, then, is to aid worship by reflecting as fully as possible the breadth of the love of God in Christ. In conclusion, we should listen to the sage words of George Hunsinger about the radically disruptive experience of divine grace:

> Grace that is not disruptive is not grace—a point that Flannery O'Connor well grasped alongside Karl Barth. Grace, strictly speaking, does not mean continuity but radical discontinuity, not reform but revolution, not violence but nonviolence, not the perfecting of virtues but the forgiveness of sins, not improvement but resurrection from the dead. It means repentance, judgment, and death as the portal to life. It means negation and the negation of the negation. The grace of God really comes to lost sinners, but in coming it disrupts them to the core. It slays to make alive and sets the captive free. Grace may of course work silently and secretly like a germinating seed as well as like a bolt from the blue. It is always wholly as incalculable as it is reliable, unmerited, and full of blessing. Yet it is necessarily as unsettling as it is comforting. It does not finally teach of its own sufficiency without appointing a thorn in the flesh.

Grace is disruptive because God does not compromise with sin, nor ignore it, nor call it good. On the contrary, God removes it by submitting to the cross to show that love is stronger than death. Those whom God loves may be drawn to God through their suffering and be privileged to share in his sufferings in the world, because grace in its radical disruption surpasses all that we imagine or think.[44]

Chapter 6

Worship

Perhaps chief among the concerns of the early Protestant Reformers was the need to reform Christian worship according to God's Word. While defining the gospel and articulating the importance of justification by faith alone were crucial polemical issues, the emphasis was always on the doxological or liturgical practice. Why this emphasis? The Reformed confessions have always acknowledged that worship is the highest calling of the creature:

Q. 1. What is the chief end of man?
A. Man's chief end is to glorify God, and to enjoy him forever. (WSC, 1, in *BC*, p. 229)

All God's works lead to worship of the all-surpassing Giver. For example, the church is a "chosen people, a royal priesthood, a holy nation, a people belonging to God, *that* you may declare the praises of him who called you out of darkness into his wonderful light" (1 Pet. 2.9, emphasis added). Even the difficult doctrine of predestination was intended to deepen Christian worship by instilling gratitude for all God has done in the hearts of the elect. In believing this, Reformed Christians have tried to follow Paul's teaching on predestination "so that we . . . might live for the praise of his glory" (Eph. 1.12). Indeed, Paul's detailed account of the eternal roots of God's saving love in Christ recurs time and again as purposed "to the praise of his glorious grace" (Eph. 1.5; cf. 1.14).

Of course, that good theology facilitates right worship means also that bad theology hinders worshipping well. P.T. Forsyth remarked: "There are few dangers threatening the religious future more seriously than the slow shallowing of the religious mind . . . And the poverty of our worship amid its very refinements, its lack of solemnity . . . is the fatal index of the peril."[1] The Protestant

Reformation arose within a context of liturgical degeneration, and Reformed theologians from Calvin onward have insisted that the human heart is a factory of idols. Thus, humans will tend toward worshipping badly by their very sinful inclination. So prophetic warnings and the continuing practice of reforming worship must be a hallmark of the church.

Jesus declared that "true worshippers will worship the Father in spirit and truth . . . God is spirit, and those who worship him must worship in spirit and truth" (Jn 4.23–24). Attitudes and forms matter. Intent and manner matter too, because worship, like all obedience, must proceed from and in faith if it is to please the Lord (Heb. 11.6; Rom. 14.23). Worship must be by faith, because God "is not served by human hands, as if he needed anything. Rather, he himself gives everyone life and breath and everything else" (Acts 17.25). Worship must be celebrated in dependent delight in the goodness of YHWH. Right intent is necessary but not sufficient for right worship. "Spirit" must be coupled with "truth," that is, faithful worship must take a lawful form guided by the Word of God. As we will see, the Reformed churches have coupled the pastoral emphasis on worship by faith with a distinctive concern for worship that is faithful to God's design.

In this chapter, the relationship between *sola Scriptura* and the reform of worship will be teased out, and then two examples will be surveyed. First, Reformed theology offered a revised doctrine of the sacraments and their role in mediating grace to partakers. Second, the Reformed churches created a culture of iconoclasm due to an emphasis on the priority of sound over sight in the divine economy.

Reforming Worship According to God's Word

Worship has been the primary purpose of humanity as is clear from Genesis to Revelation. Temple imagery gives texture to the creation account in Gen. 1 and offers the heightened hopes for the last days in Rev. 20–21.[2] As John's Apocalypse states, "See, the home of God is among mortals. He will dwell with them; they will be his people, and God himself will be with them"

(Rev. 21.3). John's Gospel portrays Jesus as the temple, the very location of God's presence (Jn 2.19, 21). The key incident in the Old Testament—the exodus from Egypt—is portrayed as deliverance from slavery and labor under the hegemonic rule of Pharoah for the sake of worship of YHWH in freedom. Time and again, the exodus is portrayed not merely as political emancipation but as purposed for worship of God (Exod. 3.12; cf. 3.18; 7.16; 8.1, 20, 25–28; 9.1, 13; 10.3, 7–11, 24–26; 12.31). In this lies a deep Christian truth: real freedom is not only from the power and pains of sin, but also for the sake of rendering due praise to God. Hence, the church is frequently called the *ekklesia*, meaning the "called out" ones gathered for God's praise (see, for example, 1 Pet. 2.9).

In the Scriptures, YHWH manifests great concern for proper worship, punishing those who wrongly innovate in this arena. Nadab and Abihu were burnt up in fire when they "offered unauthorized fire . . . contrary to his command" (Lev. 10.1–2). Korah, Dathan, Abiram, and On were killed in an earthquake when they took the task of offering sacrifice upon themselves, rather than going to the appointed Aaronic priest (Num. 16). Saul's offering was also rebuked (1 Sam. 15.22), as were the actions of David and Uzzah with the ark of the covenant (2 Sam. 6.3, 13). Similarly, King Uzziah assumed the priestly role of offering sacrifice and, thus, was struck down with leprosy (2 Chron. 26.16–19). While obvious experiments in pagan-style worship brought judgment on the Israelites (Jer. 19.5; 32.35), so did the pious development of unsanctioned Jewish practices, like *korban*, by the Pharisees (Mt. 15.1–4).

The Lutheran and Roman Catholic traditions have held to what has been called the "normative principle," wherein authorities in the church may include practices in worship services even if they are not approved in the Bible, so long as they are prudent additions to worship. In other words, as long as the Bible does not prohibit something, it might conceivably be included in a worship gathering. Reformed churches have largely responded to this approach by emphasizing that the Bible does not merely preclude certain things from Christian worship, but also provides warrant or permission for anything that will be an element of worship. In other words, to do something in a service, it must be permitted by scriptural warrant or necessary implication from the Bible. As the Westminster Confession says,

> [T]he acceptable way of worshipping the true God is instituted by himself, and so limited by his own revealed will, that he may not be worshipped according to the imaginations and devices of men, or the suggestions of Satan, under any visible representation or any other way not prescribed in Holy Scripture. (WCF, XXIII.1, in *BC*, p. 196)

The key term there is "prescribed," requiring actual permission in the Bible for a practice to be valid. If read in the context of WCF I ("Of the Holy Scripture"), this "prescription" can come in two forms: "either expressly set down in Scripture, or by good and necessary consequence may be deduced from Scripture." So prescription comes in explicit and implicit fashion. The key point, however, is that only these prescriptions are allowed in worship, "unto which nothing at any time is to be added, whether by new revelations of the Spirit, or traditions of men" (WCF, I.6, in *BC*, p. 175).

The Belgic Confession concurs: "we believe, though it is useful and beneficial, that those who are rulers of the Church institute and establish certain ordinances among themselves for maintaining the body of the Church; yet they ought studiously to take care that they do not depart from those things which Christ, our only master, hath instituted. And, therefore, we reject all human inventions, and all laws which man would introduce into the worship of God, thereby to bind and compel the conscience in any matter whatever" (BC, XXXII, in *RCSC*, p. 212). Here continental and Anglo-American Reformed churches have been at one: God alone introduces elements into worship, and God does so through the written Word. Both the Westminster and the Belgic Confessions link this restriction on human ingenuity to the fact that worship "binds" or "compels" the conscience of parishioners; in other words, the clergy and elders have authority to shape how Christians worship but only when they follow the Word of God.

Of course, there are intricacies and contingencies that must vary from time to time and that do not require express sanction from the Word of God: when to meet, how long to preach, which

songs to sing, what to pray for, whether or not to use a micro-
phone, etc. With regard to such "forms" and "circumstances," the
Reformed have maintained that wisdom is necessary, while
explicit biblical sanction is not. These contingencies are not
"elements," key components or actual practices, in the worship
service and, thus, do not require permission from God's revealed
will. As the Westminster Confession puts it, "there are some
circumstances concerning the worship of God and government
of the church, common to human actions and societies, which
are to be ordered by the light of nature and Christian prudence,
according to the general rules of the Word, which are always to
be observed" (WCF, I.6, in *BC*, p. 175). So the Bible tells us that
worship should include confession of sin, though it remains for
elders to discern prudently whether to do so in poetry (like
the Psalms) or prose (like Rom. 3). The difficulty here becomes
identifying what is an "element" needing such permission and
what is merely a "form" or "circumstance" requiring no express
prescription. The Reformed approach does not foolproof worship
services from sinful accretions, but it does encourage a habit
of mind whereby the church looks to God's revealed Word for
guidance regarding worship.

Do Reformed beliefs about worship suggest that it will
be timeless or ever-changing? Will it be staid and true or will it
evolve with the times? One key principle is stated in the Scots
Confession of 1560: "the reason why the general councils met . . .
was that good policy and order should be constituted and observed
in the Kirk where, as in the house of God, it becomes all things
to be done decently and in order." The phrase "decently and in
order" has since served as something of a mantra for Presbyterian
policy, typified perhaps by following *Robert's Rules of Order*. Of
course, this principle follows from Paul's words to the church at
Corinth: "God is a God not of disorder but of peace" (1 Cor.
14.33). The reforming process ought to follow guidelines that
provide for order and stability, honoring the continuity of God's
covenant work. Yet it is worth noting the following comments
found in the Scots Confession: "Not that we think any policy or
order of ceremonies which men have devised can be appointed
for all ages, times, and places; for as ceremonies which men have
devised are but temporal, so they may, and ought to be, changed,

when they foster superstition rather than edify the Kirk" (SC, XIX, p. 43). This clearly refers to the practice of worship as "ceremonies" are mentioned twice, and it explicitly limits the ability of the church, or any council of the church, to lay down liturgical guidelines once and for all. As Bob Dylan stated, change is a'comin.

So worship is ever being reformed. This emphasis on appropriate fidelity within each context is found in the pages of the New Testament, of course, as the apostles sought to reform Jewish liturgical practices gleaned from the Old Testament in light of the sacrifice of the Messiah, Jesus. Hebrews 10.1–4, 11–15 clearly teaches that Jesus has offered himself as a sacrifice once and for all, putting an end to the need for ongoing sacrifices as in the days of the Levitical priesthood. In other words, Jesus has proven himself to be the great high priest inasmuch as he is also the sin offering himself. Thus, Christian worship looks back to his sacrifice and does not include the ongoing slaying of animals as did Old Covenant worship. A covenantal shift or escalation has occurred, and liturgical practice must morph accordingly. Indeed, the Incarnation and the atonement actually led the apostles to identify the church's worship as participation in that of Jesus. As James Torrance has insisted, Jesus prays and worships on behalf of his people, vicariously, and the church joins in that service to God.[3] "Through him, then, let us continually offer a sacrifice of praise to God, that is, the fruit of lips that confess his name. Do not neglect to do good and to share what you have, for such sacrifices are pleasing to God" (Heb. 13.15–16). Christian worship is "through him," Christ, and involves only the sacrifice of virtuous gratitude to God (see also Rom. 12.1).[4]

Other changes have proven controversial, however, inasmuch as they follow from cultural and not covenantal developments. For example, many have suggested that male names and metaphors for God should be shirked in favor of gender-neutral or even feminine language. This has followed from the adoption of certain feminist principles involving the dangers of gendered language in not only reflecting but also shaping cultural values. The infamous Reimagining Conference was held in Minneapolis in 1993, calling for a revision of language used for God and creating a firestorm in mainline Protestant circles (including the Reformed).[5]

This feminist reform suggests that the Bible teaches the full equality of men and women, and that any language which suggests
superiority of the male (especially by identifying God exclusively
or predominantly with the male) should be removed, revised, or
replaced. A theological tenet—gender equality—is being used as
the basis for reform. Yet it becomes quite complex, because this
reform cuts against the grain of the revealed will of God, that is,
the pages of Holy Scripture. The Bible contains and even endorses
this male language (e.g., calling the first person of the Trinity
"Father"). So the feminist critique would actually apply also to
the Bible. For this reason, most Reformed theologians have been
hesitant to view this as a valid reform. While the feminist concern
about language rightly warns of the dangers of identifying God
with the male, biblical authority as well as linguistic wisdom seems
best honored by maintaining a traditional line.[6] Surely a lesson to
be learned here is that proposed reforms of theology and worship
must make sense of the whole canon of Scripture.[7]

Each case of proposed reform, then, will have to be taken on its
own terms. As the Scots Confession confesses, reform must be
brought to pass "decently and in order." Noting the dangers of
idolatry and liturgical abuse is no easy task. We do well to focus
on a couple of examples that accentuate the Reformed goal of
following closely the revealed Word.[8]

Sacramental Mediation

The sacraments, for instance, are viewed within the context of the
covenant of grace. That is, they are authorized, even commanded by
God as part of the divine-human fellowship (*koinonia*) celebrated
regularly in a corporate setting. In this view, corporate gatherings
for worship are akin to covenant renewal ceremonies, wherein the
provisions, demands, and the promises of the covenantal Lord are
voiced, and where the covenantal servant affirms their desire to
abide by these terms. In other words, worship proclaims the all-
sufficiency of Christ as well as the call for faith and witness. The
service further includes opportunities for voicing the praises and
adoration of the people as well as for offering confession and
repentance for past sins. Indeed, it is important to note that
worship is a conversational or dialogical experience, wherein the

Lord and servant commune. Examples of this abound within the pages of the Old Testament, where the prophet would read aloud the covenant words of YHWH, to which the people would respond with affirmations of commitment and/or repentance (see, for example, Neh. 8.1–6). Such gatherings shape the symbolic world of the participants, reprioritizing and renaming things that they might better serve God in faith. In times of great persecution or especially trying challenges for Christian life, the churches are to gather all the more frequently in worship so as to avoid being washed away by the ever-powerful tides of culture (Heb. 10.25).

A major part of the covenant renewal ceremony is the symbolic or sacramental sign given to demonstrate the ongoing commitment of YHWH to the people.

Q. 66. What are the Sacraments?
A. They are visible, holy signs and seals instituted by God
   in order that by their use he may the more fully disclose
   and seal to us the promise of the gospel, namely, that
   because of the one sacrifice of Christ accomplished on
   the cross he graciously grants us the forgiveness of sins.
   (HC, 66, in *BC*, p. 68)

Just as circumcision and Passover were regular practices mandated and blessed by YHWH (see Gen. 15.10–11; Exod. 13.3–10), so Jesus has instituted two sacraments: baptism and the Lord's Supper.[9]

The sacraments are also viewed as regular "means of grace," whereby God works to nurture and mature his children. Humans are concrete and material, formed of the earth. Humans see and learn and converse and interact in concrete ways. God accommodates himself to this level by using common elements for conveying divine promises. So it is sometimes said that the sacraments involve God taking an element away from its common use and putting it toward a sacred or holy use. Better put, the common use is shown to have sacred significance. It is the cleansing function of water that makes it a powerful symbol of union with Christ, just as it is the nourishing and satisfying role of bread and wine that highlights the feast to be found in Christ's presence.

The sacraments are "visible words" that consist of three parts: the word, the sign, and the thing signified. Here the Second

Helvetic Confession is clear: "as formerly the Sacraments consisted of the word, the sign, and the thing signified; so even now they are composed, as it were, of the same parts" (SHC, XIX, in *RCSC*, pp. 138–139). The promise is imaged in a sign, and God really brings the promise of the gospel to pass through this practice. With the reality coming in with the sign, then, one can say realistically that "the thing signified" is present. George Hunsinger locates this real work of grace within the broader economy of Christ's work in the Spirit:

> The mediation and attestation of Christ (a) by the church (b) in the power of the Spirit (c) through the secondary forms of God's Word thus pertain (d) to our *koinonia* with the *Christus praesens* only as he manifests himself to us in the living coinherence of his person (e) with his finished work and (f) its future consummation.[10]

Jesus continues to touch people, now reaching down from his ascended place at the Father's right hand by means of the Spirit's work through the ministry of the church and the practice of the sacraments. As Hunsinger says, the presence of Christ (*Christus praesens*) is mediated by the church, the one who administers the sacrament, and the Spirit; in other words, all this is done in faith. But Jesus does touch people.

The Reformed churches believe in the efficacy of the sacraments, and this follows from their emphasis on the work of the Spirit in a material world. Martha Moore-Keish suggests that though the "Confession of 1967" did not mention that the Spirit makes communion effective, probably because many moderns do not think of Christ really being made present in this sacrament, the more recent "Brief Statement of Faith" reinstated this emphasis.[11] In any case, here the Westminster Shorter Catechism speaks plainly:

Q. 91. How do the sacraments become effectual means of salvation?

A. The sacraments become effectual means of salvation, not from any virtue in them, or in him that doth administer them, but only by the blessing of Christ, and the working of his Spirit in them that by faith receive them. (WSC, 91, in *BC*, p. 238)

Jesus administers grace through the faithful practice of the sacraments, and he does so by means of his life-giving Spirit.

Yet the Reformed confessions, the whole theological tradition really, has minimized the philosophical and metaphysical framework used to make sense of this efficacy. Whereas Lutherans and Roman Catholics developed fairly intricate schemes by which they affirmed the physical and local presence of Christ's human body and blood in the elements of bread and wine, the Reformed have found no such detail present in Scripture.

In fact, Reformed Christology suggests that this idea of multiple local presences, that is, Jesus being present in numerous communions around the world on Sunday morning, would be quite impossible. Humans do not exist in multiple spots at once, and Jesus remains a human. In place of these Eucharistic beliefs, the Reformed have typically followed the lead of John Calvin in speaking of a spiritual presence of Christ in the Supper.

Most notable about Calvin's teaching on the Supper is its restraint. He affirms a doctrine of Eucharistic efficacy, namely, that humans are really blessed or cursed by partaking. He believes that the Mediator is really present in this practice in a special way. Yet he offers a vague explanation: humans are brought by the Spirit into the heavenly presence of their Savior. It sounds mystical, and it is, but it is more emphatically modest than the alternatives. Calvin has not made sense of Jesus' ministry through the sacrament by means of some theory to get the Savior down to earth. He has offered an affirmation of presence and grace and, then, kept from speaking beyond what the Bible says. And the Reformed tradition has majored on the role of the Holy Spirit in bringing such divine-human covenantal fellowship to pass: "This union and conjunction which we have with the body and blood of Christ Jesus in the right use of the sacraments is wrought by means of the Holy Ghost" (SC, XXI, in *BC*, p. 44). Even more poignant are the words of the Heidelberg Catechism:

Q. 76. What does it mean to eat the crucified body of Christ and to drink his shed blood?
A. It is . . . to be so united more and more to his blessed body by the Holy Spirit dwelling both in Christ and in us that, although he is in heaven and we are on earth, we are

nevertheless flesh of his flesh and bone of his bone, always living and being governed by one Spirit, as the members of our bodies are governed by one soul. (HC, 76, in *BC*, p. 70)

The same Spirit who brought the Son into the virgin's womb, drove Jesus into the wilderness, and raised the dead Messiah to new life now brings the Son and his people together.[12]

The Reformed tradition has maintained that sacraments are beneficial only for those who have faith. In other words, they do not just bless people magically or "by the working of the work" (*ex opere operato*), as tradition would have it. Communing with Jesus in his Supper occurs when one trustingly turns for nourishment to the Savior; hence, examination is necessary lest one partake wrongly. Note the assumption behind this Pauline injunction: one can partake wrongly and with ill effects. That is, the sacrament is going to do something one way or another. It is effective. But there is a great and grave difference between an effective grace and an efficacious curse, for "all who eat and drink without discerning the body, eat and drink judgment against themselves. For this reason many of you are weak and ill, and some have died" (1 Cor. 11.30). It is here that Annie Dilllard's comments about being in the presence of the only true God are pertinent:

> On the whole, I do not find Christians, outside of the catacombs, sufficiently sensible of conditions. Does anyone have the foggiest idea what sort of power we so blithely invoke? Or, as I suspect, does no one believe a word of it? The churches are children playing on the floor with their chemistry sets, mixing up a batch of TNT to kill a Sunday morning. It is madness to wear ladies' straw hats and velvet hats to church; we should all be wearing crash helmets. Ushers should issue life preservers and signal flares; they should lash us to our pews. For the sleeping god may wake someday and take offence; or the waking god may draw us out to where we can never return.[13]

Having noted the importance of faith for right use of the sacraments in worship, the issue of infant baptism (*paedobaptism*) ought to be briefly discussed as well. Reformed churches baptize the babies of communing members. Lest others misunderstand, this does not mean that these churches only baptize babies; adult converts are welcome to the baptismal waters as well. But controversy does not surround such conversions; debate involves the admission of anyone else to this initiating sacrament. Many baptistic believers (*credobaptists*) have suggested that the practice of infant baptism actually heightened nominalism in the church and misleads individuals about their eternal fate by giving them a false sense of assurance.[14]

Many have argued that infant baptism is nowhere commanded in the New Testament, suggesting that it fails to meet the requirements of the regulative principle. Others note that there are not even any instances of infant baptism recorded in Scripture, taking the so-called household baptisms to refer only to converts within a house or to exclude children of a certain young age (e.g., Acts 16.14–15; 18.8). Both these arguments are rather weak. A stronger baptistic argument has arisen, though, which should draw reflection from Reformed defenders of infant baptism. According to Baptists, the New Covenant promises found in Jer. 31 show that this covenant (1) cannot be broken, (2) is "fully internalized," and (3) includes only regenerate persons. In other words, Baptists take the New Covenant church to be a pure assembly, a fully regenerate church.[15] As baptized infants cannot be guaranteed to follow in the faith of their parents, they should not be baptized until they profess personal faith.[16] Though the Old Covenant required circumcision and membership for infants, the New Covenant is more restricted.

This newer, salvation-historical argument has greater sway than the earlier exegetical arguments from omission. Yet Reformed theology can respond aptly. The New Covenant will culminate in a pure assembly and a regenerate people of God. Richard Pratt offers a helpful analysis:

> To develop a fuller understanding of the New Testament
> perspective, we must remember that Jeremiah's new
> covenant prophecy is inextricably enmeshed with many
> other promises of Israel's return from exile . . . Instead of

happening completely and all at once, the expectations of restoration have been fulfilled and are being fulfilled over a long stretch of time.[17]

As the surrounding land-based promises of Jer. 31 show, the New Covenant is not yet fully realized in the first coming of Jesus. The climax may have begun to arrive, but the curtain has not yet fallen. When Jesus returns and rights all wrongs, the sheep will be fully separated from the goats and only the saints washed in his blood will enter his presence. As for now, things are more messy. As Pratt puts it, "prior to that judgment that Christ will render at his return, the new covenant community is not restricted to believers only. If it were, there would be no separation of people at Christ's return."[18] We ought to consider the positive argument for baptizing infants, then, as sketched by the Heidelberg Catechism:

Q. 74. Are infants also to be baptized?

A. Yes, because they, as well as their parents, are included in the covenant and belong to the people of God. Since both redemption from sin through the blood of Christ and the gift of faith from the Holy Spirit are promised to these children no less than to their parents, infants are also by baptism, as a sign of the covenant, to be incorporated into the Christian church and distinguished from the children of unbelievers. This was done in the Old Covenant by circumcision. In the New Covenant baptism has been instituted to take its place. (HC, 74, in *BC*, p. 70)

Reformed theologians would do well to offer greater clarity regarding how these covenant children are "distinguished from the children of unbelievers" exactly. They will continue to insist that the baptized can break the covenant. But in so doing they become covenant-breakers rather than those who are simply outside the covenant; you cannot be unbaptized.[19] Though some infants who are baptized will fall away from the faith and, yes, may be punished in eternity, this negates neither the practice of infant baptism nor the universal preaching of the gospel. In summary, then, B. B. Warfield offers the Reformed argument for infant

baptism: "The argument in a nutshell is simply this: God established his church in the days of Abraham and put children into it.
They must remain there until He puts them out. He has nowhere
put them out. They are still then members of His church and as
such entitled to its ordinances."[20]

Images and Aesthetics

God has prohibited certain things from worship, and much reform
involves prophetic critique of ways in which the church has capit-
ulated to idolatrous tendencies. Over time, the worship of Israel
became a lax practice of mere social conformity or even infested
with pagan syncretism. Very quickly, worship in Corinth and elsewhere degenerated into class warfare and charismatic chaos.
Prophets and apostles have responded to such situations by calling
the people of God back to the first principles of worship. The
early Reformed churches believed that similar ills had befallen
medieval churches and that a prophetic critique was required.
One key issue involved the place of images within the life of the
church, namely, images of the incarnate Son.

The Old Testament emphasizes the evils of imaging God. First,
the second commandment clearly bans such images:

> You shall not make for yourself an idol, whether in the
> form of anything that is in heaven above, or that is on the
> earth beneath, or that is in the water under the earth. You
> shall not bow down to them or worship them; for I the
> Lord your God am a jealous God, punishing children for
> the iniquity of parents, to the third and the fourth genera-
> tion of those who reject me, but showing steadfast love to
> the thousandth generation of those who love me and keep
> my commandments. (Exod. 20.4–6)

Notice that this restriction defines the right way to worship YHWH.
It is not directed against pagan worship primarily, for that was the
main point of the first commandment. In other words, even after
you make sure that you are worshiping the right God (and this

God alone), you must make sure that you do not worship in an improper way.[21] This is reiterated in the book of Deuteronomy:

> Since you saw no form when the Lord spoke to you at Horeb out of the fire, take care and watch yourselves closely, so that you do not act corruptly by making an idol for yourselves, in the form of any figure—the likeness of male or female, the likeness of any animal that is on the earth, the likeness of any winged bird that flies in the air, the likeness of anything that creeps on the ground, the likeness of any fish that is in the water under the earth. And when you look up to the heavens and see the sun, the moon, and the stars, all the host of heaven, do not be led astray and bow down to them and serve them, things that the Lord your God has allotted to all the peoples everywhere under heaven. But the Lord has taken you and brought you out of the iron-smelter, out of Egypt, to become a people of his very own possession, as you are now. (Deut. 4.15–20)

Notice that these restrictions outline ways in which Israel might wrongly confuse YHWH with the wonderful works of God's mercy (e.g., sun, moon, stars above). Specifically, do not make images of God, for God has not appeared in such an imageable fashion. Rather, God's revelation is like fire and has no discernible "form."

Some argue that this prohibition only applied until the coming of the incarnate Son, in whom we can see God. Jesus is both divine and human, so he can relate in every way that is authentically human. Humans are visible. Thus, Jesus is visible. In other words, Jesus could have been photographed had Nikon been around back in the first century. Whereas the Israelites were not yet possessors of such a divine "form," Christians can now look to the incarnate Son as an image of God. To deny this is to be a docetist (a heretic who denies the full humanity of Jesus) or a Nestorian (a heretic who denies the personal union of the divine and human natures). Whereas the Israelites were not prepared to behold the glory of YHWH, now "when one turns to the Lord, the veil is removed." Indeed, "all of us with unveiled faces, seeing the glory of the Lord as though reflected in a mirror, are being transformed into the same image from one degree of glory to another; for this comes from the Lord, the Spirit" (2 Cor. 3.16, 18).

DavidVanDrunen has offered a cogent reply to this argument.[22] He cedes the main point, yet insists that the prohibition continues now anyway. First, the iconoclastic argument needs to maintain a catholic understanding of the Incarnation. As VanDrunen suggests, this requires affirmation of the full humanity or the Son (*vere homo*). Bundled in that humanity is the capacity to be seen and, yes, to be imaged or photographed. Even now, Jesus is an embodied human that might be seen or pictured. To deny this would be to fall into the docetic or Nestorian errors, neither of which is permissible in catholic and Reformed churches.

Second, however, eschatology is informative here, because God's visibility in Christ remains future: "What we do know is this: when he is revealed, we will be like him for we will see him as he is." When will this be? The previous sentence clarifies: "what we will be has not yet been revealed" (1 Jn 3.2). This vision of the Son has not yet occurred, just as the similarity between Christ and his people has not yet occurred. In fact, the New Testament seems to emphasize that the present era in salvation history is marked by faith, not sight. We still live in the kingdom of God not yet consummated, so the constraints of Deut. 4 are still pertinent (though we now know how God will become visible, by bringing the human Jesus near to us). Thus, we are to *hope* for this beatific vision, rather than to expect it now or to try to bring it about ourselves. Sight simply does not describe our current position: "Though not seeing him, you love him, and though not seeing him now, you believe in him and rejoice with an indescribable and glorious joy" (1 Pet. 1.8). Jesus predicted this: "after a little while, you will see me no longer, and again after a little while, and you will see me" (Jn 16.16). So, as Paul says, "we walk by faith not by sight" (2 Cor. 5.7).

VanDrunen asks, "why is eschatological reserve applied to matters of seeing, such as the making of images, while it is not applied to matters of hearing, such as preaching or theologizing?" Well, preaching and theologizing base themselves "upon the pre-served record of God's revelation in Scripture, while the creating and using of images do not base themselves upon any specific revelation." Thus, he says: "preaching and theologizing would be just as problematic if they based themselves upon the general truth that God had spoken, but scripture itself was unavailable and Christians remained ignorant of any of the content of God's speech."[23] So it is not images *per se* that are unfit to convey Christ, but the fact that God has chosen for the moment to work through words (recorded in the Bible) rather than images that determines the means of grace.[24] Just as some would say that the prohibition of eating from the tree of knowledge of good and evil was some-what arbitrary, a simple test of trust in God's command alone, so this would be a prohibition based only on God's determination of ways to work.

Of course, the sacraments of baptism and the Lord's Supper are visible words given to the church for this era. We might note that churches and leaders which laud the use of images and movies and the like to meet needs for visual learning are typically those which are least interested in sacramental practice with any regularity. Obviously, this is not the case with all churches (e.g., it does not explain Roman Catholic notions of iconophilism), but it does explain much of the recent Protestant nondenominational fixation with images. Perhaps renewed iconoclasm will only be a viable proposal if held alongside robust sacramental practice, for humans are embodied creatures in a physical world.

The chief issue involved is that YHWH chose to use words and writings to communicate the "standard of sound teaching" which is a "good treasure" for the churches (2 Tim. 1.13–14). If there had been inspired photos or infallible videos, then Jesus would be rightly portrayed visually. Yet God made use of the verbal medium, and Reformed theology continues to affirm the importance of the particularity of this revelation. Indeed, God determined that a particular time and place would be fit for the incarnation: first-century Palestine. Among other things, this meant that there were no camcorders or cameras with which Jesus might be imaged. God also came down as the culmination of a plan of redemption long promised to the Jews, so that they were constitutionally bent against drawing sketches of their religious leaders or, in this case, their Messiah. Affirming the particularity of Jesus requires simul-taneous admission that we have access to him through texts and not through pictures.

Today, many Reformed churches know little about this history of iconoclasm. Presbyterian churches in America use illustrations in curriculum and video clips in sermons, depicting Jesus of Nazareth. When J. I. Packer published his bestselling book *Knowing God* in 1973, he received more feedbacks regarding his defense of the Reformed prohibition of images of God than on any other subject.[25] The issue will become even harder to engage as contemporary Western culture becomes more and more visual, especially with the dominance of web-based communications and the primacy of technology for educational practices. As this becomes an age of the eye, the Reformed emphasis on the ear and the spoken word will be more and more countercultural.[26] Perhaps Reformed iconoclasm can jolt the church into avoiding any easy identification of God with the everyday and mundane, with those images to which one can point. "As the incident of the golden calf reminds us, idolatry is motivated simultaneously by an overrealized eschatology and a demand for autonomy: to be in possession and in control of the divine, to determine their future rather than to receive it as gift."[27] Perhaps this provides an opening for reasserting the primacy of Scripture in the Christian life as popular culture dethrones the book as a central societal icon.

In conclusion, Reformed worship follows the guidance of the Word of God. Worship is the covenant renewal ceremony, so the Lord of the covenant names its terms. The Reformed churches have followed the "regulative principle" as a way to note the force of *sola Scriptura* for shaping the ceremonies of the church. We have considered two ways in which this has been teased out: a Reformed approach to sacramental mediation and the prohibition of images of God. Having considered worship, we turn next to the issue of authority in the Reformed churches in Chapter 7.

Chapter 7

Confessions and Authority

Reformed theology has a remarkable doctrine of the Holy Spirit. While many would not characterize it this way in the contemporary religious environment, such was the case from the earliest days of the Protestant Reformation. Indeed, John Calvin has been called the "theologian of the Holy Spirit" by Princeton theologian B. B. Warfield.[1] One of the most influential and truly beautiful sections of his famed *Institutes of the Christian Religion* appears in book three, which describes "The Way in Which We Receive the Grace of Christ: What Benefits Come to Us from It, and What Effects Follow," and discusses the Christian life (III.vi–x). Calvin offers in these chapters a thoroughly Spirit-empowered account of Christian existence and experience. Equally yoked to the person and work of the Holy Spirit, though, is its parallel passage—book four, which addresses "The External Means or Aids by Which God Invites Us into the Society of Christ and Holds Us Therein." Indeed, the terms "way" and "means" are conceptually linked, with book three describing the individual experience and book four placing this in its broader churchly setting. The Spirit works in individuals, that they know and love God, while this occurs through certain "external means" (see especially *ICR*, IV.i.3–4).

The Reformed tradition is not beholden to an otherworldly supernaturalism, and this is why it is not frequently identified as spiritually "charismatic" today. In the late modern era, the Spirit is identified typically with immediate religious experience or with deviations from the normal flow of history. Miracles and ecstatic speech are Spirit-filled, whereas liturgy and nature are not. Such is the outlook of the early twenty-first century. As global Pentecostalism and its charismatic offshoots represent the single fastest growing version of Christianity today, the work of the Spirit is easily cast into this charismatic mold. And, by and large,

Reformed churches remain distinct from this burgeoning charismatic movement, especially in its classical Pentecostal forms.

Yet there are other ways to view the work of the Holy Spirit, approaches that are less vulnerable to denigrating the world and its God-given laws of science and nature. As noted by a number of contemporary theologians, there is a great need for a doctrine of the Spirit that shows how the third person of the Trinity hovers over the workings of the earth and the creatures therein.[2] In other words, the Spirit's life-giving work needs to be linked to the ever-increasing capacities for work and health in the technocratic Western world. How does the Spirit's healing relate to the life support given to an accident victim in an intensive care unit? Whereas an otherworldly supernaturalist would see no link (for the Spirit only or largely works independently of immanent means), the Reformed tradition would affirm that the breath of God gives life through varied instruments. Indeed, God made humans with some dirt (Gen. 2.7). The Spirit typically works through means; grace perfects nature, rather than destroying or doing an end-run around it.

The Spirit's resting upon creaturely reality, literally giving it life, relates to the noncompetitive relationship of divine and human action as discussed earlier in the doctrine of God. The Spirit empowers humanity, rather than replacing humanity. In bringing persons to faith, the Spirit does not substitute for their own spiritual inclinations; no, the Spirit kills and makes alive their spirit, so that they desire God. Reformed theologians are compatibilists, in as much as they think the Spirit's agency and human agency are neither cooperative nor mutually exclusive, but truly concursive. Of course, if the Spirit gives life and brings about obedience and faith, Christians must ask what the Spirit has promised to do in the future. What can we expect from the Spirit? Obviously, the world has not been granted perfect life all at once, as the pain and suffering and sin around and within us demonstrate. Yet we confess that the Spirit is, in the words of the Nicene Creed, "the Lord and giver of life."

How does the Spirit do this? Furthermore, how does this apply to this chapter's title—"Confessions and Authority?" The key issue to be explored is how God makes provision for Christians to know and testify rightly about God. Chapter 1 talked about the

Word of God, the revelatory work of the triune God in making himself known by humans. Here we want to expand on that discussion by focusing on the community in which God is revealed. How does that community's life together help or hinder their knowledge of God? Specifically, we will consider how authority is exercised in the church, and what role theological confessions fulfill in exercising that churchly authority. In all these ways, the Spirit guides the church into knowing and proclaiming truth. As with justification, so with Christian community: all is of grace.

Theology in the Church

The Bible offers reflection on the way in which it is to be used. As the final authority for Christian faith and practice, it must also speak to its own interpretation. Method cannot be construed pre-theologically.[3] One key text in this regard is that transitional passage in Paul's Epistle to the Romans:

> I appeal to you therefore, brothers and sisters, by the mercies of God, to present your bodies as a living sacrifice, holy and acceptable to God, which is your spiritual worship. Do not be conformed to this world, but be transformed by the renewing of your minds, so that you may discern what is the will of God—what is good and acceptable and perfect. (Rom. 12.1–2)

Of the many treasures to be found here, consider the way in which communal transformation results in the church's worship. A plurality ("brothers and sisters") is called to offer singular devotion to God ("a living sacrifice"). To do so, they must realize that they will muck it up if left to follow the normal patterns of this sinful age. They must intentionally pursue ongoing transformation of their minds if they wish to discern God's will. How will they be transformed? "By the renewing of your minds" and "by the mercies of God." Indeed, these two means are not dissimilar, for the minds are to be renewed by reflecting together on those merciful acts of redemption that God has wrought in Christ. This imperative logically follows from the entire doctrinal argument of

Rom. 1–11, beginning with the logical inference "therefore." In light of the gospel mercies, be transformed, discern God's will, and offer yourselves in worship. All of this is meant to be pursued collectively, emphasized by the plurals throughout the text.

We should not be surprised that Paul envisions theology as the renewing of minds in community, for Jesus promised that the Spirit would reveal more about him to the gathering of his disciples. The teachings of the Upper Room Discourse (Jn 14–17) accent the churchly nature of discipleship by relaying many promises of the Spirit's truth-telling ministry in a communal fashion. One text deserves mention:

> I still have many things to say to you, but you cannot bear them now. When the Spirit of truth comes, he will guide you into all the truth, for he will not speak on his own authority, but whatever he hears he will speak, and he will declare to you the things that are to come. He will glorify me, for he will take what is mine and declare it to you. All that the Father has is mine; therefore I said that he will take what is mine and declare it to you. (Jn 16.12–15)

Many other verses refer to the illumination still to be given to the disciples (Jn 17.3, 17–20, 25–26). The Spirit is the agent of this transformation, testifying to what was taught by Christ, so much so that he can be called the "Spirit of truth" (14.17; 15.27; 16.13). Crucial for Reformed views on the church is the fact that this last testament of Jesus offers promises, assured statements of what will be given by God. Thus, the faithful will bank on these means as worthy of the church's full attention, organizing her polity around them.

Figuring out context is important for thinking Christianly. Surely the rise of contextualization, the linguistic turn, and the awareness of historical situatedness have shone a light on this truth. One danger of postmodernity, however, is that it may suggest that all our beliefs are true only for our particular group or clique, our ethnicity or denominational tradition. Yet we need to realize that there are narrower and wider contexts. Surely the most important contexts are fairly wide: (1) we are human, (2) we are sinful, and (3) we are being redeemed in Christ. The most important context for Christian theology, then, is not one's socioeconomic class or gender, but the economy of salvation and the promises of God for the church's corporate life. That is, the context within redemptive history, as described for us in the Bible, surveys the lay of the land in which we do our theologizing. Jn 14–17 describes the context of the church's theological practices, offering promises and sketching expectations for this communal work.

This concern to root theology in the practices of the church has been expressed by the term "means of grace." Certain means, or instruments, have been set apart by God for the betterment of humanity. They are the divine *modus operandi*, that is, the normal course of action. While God can and does work through the miraculous (the bolt of lightning bringing light), more frequently he employs the normal and seemingly mundane path outlined in his Word (the electrical grid transmitting electricity). Reformed theologians have been committed to the fact that theology, the very knowledge of God, is by grace alone. That is, humans do not have innate capacities for knowing God that have been created apart from God's kindness. The question then becomes: how and where does God typically give such knowledge? Whereas many pietists would point to personal acts of devotion (the so-called quiet time) and many modern liberals would point to societal progress (activism and the spirit of the age), Reformed believers see the churchly means of grace as participation in the proclamation of the Word and the practice of the sacraments. Through these acts, the church grows in knowing God. We must go to find God where God has deigned to be known. Most important for our present purposes, these means of grace are communal and not merely individual. The church communes with Christ Jesus at the table, just as the whole people of God are addressed by the preached Word. Indeed, the communion of saints confesses the Creed together.

Authority and Tradition

According to the second of the Ten Theses of Berne (1528):

> The Church of Christ makes no laws or commandments without God's Word. Hence all human traditions, which

are called ecclesiastical commandments, are binding upon us only in so far as they are based on and commanded by God's Word. (in *RCSC*, p. 49)

This Reformed confession acknowledges the reality of both God's Word and human traditions or ecclesiastical commandments. Indeed, both are binding upon us. The question becomes the way in which these two are binding, their relationship to each other, and so forth. More recently, Kevin Vanhoozer has suggested that this relationship can be construed as the script (Scripture) and its performance history (tradition), each needed in its own way for rightly performing the church's role in its contemporary setting.[4] The script is the starting point and guide, but the audience pays for performance of that script. So today's churches join with previous casts in putting flesh on this story by playing their parts. Thus, there is a tradition of acting out a part. No understudy would want to play a role without recourse to the performance of the previous star; literally, one studies under this person. So it is with the ongoing practice of discipleship and formation; the church is being reared by her ancestors. Tradition is necessary for the flourishing of the church's attention to the canon of Scripture. In considering this, we must look to the formal principle of the Reformation itself (*sola Scriptura*) to see the distinctively Protestant approach for linking Scripture and tradition.

Reformation historian Heiko Oberman has described the differing approaches to the Christian tradition by the Roman Catholic Church and the magisterial Reformers.[5] Each community sought to lay claim to continuity with the church's past. Indeed, only the Anabaptists were laying claim to novelty and a rupture with the heritage of the saints.

Contrary to the odd interpretations of some, *sola scriptura* is not *nuda scriptura*, and the Reformed never intended to deny the importance of interpreting the Bible or of coming to a common mind about its teaching for faith and practice, thereby forming or continuing a tradition.[6] This affirmation of tradition is exactly why the Reformers made such effort to show their theology as rooted in the writings of the early church fathers; in particular, Calvin added numerous citations from Augustine of Hippo as his *Institutes* enlarged from one edition to the next. The goal was to show that the Roman Catholics were not the only ones who wanted to claim continuity with the church's doctrinal heritage. While even Augustine was not always agreed with (e.g., his doctrine of justification was viewed as flawed or, at best, underdeveloped), the Reformers did exemplify the practice of theology as an exercise in critical traditioning.[7]

Oberman describes the Roman Catholic approach to tradition as "T2." In this view, there are two relatively equal sources that guide Christian faith and practice: Scripture and tradition. It is worth noting, of course, that the Roman Catholic Church has never denied the authority of Scripture. The crucial observation to be made here is that the Roman model supplements the Bible with another source for theology: the church's own doctrinal decisions. So tradition is an independent source in its own right, and the church may mandate certain practices or beliefs that are not derived from the pages of holy writ (e.g., the perpetual virginity of the blessed virgin Mary). The magisterial authority of church councils and the Roman Pontiff enjoy a wider sphere of influence, in as much as they can be sources, and not merely conduits, of revelation for the church.

By contrast, Oberman terms the Protestant approach to tradition "T1" and refers to it as a single-source view. Again, Protestants deny neither the necessity nor the value of tradition; it cannot and should not be avoided. So, for example, the Protestant churches retain the ecumenical creeds as valued judgments regarding the doctrines of the Trinity and the Incarnation. To the ancient creeds are added later (Reformation and/or modern) statements of faith specific to a given denomination. Yet Protestants subsume the authority of such traditions under the all-encompassing rule of Holy Scripture. We will consider one modification of the Apostles' Creed at the end of this chapter, wherein its words were retained even as the meaning of one key phrase was revised along biblical lines. The key emphasis is related to the regulative principle, discussed in the last chapter, namely, that only what is "either expressly set down in Scripture, or by good and necessary consequence may be deduced from Scripture" is authoritative, "unto which nothing at any time is to be added, whether by new revelations of the Spirit, or traditions of men" (WCF, I.6 in *BC*, p. 175).

A helpful way of noting this distinction is to say that whereas the Roman Catholic Church views tradition in a magisterial light, the Reformed churches consider tradition to be appropriate in a ministerial function. For the creature of the Word, tradition is valuable only in as much as it rightly gives the Word to the people of God. In this regard, the doctrine of papal infallibility has proven to be a major ecumenical stumbling block: Reformed Protestants see such an (admittedly infrequent) occurrence as impossible at this time in redemptive history, that is, God has simply not promised to give assurance of such perfection in this life prior to resurrection and glorification.[8] Here it is important to note that the material and formal principles of the Reformational protest are related: the Reformers believed that the church is justified yet sinful, just as individuals are. A real declaration of vindication and rightness does not translate into immediate, empirical results that would suggest such an attainment. Though the church looks flawed and failing, she is holy and right in Christ Jesus.

The Westminster Confession of Faith illustrates the two key claims about church tradition within the Reformed faith:

> It belongeth to synods and councils, ministerially, to
> determine controversies of faith, and cases of conscience;
> to set down rules and directions for the better ordering of
> the public worship of God, and government of his Church;
> to receive complaints in cases of maladministration, and
> authoritatively to determine the same. (WCF, XXXIII.2,
> in *BC*, p. 210)

Here, first, the importance of tradition is underlined as the conduit by which Christ rules his church. Christ ministers grace to his people through the work of the gathered church, especially her ordained officers and teachers.

> All synods or councils since the apostles' times,
> whether general or particular, may err, and many have
> erred; therefore they are not to be made the rule of
> faith or practice, but to be used as a help in both.
> (WCF, XXXIII.3, in *BC*, p. 210)

Ecclesiastical realism leads, secondly, to confession of the flawed nature of churchly authority. Tradition is not God's Word and, thus, is not guaranteed to be right and true. The people of God are to honor this authority "if consonant to the Word of God" (WCF, XXXIII.2, in *BC*, p. 210). The church is viewed as the new Israel, grafted in to the sinful yet redeemed people of God and always in danger of grumbling or pursuing idols of her own making.

Amy Plantinga Pauw has termed this ecclesiastical realism as belief in the "graced infirmity of the church." According to her, "a Reformed narrative of the church has no Eden. The church on earth has always existed 'after the fall,'" so that "Reformed ecclesiology is marked by a stark recognition of the church's fallibility." This is not merely a belief about the present *status quo*, either; "because there is no Edenic church, Reformed theology rejects restorationist wistfulness for pre-Constantinian or premodern forms of ecclesial existence."[9] While the texts of Scripture should be affirmed as fully trustworthy, the churches described in the pages of the New Testament are not at all infallible. There has not been, is not, and will not be a perfect church this side of Eden, not until God perfects the saints. This realism is apparent when Pauw points to the "anti-donatist" streak in Reformed ecclesiology, namely, the belief that the church's well-being is not dependent upon the piety of the pastor or elders. God works in and through sinful leaders, just as God was able to speak to Balaam through a donkey or to rule over Israel by a murderous adulterer (David) or to guide the church by a former persecutor (Paul). Whereas, the Donatists believed that lapsed priests had never really ministered God's grace in the first place, Calvin affirms that God promises to work through his ministers, sinful though they are: "When a puny man risen from the dust speaks in God's name, at this point we best evidence our piety and obedience toward God if we show ourselves teachable toward his minister, although he excels us in nothing" (*ICR*, IV.iii.1).[10]

More widely, Reformed theology has affirmed the distinction (though not separation) of the visible and the invisible church.[11] The invisible church is the end game, the final and perfected communion of all the saints saved by God. They exist in time, though their identities are only perfectly known by the watchful eye of God. From a human vantage point, their identity is mixed with others, who profess faith but will be found wanting on the day of judgment (e.g., Mt. 25.31–46). As John Webster says, "knowledge of the church cannot be derived in a straightforward way by deduction from its visible phenomena and practices," because its visibility is a "spiritual visibility."[12] While "the visible attests the invisible," the fact that this ragtag bunch of persons is the body of Christ is a truth grasped only in faith, by looking to God's promise beyond the all-too-apparent experiences of the everyday.[13] The holiness of the church, we might add, is visible, but only to the eye of faith that would peer through an eschatologically deepened lens (looking to what God has promised to fulfill in his good time, but is only provisionally evident now).

So, confessions and creeds and church authority are provisional, strictly speaking, because they are fallible and finite. Webster clarifies what is meant by "provisionality":

> To say that the creed is conditional or penultimate is worlds apart from the idea that the creed is merely one not-very-good attempt at pinning down a God whom we cannot really know. The creed is *confident* of its object; it *knows* this God. To talk of the provisionality of the creed is not an expression of skepticism; it is not the antithesis of earnestness; it is not an attempt to undermine genuine confession. It is simply a sober consequence of the fact that sinners—even redeemed sinners—cannot comprehend God's revelation. It simply acknowledges the constantly self-reforming character of the church's thought and speech. Reformation is needed not so we can keep step with the world—why on earth would we want to do that?—but so we can make sure that we are properly out of step with the world and therefore trying to keep pace with God. Once again, this isn't a matter of promoting the instability of having everything open to revision all the time; such an attitude risks denying the reality of the gift of the Spirit to the church. All we are saying is that the creed is not God's Word, but ours; it is made, not begotten.[14]

So the act of confession, and its legal authority in guiding the church, must be viewed within the economy of the Spirit's grace.

The church is led into the truth and has been promised the truth—though not yet in its fullness, for now we see darkly.

To summarize basic Reformed beliefs about churchly authority, we can look to the nineteenth-century Scottish historian, William Cunningham, as he describes the ecclesiology of John Calvin. Five principles are found in Calvin's teaching about the way that the church is run:

1. That it is unwarrantable and unlawful to introduce into the government and worship of the church anything which has not the positive sanction of Scripture.
2. That the church, though it consists properly and primarily only of the elect or of believers, and though, therefore, visibility and organization are not *essential*, as papists allege they are, to its existence, is under a positive obligation to be organized, if possible, as a visible society, and to be organized in all things, so far as possible—its office-bearers, ordinances, worship, and general administration and arrangements—in accordance with what is prescribed or indicated upon these points in the New Testament.
3. That the fundamental principles, or leading features, of what is usually called Presbyterian church government, are indicated with sufficient clearness in the New Testament, as permanently binding upon the church.
4. That the church should be altogether free and independent of civil control, and should conduct its own distinct and independent government by presbyteries and synods, while the civil power is called upon to afford it protection and support.
5. That human laws, whether about civil or ecclesiastical things, and whether proceeding from civil or ecclesiastical authorities, do not, *per se*—that is, irrespective of their being sanctioned by the authority of God—impose an obligation upon the conscience.[15]

According to Cunningham, Calvin here affirms the regulative principle, the distinction between the visible and invisible church, a Presbyterian polity that focuses on government by plurality and with checks and balances, the freedom of the church from civil control so that it can be governed only by God's Word, and all authority in life (whether religious or secular) binding only when guided by God's Word. Each tenet can take slightly different forms in certain Reformed contexts—for example, many Anglicans have been Reformed even while affirming an Episcopal polity[16]— though these have been guiding principles of the mainstream Reformed tradition. A lengthier introduction to Reformed ecclesiology would focus on these issues of governance; for the sake of brevity, however, we must move on to focus solely on the issue of confessions as an exercise of theological authority.[17]

Context and Witness

Confession has been the crucial category for Reformed thinking about church authority. Reformed churches confess. And to aid in this endeavor, they write confessions that will guide this vocal testimony. A crucial principle has been that confession and testimony are responsive activities. In testifying or witnessing, one does not create truth or fashion the self and its identity. Rather, one speaks of what one has seen. Karl Barth often suggested that John the Baptist was the best image of this activity, pointing to the Messiah and saying, "He must increase; I must decrease." In confession, the Christian stands with the church and speaks of the wondrous works of God. Confession is an act of praise and of witness.

Confessions are written forms of confession, prepared by church authorities and legally binding upon those churches. Confessions are an extension of pastoral authority, wherein the elders of a Reformed church exercise leadership in shaping the form of the church's common life according to the Gospel. Of course, this pastoral authority is itself an extension of the sovereignty of the Word and his written words in Holy Scripture. Thus, pastoral authority is derived and secondary, whereas that of Jesus Christ is intrinsic and primary. The principle of this mediation is the Holy Scriptures, wherein Jesus's rule is passed along to his apostles and their followers. We must remember that Reformed theology affirms the "priesthood of all believers"— that every Christian has access to Christ, the great high priest, and thus can turn to God in faith apart from any other formal mediator than Christ—without undoing the judicial role of church authorities. Reformed churches have a realistic view of such authority, noting its flaws and tendencies to overreach. Hence, most Reformed churches call for multiple elders to govern the local church as well as multiple layers of government (with higher and lower courts for review). In fact, the United States of America is guided by constitutional principles largely borrowed from Reformed ecclesiology, wherein there is a balance of powers. Such "checks and balances" are intended to lean against the tendency of humans (whether the pastor or the majority) to use power wrongly.[18]

Church authority takes many forms, but central among them is the official proclamation of church doctrine and practice. In this act, the elders of the church gather together and come to a common mind regarding the teaching of Scripture, the very nature of the gospel itself as well as its necessary implications for contemporary issues. Confessions then are formal texts that serve as rules for the theological beliefs of pastors and elders; for example, many Reformed pastors have been required to affirm their belief that the Westminster Standards reflect the teaching of the Bible. In various denominations, other confessional texts serve in this role (e.g., the three forms of unity in the Dutch Reformed churches: the Belgic Confession, the Heidelberg Catechism, and the Canons of Dordt).

That confession involves attestation or witness means that confession ought not be a simple power-grab. Surely, confessions involve power. When the Nicene-Constantinopolitan Creed was adopted, Arians were no longer welcome in the orthodox churches. Power was being employed to rule the church. Yet the church has confessed that this judicial exercise has been a tool of the Spirit of Christ to reign over his body.[19] Indeed, Webster says that "a creed is not a program, a platform, a manifesto to mobilize our forces. It is an amazed cry of witness: 'Behold, the Lamb of God who takes away the sin of the world!' (Jn 1.29 NASB). Confession is attestation, not self-assertion."[20] The Spirit does judge, but that is a part of the miraculous work of bringing life into a dying world. Again, Webster is helpful: "Truth is a miracle; truth is the creation of the Holy Spirit. The notion of heresy and the practice of anathematizing are ways of following or being caught up in the miracle of truth. They are spiritual practices, aspects of the transformation of human knowledge and government by the coming of the Word of God."[21]

The modern West, of course, has largely decried any authority with regard to faith and practice. As Roger Lundin has eloquently traced it, the nineteenth century saw the demise of religious and cultural authority along with the rise of the pragmatic and aesthetic.[22] The Reformed tradition has actually spurred some of this trend, by emphasizing the need for power and authority to be reformed. Yet the Reformed battle with idols has become thoroughgoing iconoclasm, wherein any power is viewed as violent and wrongly so. Against this exaggeration of Reformed teaching, the place of the preaching of the Word stands as a symbol. Whereas modern culture and communication studies, in particular, would suggest that sermons ought to be replaced by dialogue and conversation, the Reformed confessions highlight a biblical emphasis on God's promise to work through the proclamation of the Word in monological form. The sermon really is the Word of God (see *ICR*, IV.i.6), by God's grace, according to the teaching of the Reformation-era confessions and theologians as recent as Karl Barth or Michael Horton.[23] Again, this is not a mere power-play; by faith, the Reformed churches believe that God has promised to work through the pastor's proclamation of the Gospel.

When do churches confess? Various issues have called for theological engagement from the authorities of Reformed bodies. At a certain point, churches believe that a *status confessionis* exists, wherein the church must take sides to be true to the gospel. Again, the church is employing power and exercising authority in confessing that God's gospel leads to particular implications for faith and practice. The challenge, then, is to make sure that such confessional acts and texts are truly rooted in the gospel, not merely the *status quo* or the secular projects of church members. Reformed churches have even disagreed on when a *status confessionis* exists. A number can be listed:

- The Genevan Confession addressed the early cries of the Reformation, highlighting the nature of the gospel and true worship.

- The Canons of Dordt responded to the protests of the Arminians amongst the Dutch Reformed churches, focusing on the atonement and predestination.
- The Westminster Standards and the Westminster Directory for Public Worship were prepared to guide the restored Protestant leadership of the Church of England.
- The Theological Declaration of Barmen was penned by Reformed and Lutheran leaders as a rebuke of the evils of German National Socialism (the Nazi party) and the complicity of the German churches in the rise of the Third Reich.
- The Confession of 1967 addressed issues of war and peace, racial reconciliation, and sexual politics in the turbulent 1960s.
- The Belhar Confession spoke out against the heresy of Apartheid in South African Dutch Reformed churches.

More could be listed, to be sure, but these examples prove the point: very different situations have led Reformed churches to confess the faith. Churchly authorities have seen fit to confess authoritatively on a variety of issues, claiming that the written Word speaks to these issues in explicit and binding fashion.

So Reformed churches are confessing churches. R. Scott Clark, a historian at Westminster Seminary in California, has written a recent book entitled *Recovering the Reformed Confession: Our Theology, Piety, and Practice*.[24] His concern involves the absorption of many conservative Reformed persons into the broader evangelical movement, which is relatively minimal with regard to confessional expectations. Evangelicals hold a few key distinctives in common, though they differ over sizable issues, such as the sacraments, church order, soteriology, etc. By and large, evangelical institutions do have statements of faith, though they tend to leave out many contentious issues and have been criticized by many as fostering a lowest-common-denominator theological unity.[25] In many ways (though perhaps to a lesser degree), evangelicals have followed the ecumenical model of the liberal World Council of Churches, wherein mission is seen as uniting, while doctrine divides. Churches can partner together in fighting social ills or in spreading the gospel, but theological expression of the nature of the gospel cannot be teased out in much detail (or else these constituencies would splinter and lose their luster).

Clark believes that many Reformed churches have moved to downgrade their confessional identity, and they need to pursue a reinvigorated confessional life, remembering that Reformed churches are gatherings of God's people around God's Word. Indeed, Reformed gatherings are ordered communities, witnessing to a common confession. Clark's concern is interestingly related to the rise of the so-called new Calvinism in America, wherein several partnerships are writing contemporary confessions and teaching scores of young adherents to identify confessionally with like-minded witnesses to the gospel. The Alliance of Confessing Evangelicals gathers around the "Cambridge Declaration," while the groups known as "Together for the Gospel" and "The Gospel Coalition" similarly make use of theological statements to define their identity. These are all parachurch organizations and, especially since they do not agree on all the particulars of traditional Reformed theology (e.g., infant baptism), they do not fit Clark's prescription. Nonetheless, there is a remarkable development to be noted, a turn to confessional Christianity amongst many who want to identify with the Reformation tradition in some form or another.[26] Perhaps these organizations will bring about a revival of conservative confession-writing by actual Reformed denominations to match the large group of recent confessions written by mainline Reformed bodies (e.g., the "Confession of 1967," the Theological Declaration of Barmen, the Belhar Confession).

Diversity and Pluralism

When he took up his first teaching post as honorary professor of Reformed doctrine at the University of Göttingen, Karl Barth offered a series of lectures on the Reformed confessions. As he articulated what distinguished the Reformed confessions from those of the Roman Catholics, the Lutherans, and modern Christianity, Barth focused on the local and plural nature of the Reformed statements. Each church—that is, each country or major city—would offer its own testimony to God's Word. There simply was nothing like the Formula of Concord, which bound all Lutherans after 1560, in the Reformed world. Barth construes confession as an event, not a static *status quo*, suggesting that confession must time and again be tested by the Word.[27] Indeed, according to Barth, "the only thing one cannot do is to argue to oneself or to others that *one's own* confession is *the* Reformed confession. Reformed confessions, as long as and to the extent that they are Reformed, will always be *many* and not *one*."[28] Shirley Guthrie and many contemporary theologians have taken this to be the distinctive feature of Reformed confessions, what Guthrie terms "the religious relativism" of this heritage (see his *ABR*, p. 19).

Barth's observation can be traced back to the wishes of the early Reformed leaders. Heinrich Bullinger and Leo Judae signed the First Helvetic Confession, saying this about its authority:

> We wish in no way to prescribe for all the church through these articles a single rule of faith. For we acknowledge no other rule of faith than Holy Scripture. We agree with whoever agrees with this although he uses different expressions from our confession. For we should have regard for the fact itself and for the truth, not for the words. We grant to everyone the freedom to use his own expression which is suitable for his church and will make use of this freedom ourselves, at the same time defending the true sense of this confession against distortions.[29]

Reformed churches have taken these words to heart, especially in the sixteenth and twentieth centuries, periods when they wrote numerous confessions. For example, Lukas Vischer has collected well over 30 confessions from the twentieth century alone in his book *Reformed Witness Today: A Collection of Confessions and Statements of Faith*.[30] Reformed denominations and associations have been at the forefront of confessional writing in the last few decades.

Biblical teaching about the nature of humanity and the divine intent behind diversity seems to corroborate this penchant. Clearly, dispersion to varying localities was intended by God; the very first chapter of the Bible offers the mandate that Adam and Eve are to spread their dominion over the whole earth, moving outward from Eden. One assumes they would do this by propagating and commissioning their children and their children's children each to find their own home, gradually encompassing the whole earth. Difference and geographic particularity are here implied to be a harmonious way of blessing the world, a necessary result of spreading out over the globe in obedience to God's calling. Only a few chapters later does disharmony reach epic proportions, in the story of Babel. But the Abrahamic promise involves expectation of a revived harmony amongst diverse peoples: the Israelite offspring and the nations. Eventually, Jesus tears down the dividing wall, and the Spirit's appearance at Pentecost makes a difference (in linguistic terms) to be of a peaceful and harmonious nature again. In the vision of the New Jerusalem (Rev. 21.22–27), the glory of God does not do away with the glory of the kings of the nations, but perfects them in the presence of God. Difference is intended by God, stricken by sin, redeemed in Christ, and eventually perfected by the Spirit. Thus, we should not be surprised that different ways of voicing creation's praises arise from churches in various times and places (even within the same Reformed tradition).

Obviously, some doctrinal statements have wider and longer influence than others. Scottish theologian Andrew McGowan offers his reflections on the enduring influence of the Westminster Standards in English-speaking Reformed churches today:

> I greatly value the *WCF* and am entirely commited to the federal theology. I spoke confidently and without mental reservation when I affirmed my belief in its theology at my ordination. But yet I look forward to the day when there will be a new Confession of Faith which holds the same federal theology as that of the *WCF* but which expresses that theology in a way which takes into account the lessons learned within the tradition since 1647, and which deals with the issues of today, and not those of the seventeenth century. A Confession, for example, which would speak more specifically about regeneration, about the Person and work of the Holy Spirit, about mission and evangelism. More importantly, it would be a Confession which points out the errors of liberal theology, of relativism, of pluralism and of the New Age movement rather than simply the errors of Roman Catholicism.[31]

McGowan's point is only underlined by the late David Wright, professor of church history at the University of Edinburgh:

> If the Reformation confessions and catechisms did not suffice in the subsequent century, why should Westminster's handiwork do so over three centuries later? It is as if we were to conclude that the King James Version of the Bible could not be significantly improved upon—and at the same time forget that several high-quality English translations had been published in the century before 1611.[32]

Clearly, just as churches continue to revise translations of the Bible, so they should continue to refine their commentary on its teaching regarding Christian faith and practice, that is, their confessions of faith.

Perhaps, then, the Presbyterian Church (USA) has found the right path, adopting a *Book of Confessions*, including statements ranging from ancient creeds to Reformation and post-Reformation confessions and catechisms into the modern realm with witnesses like the Barmen Declaration and the Brief Statement of Faith. Such an approach to confessional authority allows for the ancient and Reformation-era confessions to have their say, yet it supplements these classic texts with modern declarations. Such an approach surely manifests that no single churchly text can encompass the truths of God's Word. This format also suggests that varying contexts call for different responses from the church. Perhaps this approach best witnesses to Barth's concern that no single confession be taken as *the* Reformed confession. Many have argued this.

Are there weaknesses, however, to this approach? The *Book of Confessions* contains documents that seem to contradict one another.[33] Indeed, the very documents differ with regard to what they envision a confession doing, how such a statement ministers God's Word to the people of God. William Placher proposed that there were three different views regarding how the Bible is authoritative for the church, each with precedent within the Reformed confessional heritage.[34] Placher's useful taxonomy only highlights a reality of the PC(USA)'s theological identity: it is fragmented, and this fragmentation is implicit in its very confessional collection. The Theological Declaration of Barmen and the Confession of 1967 both exemplify, in various forms, Barthian theology, which largely shirks certain classical tenets of the Reformation and post-Reformation confessions (especially the Westminster Standards). Of course, the Westminster standards are still in this collection, right there alongside the universalistic tones of the Declaration of 1967 and the criticism of any natural theology in Barmen. Cognitive dissonance ensues should any reader try to read these together. How do these function, then, in guiding the theological identity of this denomination, her ordained officers, and their teaching? One may opt for any of the theologies within the text, any of the three positions in Placher's taxonomy, and claim to be receiving the *Book of Confessions* as a subordinate standard for Christian faith and practice. Loss of coherence is a danger.

Some have proposed a way to deal with such possible incoherence: naming certain essential tenets that must be affirmed by candidates for ordination and, hence, must guide the teaching ministry of the church. Indeed, this is required by the third ordination vow found in the PC(USA) *Book of Order*: "Do you sincerely receive and adopt the essential tenets of the Reformed Faith as expressed in the confessions of our church as authentic and reliable expositions of what Scripture leads us to believe and do and will you be instructed and led by those confessions as you lead the people of God?"[35] Some list of "essential tenets" or, in an earlier era, "fundamentals" has not proven successful as an easy solution.[36] In this regard, debates within the Church of Scotland have proven indicative. Many theologians, having grown frustrated with certain aspects of the federal theology of the Westminster Standards, proposed the adoption of a book of confessions, including ancient creeds and more recent statements. This would be accompanied by a "Declaratory Act," which would note the essentials to be gleaned from each of these (somewhat contradictory) texts and confessed together. In David Fergusson's words, "it was defeated by an alliance of those on the right who resented any further loosening of our doctrinal standards, and those on the left who perceived a threat to liberty of opinion."[37] John McIntyre argued that adoption of such a collection would lead to further theological confusion, in reality allowing the "Declaratory Act" to be the only actual confessional standard and essentially undoing the function of the book as a whole.[38] In other words, under the guise of bringing in supplemental standards, the creation of such a book that will be interpreted by means of a list of essential tenets (not explicitly stated in one of the confessions) results in those tenets being the standards and the various confessions (classic and contemporary) being mere illustrations or historical documents. By and large, in actual practice, it has been left up to each governing body (presbytery or classis) to determine the essential tenets, which cannot be written down and published abroad.

As Colin Gunton highlighted, Reformed churches must remember that the Reformation was innovative in certain respects—giving newfound clarity to doctrines such as justification, Scripture, and worship. It would be odd, then, for this reformation or revolution to become an utterly enduring *status quo*, rather than a place from which to see further and pursue reform.[39] We should note a drastic example of reform that has proven largely influential in all Reformed circles, from the revisionary and liberal to the most conservative and traditional. The extent to which Reformed churches have shown themselves willing to revise their doctrinal affirmations can be most fully seen in looking at the Apostles' Creed and the claim that Christ "descended into hell."[40]

The so-called Apostles' Creed affirms many core beliefs of the Christian faith, among them the truth that Christ "descended into hell." Historians are largely agreed that the early church must have understood this to refer to a journey made between Good Friday (crucifixion) and Easter morning (resurrection), when Jesus journeyed to an underworld of some sort. There were many takes on what this underworld was (whether a holding pen for saints awaiting resurrection or a place of punishment) and there were various views on how Christ went there (whether in body or merely in soul). Christians even disagreed regarding the purpose of this journey (to save some who were there or to proclaim his triumph over them). John Calvin argued that exegesis of the biblical passages traditionally linked to this doctrine was flawed, and so he suggested a reinterpretation of this creedal tenet (see his *ICR*, II.xvi.8–12). For Calvin, the descent to hell occurred prior to the death of Jesus, rather than during what has been called "holy Saturday." Calvin's temporal change was matched by a geographic shift: no longer was the descent a trek to a place other than this world, but it was now viewed as a way of describing Christ's human life and especially his suffering on the cross as a spiritual event: suffering God's wrath in our place. As he puts it so eloquently:

> The point is that the Creed sets forth what Christ suffered
> in the sight of men, and then appositely speaks of that
> invisible and incomprehensible judgment which he
> underwent in the sight of God in order that we might
> know not only that Christ's body was given as the price of
> our redemption, but that he paid a greater and more
> excellent price in suffering in his soul the terrible torments
> of a condemned and forsaken man. (*ICR*, II.xvi.10)

Calvin is clear that he takes the descent clause of the Creed to be a spiritual qualification of the immediately prior clause, which addresses the physical death of Jesus. His death had spiritual significance. He argues on the basis of exegetical work, showing the flimsy nature of the traditional reading and the superiority of his own articulation, especially by pointing to the "cry of dereliction," when Jesus experienced the abandonment of the Father on the cross (see Mk 15.34).[41] While Calvin's view of the descent is not entirely without precedent (partially prefaced by Nicholas of Cusa in a sermon on Ps. 30.11), he has pointedly shown a willingness to buck tradition by refashioning a creedal claim. He does not abandon it, as many modern biblicists have, but he recasts its meaning to fit the biblical material.

Nevertheless, the enduring legacy of the Reformed reformation cannot simply be reduced to its formal principle: reform by Scripture alone. Many have been tempted to sever the formal from the material, taking the Reformed tradition as a constantly revolutionary process. Even in the nineteenth century, William Cunningham could reflect back on years and years of this turning of the Reformed principle against the Reformers themselves.[42] But cultural and religious iconoclasm is not the Reformed vision or the practice of reforming church practice. It must also be guided by the material principle and key theological tenets of the

Reformed identity: justification, predestination, etc. While there may be no hermeneutical or ecclesiastical safeguard that can keep the church from the danger of doing away with tradition, surely the doctrinal chaos of many Reformed churches is far from ideal. Conservatives too must be vigilant, resisting the urge to allow anything to have even functional infallibility in the practice of theology. Just as the Reformers insisted that the Pope and church councils were never infallible (against Rome), so today Reformed churches must add to that Reformational protest an insistence that neither academically pedigreed scholars (the Ph.D.) nor Protestant confessions (the Westminster Standards) can be infallible. Reformed theology is committed to the sole final authority of the Bible, to be read amongst the church and under the authority of her official confessions. We trust that God works through these means, yet we remain ready to be shown idols of our own making that must be reformed by the Word. We will let John Webster have the last word here: "Theology does not start *de novo*; but citation of the past will not suffice for a church in which reformation is not an inherited condition but an event."[43]

Chapter 8

Culture and Eschatology

The Reformed trad ition is no stranger to engaging the public square. Indeed, Max Weber's famed thesis regarding the "Protestant work ethic" and the "spirit of capitalism" really flows from a particular interpretation of the Reformed corner of the Protestant world. Weber suggested that the religious ideals and practices of the Calvinist churches encouraged the rise of the capitalist economy.[1] His thesis has received criticism through the decades, yet it remains influential in many quarters of religious studies. So here is a claim that some form of Reformed faith and practice can have massive effects on economic culture, even that well beyond the bounds of any Presbyterian or Reformed church membership. Certain notions of vocational and financial praxis may have spilled over from the stream of Reformed theology.

More recently, David Hall has provided an acronym ("DARCL") for the major points of what he calls "political Calvinism." That is, he believes these emphases have been pushed by Reformed convictions. The 5 tenets are as follows:

1. Depravity as a perennial human variable to accommodate;
2. Accountability for leaders via a collegium;
3. Republicanism as the preferred form of government;
4. Constitutionalism needed to restrain both the rulers and the ruled;
5. Limited government, beginning with the family, as foundational.[2]

Indeed, there is much to be said for the influence of Reformed theology upon the founding principles of the American Republic. To affirm this is not to make any claims regarding the religious or theological beliefs of the "founding fathers," only to point out that certain Reformed doctrines held a large cultural cachet in the modern era. At the 2006 meeting of the American Academy of Religion in Washington, D.C., the Reformed Theology and History Group was able to spend several hours considering the relationship of Reformed theology to, or, even more strongly, its influence upon, the political character of American government, under the banner, "What hath Washington, D.C., to do with Geneva?" In this case, it was shown that political philosophies and practices have been related to theological tenets deep within this churchly heritage.

If Reformed theology has had effects (good and bad) in the realms of economics and politics, we must inquire about the teachings regarding culture and human history in various Reformed contexts. John Webster has suggested:

> [B]y the grace of God it is given to the church (and therefore to its theology) to discern the situation of humanity faithfully and truthfully—in faith, not in sight, but nevertheless in truth—and therefore to see the human situation now as that stretch of human history which lies between the first and second advents of Jesus, in whom and for whom all things are created and perfected.[3]

Theology is about God, and all things in relation to him. Because theology speaks of this world and this time, one's doctrinal commitments are going to have social, political, economic, and artistic ramifications. In this chapter, issues of ethics and culture will be addressed, especially by showing how they are viewed within theological categories such as eschatology and law. To show areas of major influence, we should briefly survey the high points of redemptive history that shape how culture is to be viewed in light of God and his works.[4]

Creation

Reformed churches have sought to affirm the classical Christian doctrine of creation, namely, that God made the world *ex nihilo* ("from nothing"). While debates have raged about issues of science and history, the more central theological concern has been upheld:

God made the creation. More specifically, God made a physical world; in so doing, God declared this material world to be "good" (Gen. 1.4, 10, 12, 18, 21, 25, 31). The great danger perennially to be avoided has been Gnostic dualism: the elevation of the spiritual at the expense of the physical or material. At the time of the Reformation, this was a major cultural and churchly issue, precisely because dualism had been normalized and even institutionalized. For example, standard views of the blessed hope (eschatology) in the Middle Ages involved a relatively gnostic bent.[5] We can see this by looking to the best of the medievals, Thomas Aquinas, who did manage to honor the hope of a resurrected body. But even Aquinas could only point to a negative use of this resurrected body: it is useful in this glorified future only because it will no longer distract humans from their ultimate task of the beatific vision, a spiritual apprehension of God. Ever so gradually, and not really until the late Modern Age, these spiritualized hopes and aspirations were placed in a wider perspective, so that the goodness of resurrection *bodies* and the full panorama of human activities (including labor) could be honored as part of the New Jerusalem. Creation is good; physicality and sociality are essential to being human. Thus, the new creation will also involve materiality; indeed, it will be the perfection of every aspect of created reality.

Another way to put this is to say that spirituality (or life with God) is not about a flight from earthly life. Shirley Guthrie says it well:

> Any spirituality, including supposedly Christian spirituality, that retreats from the world into the self-serving piety of a private religious life is a false spirituality that flees rather than seeks God. True Christian spirituality cheerfully and confidently plunges into the life of our dirty, sinful, confused world, for there is where we meet the Spirit of the triune God who is present and at work not to save people *from* but *in* and *for the sake of* that world—the world that was and is and will be God's world. (*ABR*, p. 86)

Guthrie expands on this as well, showing how truly Christian spirituality observes daily affairs as divinely given. So there is no chasm or divide between the earthly and the heavenly; rather, heaven comes to earth. Or, to be more precise, we pray and expect that things *will be* on earth as it is in heaven.

This earthly spirituality is still *spirituality*, however, so the emphasis upon earthiness cannot be seen as a form of naturalistic reductionism. Life on earth is still aiming at life in the new heavens and new earth, toward life with God. In the modern era, many have minimized or denied this transcendent perspective on life, seeing all things as natural(istic) and even reductionistically so. Charles Mathewes has given a sharp rebuttal of this mini- malistic portrayal of cultural engagement. While his "theology of public life" is not Reformed but more generally Augustinian, his assessment of the modern malaise accurately describes tensions felt by many Reformed churches, a gravitational pull toward viewing religious language as ornamental and expressive talk to describe solely natural and political ends.[6] Spiritual language and practice become merely instrumental in getting people to ends that are pursued for other reasons. Against such "domestication of transcendence," to use William Placher's phrase, humans were created as not only physical but also spiritual beings: see, for example, the twofold nature of the creation account in Gen. 2.7. All told, a theology of engagement with the world in all its intricacies cannot be played off against the spiritual life, but must be viewed within the covenantal structure given by God.

This key point is accented by the blessed mandate given later in Gen. 1, commanding Adam and Eve to be fruitful and multiply, to spread out and have dominion, to extend God's glory over the whole globe (Gen. 1.28–30). Sandwiched as it is between divine declarations of creation's goodness, this calling suggests that familial, social, political, and economic activities are part of God's good intentions for the world. The goodness of normal life experience in all its physicality and sociality has not always been appreciated; witness the *status quo* in late medieval Europe on the cusp of the Protestant Reformation. For example, the laity viewed the celibate clergy or other religious orders as enjoying a higher calling, in as much as they were removed from family ties, the marketplace, the battlefield, and other material realms of interaction. Luther and the other Reformers responded boldly (e.g., Luther married a nun), giving honor and respect to so-called secular vocations as being good and worthy of respect. Culture and work, then, are given real spiritual worth, precisely as culture and work. They are not merely instrumental (though there are surely instrumental uses: for example, farming provides food that keeps people alive long enough to come to know and love Christ), since they are required by God even before they fall into sin and the need for redemption. Many Reformed types continue to turn to this "cultural mandate" as grounds for their engagement of culture from a theological perspective.

Fall

Just as the whole spectrum of created reality is good, so Reformed theologians have affirmed that every nook and cranny of creation have been distorted by sin. Sin and death limit the potential of culture, in as much as they skew the desires and abilities of cultural agents, who now pursue the wrong rather than the good. So the Genesis account moves eastward from Eden to bad blood in the family, to the evils of society that result in the flood, and eventually to the debacle of Babel. These later stories offer communal and societal manifestations of sin's curse. Perhaps no person has so emphasized the effects of sin upon the broad parameters of modern society as did the late Reinhold Niebuhr. Many have challenged his defenses of democracy and American policies as a Constantinian confusion of church and state, yet it must be noted that Niebuhr at least attempted (if not succeeded) in suggesting that, for example, democracy was ideal as the least evil system for government, in as much as it best minimizes the heinous nature of any and every evil human participant. Though there can certainly be healthy debate regarding the degree to which he faithfully or rightly promoted certain social and political practices, he was attempting to do so in light of the gospel construed from a Reformed perspective (especially by honoring the doctrine of original sin).[7]

Of course, the doctrine of total depravity has been under attack ever since the Enlightenment age, in which sin has been viewed as a force able to be extricated from humans, who are really and essentially good. Many revisionist figures within the Reformed churches have echoed the Arminian maxim that responsibility presupposes ability; such presuppositions led to the distaste of many in mainline Reformed denominations for the classic orthodoxy of the post-Reformation era (e.g., the Westminster standards). Still, this teaching from Protestant orthodoxy remains the confessional heritage of the Reformed churches, and it starkly opposes the cultural optimism of modernity. Whereas many thought industrialization and urbanization would bring the kingdom of God (hence, naming a new mainline periodical on the cusp of the twentieth century *The Christian Century*), the doctrine of total depravity mellows any such expectations on this side of Christ's glorious return.

Common Grace

Scottish theologian John Murray, the most impressive of the theologians from Westminster Seminary in Philadelphia, observed:

> [I]f we appreciate the implications of total depravity, then we are faced with a series of very insistent questions. How is it that men who still lie under the wrath and curse of God and are heirs of hell enjoy so many good gifts at the hand of God? How is it that men who are not savingly renewed by the Spirit of God nevertheless exhibit so many qualities, gifts and accomplishments that promote the preservation, temporal happiness, cultural progress, social and economic improvement of themselves and of others? How is it that races and peoples that have been apparently untouched by the redemptive and regenerative influences of the gospel contribute so much to what we call human civilization? To put the question most comprehensively: how is it that this sin-cursed world enjoys so much favour and kindness at the hand of its holy and ever-blessed Creator?[8]

Perhaps Murray's question can be most useful when made very specific. Consider the scores of celebrities in the news, combining materialistic and hedonistic excess with a globe-trotting, philanthropic lifestyle of mercy. How is it that Hollywood sex symbols, who exhibit no manifestation of Christian salvation, are inclined

161

to adopt children from situations of terrible plight and need? From where does this good come? If we confess original sin, from where do pagan beauty, truth, and goodness emerge?

Grace is the first answer, that is, any goodness is surely an undeserved gift from God (Jas 1.17). The Bible speaks of various types of grace, two of which are especially pertinent. First, there is obviously a redemptive grace that is poured out on those who will be redeemed by God. This type of grace is the presupposition of Murray's position, as it is essential for turning the sinner's desires toward the good of the Gospel. Second, there is grace that does not result in salvation *per se*, even as it leads to good works in the here and now. God's restraining and invigorating grace allows for good things to flow from unredeemed people: see the gifting of Cain, so that he could build a city (Gen. 4.12, 15) or the covenantal promise given to Noah (Gen. 8.21–22; 9.9–11). In both cases, God is not dealing with the problem of their sins, but is only maintaining and guarding their continued earthly existence. God also keeps certain pagans from acting in evil ways at certain points: consider the sexual restraint of Abimelech (Gen. 20.6) or the guidance of Sennacherib's military (2 Kgs 19.27–28), both of which are enabled by God. Countless Psalms reference the manifestation of God's glory in the beauty of the creation; even more so, the Psalms speak of God's provision of food and drink for the righteous *and the wicked* (Pss. 659–10; 104.14–15, 24, 27–30; 145.9). John Murray, accordingly, calls these divine blessings "common grace": "every favour of whatever kind or degree, falling short of salvation, which this undeserving and sin-cursed world enjoys at the hand of God."[9]

Finally, common grace must be understood as only one form of God's grace. This must be clearly affirmed, precisely because many modern pluralists would treat all grace as a generic experience: so New Age de-stressing and Lutheran sacramental practices are common in conveying grace and in aiding human flourishing. Such pluralism can suggest that spirituality can be practiced apart from religion or any churchly form of piety. But Shirley Guthrie's warning is apt: "people who are too spiritual for the church are also too spiritual for the triune God who promises to be present and at work in this all-too-questionable Christian community" (*ABR*, p. 89). Redemptive grace is only found in the Christian community, and common grace's usefulness does not mitigate the importance of moving on to partake of such higher gifts. In conclusion, Reformed churches see God giving blessings to the righteous and the wicked, that is, commonly aiding culture and society; however, these graces are not themselves redemptive.

Redemption and God's Kingdom

The novelist Marilynne Robinson states, "Wherever you turn your eyes the world can shine like transfiguration. You don't have to bring a thing to it except a little willingness to see. Only, who could have the courage to see it?"[10] "Transfiguration" involves the presence of grace amidst the everyday, heightening its meaning and significance. Robinson claims that these heights are "wherever you turn," there in the everyday and mundane. Indeed, Robinson's novel *Gilead* may be one of the most beautiful Reformed ruminations on the world, even as it draws on a long tradition of thinking about all reality in light of God. The whole world is God's theater, Calvin used to say, wherein the drama of divine blessing plays out anew each day. Gradually, the luminescence of the Son's light beckons our attention. So the so-called nature psalms speak of the rocks and trees, the valleys and the mountains, all voicing creation's praise of God. Albeit too slowly, we see and learn more and more of God and his blessings for the world. The key theological principle is this: grace perfects, rather than destroys, nature.

Salvation does reshape cultural practices, then, because God's redemptive works give newness to every facet of human life. For example, whereas Babel represents the undoing of human society, with difference becoming an occasion and expression of pain and divergence, the gift of the Spirit at Pentecost involves the harmonizing work of making difference work. Language and conversation are no longer realms of frustration and sin, but they are "transfigured" here by the Spirit. By the end of Luke's writing, they have served as the means by which the gospel moves outward from the Jews in Jerusalem and reaches the center of a Gentile empire: Rome (Acts 28.31). The Spirit does not do away with talking, even with doing so in different languages, but provides for this cross-cultural speech being graced and effective. Salvation and grace re-make, but do not destroy, nature and culture.

The real issue involved in the relationship of Christianity and culture, therefore, is the way in which eschatology and salvation relate. How does the redemption brought by Christ play itself out over the course of the plan of God? In what time and at what pace will these things happen? In asking this, we are entering a new doctrinal subject: eschatology, the study of the "last things."

Eschatology did not become a major doctrinal topic in its own right until the late modern era, wherein the discipline of history was developed and required a methodological framework. This comparative claim cannot be taken too strictly, for eschatological beliefs have always been professed by Christians. The Apostles' Creed affirms the resurrection of the body and other such expectations, and John Calvin's first theological book (*Psychopannychia*, written in 1534) dealt with the issue of "soul sleep" and the intermediate state. So the future always has been considered by Christians. But there is a sense in which eschatology has changed in the modern era. Whereas the Westminster Confession of Faith addressed the intermediate state (ch. 32) and the last judgment (ch. 33) in its seventeenth-century context, more recent eschatology has emphasized the eschatological nature of *all* of history: in other words, offering a broader philosophy of history and where it is going.[11] Today the greatest exuberance for eschatology is surely found in the apocalyptic visions of dispensationalism and the "Left Behind" culture of American fundamentalism. The detail of such proposals strikes the studious as altogether immodest. Amy Plantinga Pauw admits, however, that "Reformed eschatology has not always been modest. From the elaborate covenant dispensations of Johannes Cocceius to the vivid apocalyptic speculations of Jonathan Edwards, Reformed theologians have sometimes combined epistemological confidence with a fertile imagination in their reflections on the last things" ("Some Last Words about Eschatology," in *FWERD*, p. 221). Surely a theology reformed by the Word of God, bound to its teaching, remains an aspiration and not a possession.

Perhaps the greatest danger of such exuberant eschatologies is that of social quietism. Historian Mark Noll has shown how the rise of dispensationalism led to the dearth of investment from fundamentalism and much of early neoevangelicalism in any life of the mind, that is, in developing a unique intellectual tradition.[12] Noll's observation could be widened, in as much as an expectation that an imminent return of Jesus to bring his millennial kingdom would lead many persons to avoid all sorts of cultural engagement. Precisely because this eschatology minimizes the permanence of human society, it tends to invest its energies elsewhere.[13] While the historical argument is probably overstated (e.g., one key emphasis of nineteenth- and twentieth-century evangelicalism was its activism, according to David Bebbington), one can see how these eschatological theories could easily mislead one to abandon cultural engagement.[14] Hence, fundamentalism has gained a reputation as culturally separatist.

How might a Reformed approach to eschatology properly take shape? Amy Plantinga Pauw highlights major concerns:

> Eschatology is not simply a set of brave moral imperatives that human beings adopt in the hope of a better world. Eschatological convictions are grounded in God's continuing faithfulness to the creation that was declared "very good." They take their direction from the new thing God has already done in Jesus Christ. These convictions are alert to the present movements of the Spirit in both familiar and unexpected places. The fact that "God is not through" means there are still many surprises in store; but our eschatological convictions are shaped by the trust that what lies ahead will not contradict the creative, redemptive, and transformative grace already revealed by the triune God. ("Some Last Words about Eschatology," in *FWERD*, p. 222)

She hits the crucial points: the world is yet to be made fully right, surprises are still to come, but all that comes will fit with what we have seen already in the life of Jesus the Christ. While eschatology is not merely a way of prodding believers along to obey, the doctrine of the last things should inspire radical human action. This moral imperative flows from roots in divine action: the expectation that the gospel of Christ is still playing itself out fully. Or, to use a phrase taken from Emilie Townes, "God is not through" with the world yet.

By and large, then, the Reformed churches have offered what can be called "amillennial" readings of the New Testament.[15] Whereas dispensationalists and "classic premillennialists" interpret Rev. 20 as foretelling of a thousand year reign between Christ's second and third comings, amillennialists take this to be a literary figure that describes life nowadays. The kingdom of God (sometimes called the kingdom of Christ) has been inaugurated in the life and ministry of the Christ. So the millennium—this time of Christ's rule over all the world—has really begun. Yet the kingdom has not yet been fulfilled or consummated: "God is not through" with setting the world right. In this view, then, eschatology is a present-day reality: we are living in the last days. But this insertion of present-day life (and, thus, our cultural and social engagement within it) in the "last days" does not equate with a dispensationalist view of the "imminent return" of Jesus in judgment. With a few notable exceptions, Reformed theologians have not joined their dispensationalist brethren in trying to read the times, identifying social, political, moral, and other events as prophesied directly in the New Testament.

The second most frequent eschatological position amongst the Reformed has been called "postmillennialism," a view that the world is moving toward perfection gradually. At a certain point of moral progress (enabled by the grace of the Spirit), Jesus will return in glory. So Christ returns after a millennium of positive growth, when the kingdom has been prepared for his physical presence and reign. Certain commissioners thought the Westminster Assembly of the 1640s kick-started the progress of the gospel toward the millennial kingdom.[16] Some postmillennialists have been led to propose theonomic morals as a means to bring about this return of Christ, supposing that reinstitution of Mosaic theocracy would speed the moral progress and bring about the millenium. Granted, most theonomists (also called Christian reconstructionists or dominion theologians) believe that mass conversion must precede the institution of Old Testament law as secular government policy, but their position has still received widespread criticism for denying any substantive difference between the creational and redemptive realms. Though theonomy has been a maligned position, it continues to be affirmed by some marginalized voices in the tradition.[17]

Oftentimes, amillennial eschatology is characterized as pessimistic, with the kingdom of Christ looking *like this* sin plagued world and nothing better, over against the more optimistic picture of a future millennial era, wherein earthly life will be more in line with Christ's rule. Yet terms like pessimism and optimism are not very helpful. First, all are optimistic, in as much as all Christians look toward a "blessed hope": eternal life with God in the new heavens and new earth. Second, everyone is also pessimistic in so far as that simply means awareness of present sinfulness. Attitudinal terms (optimistic and pessimistic) stand in poorly for moral terms (good and bad); at best, they are confusing. More importantly, though, is the issue of confidence and its relationship to realism. Both positions support Christian confidence that history is moving toward a fulfillment that is good: judgment and renewal by Christ revealed one day in all his glory. At the same time, both positions can honor the realities of our experience, with their ills and sins. The real difference between the two positions is much more narrow than frequently thought and is largely exegetical, rather than attitudinal. In fact, Richard Gaffin has argued that what is now known as amillennialism might have been known in the past as a subset of postmillennialism.[18] Whether taking amillennial or even postmillennial form, Reformed churches believe that Christ's kingdom has been inaugurated but not yet fulfilled. Thus, culture and society are now within the realm of grace and have the hope of improvement, but must also be viewed realistically as they are still suffering the pains of sin. As Michael Horton says, "In this era of common grace, neither salvation nor judgment is fully consummated."[19]

Having considered eschatology briefly, we should now turn more directly to questions of cultural engagement. Perhaps useful as a framework within which to consider various options or approaches to these issues, we can look at how Richard Niebuhr proposed five ways that Christians have envisioned the relationship of Christ and culture:

1. Christ *against* culture (e.g., monastics, Anabaptists, and fundamentalists);
2. Christ *of* culture (e.g., Gnostics and liberal Protestants);
3. Christ *above* culture (e.g., Thomists);

4. Christ and culture *in paradox* (e.g., Martin Luther);
5. Christ *as transformer of* culture (e.g., John Calvin).

D. A. Carson has shown that Niebuhr's categories are reductionistic and, more fatally, that this whole notion of finding discrete, singular approaches to culture within the Bible is flawed.[20] Carson suggests that various texts emphasize different doctrinal concerns, but a proper approach would somehow honor each strand as part of a multi-faceted whole (with the exception of the second strand, which Carson argues is not at all Christian). Carson's observations are helpful, but we can note that Niebuhr did highlight various emphases in negotiating social engagement. Furthermore, he acknowledged that there rarely (if ever) are persons or groups who fit perfectly into any one type.

What is Niebuhr's assessment of these five viewpoints? George Hunsinger has given a useful summary:

Roughly speaking, Niebuhr evaluated the substance of his five types as follows:

- The sectarian type of cultural withdrawal (Christ against culture) was too antagonistic and severe, as well as too naïve about the possibilities of Christian escape from original sin.
- On the other hand, the accommodationist type (Christ of culture) was much the reverse, being too untroubled (ultimately) about the status quo and its possibilities for improvement.
- In turn, the synthetic type (Christ above culture), by presuming to build from culture to Christ, was at once too credulous about culture and too conciliatory about Christ, lacking an adequate sense of divine judgment.
- Meanwhile, like the sectarians, the dualists (Christ and culture in paradox) were too pessimistic about prospects for cultural betterment.
- Only the conversionists (Christ transforming culture) struck a proper balance between judgment and hope, being neither as suspicious toward culture as some (sectarians and dualists) nor as sanguine about it as others (accommodationists and synthesists).[21]

Niebuhr suggests (in an understated way) that the fifth type is the Reformed and also the correct approach. He does so merely by holding back from criticizing it as he does the others. Thus, having noted already Carson's broader concerns regarding the typology, we should focus on this idea of Christianity transforming culture, especially since Niebuhr suggests that John Calvin is the exemplar of this type. Specifically, we will consider how culture should be engaged by churches and by individual Christians. While Niebuhr makes some accurate observations about involvement in various realms of human society by Reformed Christians (and those influenced by their cultural leadership), his analysis overlooks some crucial distinctions within this theological tradition. Here one of Stanley Hauerwas' observations about Niebuhr is pertinent: Niebuhr is addressing the establishment elites of mid-twentieth-century America, presuming a certain identification between this citizenry and the mainline church. Of course, we now live and move and have our being within a post-Constantinian or, better yet, post-Christendom era, wherein we can no longer assume the social dominance of mainline Christianity within the broader culture of America, much less in other Western countries. Niebuhr's writings do not show much concern to distinguish between particular Christians and the life of Christian communities or organized churches, so we must pursue such distinctions further.

The Culture: Engaged by Churches and Christians

As with Other places in this book, stories from the American Presbyterian heritage can serve as representatives of broader Reformed trends. Here we can look to two different approaches to relating church and culture, each rooted in modern American history.

First, the theological principle that guarded the Southern institution of slavery was the doctrine of the spirituality of the church. James Henley Thornwell, who taught at Columbia Theological Seminary in Georgia and founded the *Southern Presbyterian Review* in 1846, defined the church as a "spiritual body" aimed at the "gathering and perfecting of the saints." As the church's doctrine and authority related to spiritual matters, she could not claim to rule on secular matters of government.

In Thornwell's words here is the positive constitution of the Church:

> The Church of Jesus Christ is a spiritual body, to which have been given the ministry, oracles and ordinances of God, for the gathering and perfecting of the saints in this life, to the end of the world. It is the great instrument of the Savior, through which, by his eternal Spirit, He dispenses salvation to the objects of His love. Its ends are holiness and life, to the manifestation of the riches and glory of divine grace, and not simply morality, decency and good order which may to some extent be secured without faith in the Redeemer, or the transforming efficacy of the Holy Spirit.[22]

Thornwell understands this mission as being limited:

> The Church is exclusively a spiritual organization, and possesses none but spiritual power. It is her mission to promote the glory of God and the salvation of men from the curse of the law. She has nothing to do with the voluntary associations of men for various civil and social purposes, that are outside of her pale ... The Church deals with men *as men*, as fallen sinners standing in *need of salvation*; not as citizens of the Commonwealth, or philanthropists, or members of society. Her mission is to bring men to the Cross, to reconcile them to God through the Blood of the Lamb, to imbue them with the Spirit of the Divine Master, and then send them forth to perform their social duties, to manage society, and perform the functions that pertain to their social and civil relations.[23]

He best expresses the spirituality of the church as rendering the church politically insignificant here:

> The provinces of church and state are perfectly distinct, and the one has no right to usurp the jurisdiction of the

other. The state is a natural institute, founded in the constitution of man as moral and social, and designed to realize the idea of justice. It is the society of rights. The church is a supernatural institute, founded in the facts of redemption, and is designed to realize the idea of grace . . . The state aims at social order; the church at spiritual holiness. The state looks to the visible and outward; the church is concerned for the invisible and inward . . . The power of the church is exclusively spiritual.[24]

This "Address" then defends the silence of the church in condemning slavery. As the Bible nowhere condemns it, the church has neither the right nor the authority to condemn it.[25] Morton Smith notes that Thornwell was not entirely consistent in his distinction between the natural order of the state and the supernatural order of the church. Thornwell considered the United States to be a Christian people, and thus he thought it appropriate to acknowledge Jesus as head of the nation. Though he was challenged that this was an inconsistency, he nonetheless maintained the stance alongside his proslavery argument by way of the spirituality of the church.[26]

Though Charles Hodge of Princeton, a contemporary of Thornwell, was not a thoroughgoing abolitionist, he nonetheless disagreed with Thornwell's doctrine of the spirituality of the church, asserting that it consigned the church to silence regarding all social evils. The difference between Hodge and Thornwell extended to other issues, all related to their views of the church, theological method, and the principle of *sola scriptura*. For example, Thornwell asserted that Presbyterians could not form mission boards or agencies because the Scriptures nowhere affirm such a function of the church. Hodge suggested that this was rigid biblicism and noted its logical implications: namely, all forms required Scriptural warrant, and all forms prescribed in Scripture would be treated as essentials. Thornwell agreed with this assessment of his methodology and ecclesiology, for he argued that Presbyterian polity was essential to the Gospel.[27]

How can we summarize Thornwell's and, therefore, the Southern Presbyterian argument? According to Smith, "Thornwell's basic argument was that the Church should not add anything that is not specifically or by good and necessary inference derived from Scripture."[28] Or, in Thornwell's own words:

> The power of the Church is purely ministerial and declarative. She is only to hold forth the doctrine, enforce the law, and execute the government which Christ has given her. She is to add nothing of her own to, and to subtract nothing from, what her Lord has established. Disceretionary power she does not possess . . . The great error of the Church in all ages, the fruitful source of her apostasy and crime, has been a presumptuous reliance upon her own understanding.[29]

The spirituality of the church did not pass away with the Confederacy. Rather, this perspective on the church's relationship to culture continued in the Southern Presbyterian churches, in admittedly mellowed form, throughout the middle of the twentieth century. During the Civil Rights movement, many leaders and congregations objected to the denominational support of social and political goals. And, so, very recently claims like that of Morton Smith can be found, understanding the doctrine of the spirituality of the church to flow directly and necessarily from the formal importance of *sola Scriptura*.[30] The church only ministers the Word of God, and it cannot speak authoritatively on issues not directly addressed by that scriptural text. This has led to quietism on many moral and cultural issues.

Second, though, many twentieth-century Presbyterians have opted for a very different approach to relating faith and culture. While there are numerous parallels within broader American evangelicalism, we will focus on events in the mainline Presbyterian world. Two statements from the last few years illustrate this other approach. First, the Presbyterian Church (USA) offers an official statement on the way forward in the Israeli-Palestianian conflict, written by Stated Clerk Gradye Parsons, in which a two-state solution is reaffirmed, certain Israeli settlements and the building of a protective wall in the West Bank are termed illegal, and fighting is called to end as it cannot be justified.[31] This statement confirmed policy positions adopted by the 218th General Assembly that had gathered the previous summer in San Diego. Second, one can

look to a webpage with the headline: "Burger King hears from
farmworkers and PC(USA): Protesters march through Miami
to picket headquarters of fast-food giant." Here, the previous
Stated Clerk of that denomination, Clifton Kirkpatrick, posted
an official letter lending support to the protests of migrant
workers seeking higher wages from the fast-food chain Burger
King.[32] The denomination supported the Coalition of Immokalee
Workers, a farmworkers organization striving to persuade Burger
King to pay a penny more per pound of tomatoes bought. The
denominational General Assembly had called for a 2002 boycott
of Taco Bell restaurants for similar reasons, the protest lasting for
4 years until the farmworkers organization won a similar penny-
per-pound increase from the fast-four chain. These two examples
represent a whole host of occasions on which mainline Reformed
churches take policy positions and lobby regarding social,
economic, and political issues.

Perhaps this mainline activism is rooted in nineteenth-century
abolitionist theologizing, just as much opposition to the Civil
Rights Movement was continuous with the earlier emphasis on
the spirituality of the church. Another influence might be the
way in which Karl Barth's writing of the Theological Declaration
of Barmen was seen by many neoorthodox members of the
American Reformed churches as a high point in early-twentieth-
century theology, with Barth standing virtually alone against the
Nazis and their supporters in the German establishment churches.
Ironically, of course, the Barmen Declaration is primarily a protest
of the Nazis' conflation of Christ with a political movement,
that of the National Socialist Party. It does not speak out against
the Nazis' anti-Semitism or Nazism as a particular ideology
so much as it speaks out against the merging of any ideology
with Christianity.[33] In practice, though, this meant that many
affirmed Barmen as a way to oppose this right-wing German
movement and to fight fascism in numerous locations. Similarly,
many Reformed churches wished to deal with other political
movements and social issues.[34]

The activistic approach was manifested especially in the Confession of 1967, approved by the United Presbyterian Church (USA),
the Northern Presbyterian denomination. The entire confession
focuses on reconciliation as a key doctrine, setting it in twofold

form: God's work of reconciliation followed by the ministry of reconciliation. It concludes with an eschatological analysis of how reconciliation is realized already, but not yet completely. Its finale gives a matchless depiction of how Reformed eschatology affects ethics: "With an urgency born of this hope, the church applies itself to present tasks and strives for a better world. It does not identify limited progress with the kingdom of God on earth, nor does it despair in the face of disappointment and defeat. In steadfast hope, the church looks beyond all partial achievement to the final triumph of God." Furthermore, this reconciliation "embraces the whole of man's life: social and cultural, economic and political, scientific and technological, individual and corporate" (C-67, III, in *BC*, p. 330). In these comments, the confession mirrors much earlier Reformed thinking on eschatology and culture. But the confession also speaks to the church's role in pursuing the fulfillment of the kingdom: "The church, guided by the Spirit, humbled by its own complicity and instructed by all attainable knowledge, seeks to discern the will of God and learn how to obey in these concrete situations" (C-67, II.4, in *BC*, p. 327). In many ways, the church was taking positions on issues like the war in Vietnam, specific policies in the Civil Rights Movement, etc. These would fall under the confessional category of "concrete situations" to be addressed by the church.

So one story shows a church that will not address any social ills, even the evils of chattel slavery, while the other tale portrays a church speaking authoritatively, even lobbying, with regard to very detailed political action plans. For the Old Southern Presbyterians, it was as though culture, at least concern for racial relations, was not addressed by the Word of God. For mainline activists, God clearly spoke about social issues, even down to the details of how much migrant workers should make per hour. Neither approach represents the classical Reformation tradition, however, so contemporary issues might be served best by looking backward for more nuanced approaches to issues of cultural engagement. Four key points should be observed.

First, Christian faith has cultural implications. We see this throughout the New Testament. For example, justification by faith alone undergirds ethnic harmony within the people of God (see Gal. 2–3). Similarly, the doctrine of Christ's resurrection threatens to undo various economic and political practices that developed around idol worship in Asia Minor (Acts 17 and 19). This has been affirmed throughout Reformed history too, perhaps made famous by Kuyper's famed statement that there is not a single place not claimed by Christ. The key doctrinal point is the sovereignty of God over all the heavens and the earth; as the Lord and Creator of all, God claims the right to mandate how life will be lived in every arena. The buck stops, ultimately, with God.

Second, we must distinguish between the rights and responsibilities of the Christian and those of the church. Niebuhr failed to note this. In other words, we must ask how churches exercise authority over particular Christians and what tasks churches are called to pursue corporately. Here is a confessional belief that the church's work differs from that of individuals (who are members of that corporate body):

> Synods and councils are to handle, or conclude nothing, but that which is ecclesiastical: and are not to intermeddle with civil affairs which concern the commonwealth, unless by way of humble petition in cases extraordinary; or, by way of advice, for satisfaction of conscience, if they be thereunto required by the civil magistrate. (WCF, XXXI.4)

A difference between civil and ecclesiastical matters is noted, with churchly involvement focused on the latter. Still, there is affirmation of the extraordinary circumstance, in which civil affairs are to be addressed by a synod or council. Such exceptional involvement is still called "intermeddling," suggesting that it is abnormal or exceedingly rare. The church hierarchy should not be dictating the way the monarch or congress should manage the state. By implication, then, pastors and local church leadership would likely speak to societal or political issues only with rarity and great care.

A theological basis for this warning can be found in the doctrine of the two kingdoms. Drawn from Augustine's *City of God* and affirmed by the Lutheran "two kingdom theology" plus many Reformed adherents, this approach sees two spheres in the world (see, for example, *ICR*, IV.xx.1–3).[35] The "city of God" involves creation as related to God in covenantal terms. Elders and pastors offer leadership and guidance in this arena. The "city of Man," by contrast, entails creation as immanently considered, a human polity or commonwealth. This realm is governed by cultural and political leaders, especially those in official office. According to this affirmation of two kingdoms, God has appointed differing authorities for each sphere, and they are not to cross the dividing line. Caesar is not to direct the church, nor is any pope or council to command the state. So Reformed pastors ought not speak for or against civil issues *unless directly mandated by the Word of God*. This is an application of the *sola Scriptura* principle, a permutation of the spirituality of the church doctrine, that restricts the powers and callings of the church to those things stated by the written Word.[36] Again, the church cannot act in ways that are merely not prohibited; the church regulated by God's Word can only speak where God has first spoken. Remember that this is a limit on churchly speech, not on the thought-processes or public actions of individual Christians, who will of necessity form opinions and act on a whole host of public and social issues.

Third, we must also distinguish between ethical principles and specific policies regarding society, family, politics, etc. This distinction is best illustrated by looking to the very issue that has so marred the spirituality of the church doctrine: racial relations. Surely we can distinguish between advocacy of racial equality and the pursuit of that goal by particular policies (be they constitutional amendments or new forms of enforcing the law as it already stood). While the Bible speaks to the reality of racial equality, then, Christians might differ in their assessment of what social and political means will most prudently get us to that goal. Thus, a preacher should address racism and its judgment by the gospel as this cultural issue appears throughout the Bible (e.g., Eph. 2.11ff.), yet refrain from addressing the value of a particular law (which may or may not be viewed as not only moral, but also politically expedient and wise). To turn to examples from earlier in this chapter, while pastors may speak to the need for farmworkers to be treated rightly and justly, there still might be room for debate as to the exact demands of the Coalition for Immokalee Workers. While the Bible addresses just economic practices, one is going to have a hard time showing that it plainly speaks to adding a penny-per-pound to a particular industry's purchase of tomatoes.

Fourth, we must be reminded that the church is a gathering of persons who are not at all similar. In fact, the body of Christ is portrayed by the apostle Paul as being harmed if all its members are of one sort: diversity is a benefit, not a cost. While all should be united to Christ by faith, guided by the divine law, and empowered by the divine Spirit, this does not mean that all should be of one nationality, political party, or philosophical persuasion. Virtually every arena of cultural engagement requires observation, assessment, and application of seemingly minute details, so we should not be surprised to find differing viewpoints within the Christian community. As Michael Horton argues, "The church is the *place* where sinners are receivers, yet it is also the *people* who are scattered to fulfill their common calling. In the latter, the church has dominion. It cannot command the covenant community to embrace particular political ideologies, policies, parties, or politicians."[37] As in all things, the church too must be reformed and regulated by God's Word. The community of the saints will pursue the ever-increasing fulfillment of God's kingdom by works of witness and mercy, yet it will not allow its zeal to inflate its claims for authority or dominion. Christ is King of all and will be shown to rule, not only in his church but also over all kingdoms. The blessed hope is when this reign is fully public and acknowledged the world over.

The Always Being
Reformed Church

The previous chapters sketch the doctrinal distinctives and emphases of Reformed churches, surveying centuries past as well as varieties present.

Again, this book has limits. It surveys the entirety of Reformed theology, primarily within the Western world. While its author would, undoubtedly, be identified as a member of a conservative, confessional Reformed denomination, this book is not only an account of conservative Reformed theology. Such an account is well worth doing; for now, I would point the interested reader toward an excellent book recently released by Sean Michael Lucas, *On Being Presbyterian: Our Beliefs, Practices, and Stories.*[1] Similarly, those wishing greater depth with regard to liberal (or, to use my preferred term, revisionist) Reformed thought should look toward Shirley Guthrie's *Always Being Reformed*, with which certain chapters have interacted a great deal. The present book, in contrast to these two texts, surveys both conservative and liberal approaches to Reformed faith and practice, attempting to state honestly the similarities and differences. Surely, it is too simplistic to think that these two categories—liberal and conservative—accurately reflect the panoply of viewpoints and interests involved in various Reformed denominations, but one must start somewhere manageable in an introductory text of this sort.

Many would argue that only conservative or only revisionist churches can really claim the title "Reformed." The others have ceased being judged and renewed by the Word of God, they say, or have given away their heritage in an iconoclastic zeal, protest the others. I reject both claims from an historical perspective. There remain churches that are recognized by most observers as "Reformed," largely because they claim this title for themselves.

While I would argue theologically that many cannot do so coherently, I cannot fool anyone into thinking that my theological reflections are sociological reality. There really are conservative denominations located next door to mainline denominations. Again, my historical assessment cannot be taken as reflecting theological disinterest. There are many who must be called "Reformed" historically who may very well not be Christian (much less, say, Presbyterian) in a theologically robust way. The point to be made here is that one must read this book in the right realm of discourse. Of course, my prescriptions and assessments appear at a few points, but I have tried to note where this is occurring and differentiate this from the historical analysis.

Neither is this book an apologetic for the Reformed churches and their theology. Again, such a goal is well worth pursuing, with further work in this area needed in our day. Such a proposal, however, would require a great deal more in the line of biblical and philosophical argument, with a bit more depth in historical excurses on key topics. Instead, this book introduces Reformed doctrine. If it proves captivating, it will have simply shown that careful dogmatic work can make for good apologetics on its own terms. That is, one does not need to do something more than good, biblically faithful theology to give an account for the particular hope one holds. As Karl Barth said, good dogmatics is the best apologetic. Of course, apologetics can function well as a distinct literary genre with very narrow pragmatic purposes, if done in a way that honors its theological roots. Ironically, Barth and his vehement Reformed critic, Cornelius Van Til, are basically in agreement on this point.

All things considered, then, Reformed doctrine can be usefully surveyed by focusing on a few key theological subjects: Word, covenant, God, Christ, faith, sin, grace, etc. Understanding the faith and practice of the Reformed churches requires paying careful attention to resources from the past as well as continuing debates and reformulations in contemporary works. Reformed theology is always being reformed. Note the passivity there: it is always "being reformed" by the life giving, sanctifying work of the triune God. It is not merely that Reformed theology is constantly self-correcting, as any good human activity or praxis should be. No, Reformed theology is done in the hope that God continually kills and makes alive the reason of those who are in Christ Jesus.

Notes

Introduction

1. George W. Stroup, "Reformed Identity in an Ecumenical World," in *Reformed Theology: Identity and Ecumenicity* (ed. Wallace M. Alston, Jr., and Michael Welker; Grand Rapids, MI: Eerdmans, 2003), pp. 257–270.
2. Augustine, *Confessions*, xi.17.
3. For a brief account of popularized "Reformed theology" or "Calvinism" in the USA, see Collin Hansen, *Young, Restless, Reformed: A Journalist's Journey with the New Calvinists* (Wheaton, IL: Crossway, 2008). Hansen offers very little clarity regarding definitional debates (but see pp. 110–114).
4. *Contra* the preference of Richard Mouw, *Calvinism at the Las Vegas Airport* (Grand Rapids, MI: Zondervan, 2004), pp. 18–21. Mouw notes that terms need to distinguish helpfully that which needs distinguishing; unfortunately, he does not show how "Calvinist" accurately does so.
5. Richard A. Muller, "How Many Points?" *Calvin Theological Journal* 28, no. 2 (1993), p. 427.

Chapter 1

1. Ten Theses of Berne, 1528, I, in *RCSC*, p. 49.
2. John Calvin, *Sermons on the Ten Commandments* (ed. Benjamin W. Farley; Grand Rapids, MI: Baker, 1980), p. 67.
3. Walter Brueggemann, "Foreword," *Journal for Preachers* 26 (Easter 2003), p. 1.
4. T. F. Torrance, *The Hermeneutics of John Calvin* (Edinburgh: Scottish Academic Press, 1988), pp. 91–92.
5. See, for example, his "*Theologia Reformata et Semper Reformanda*," in *Toward the Future of Reformed Theology: Tasks, Topics, Traditions* (ed. David Willis and Michael Welker; Grand Rapids, MI: Eerdmans, 1999), pp. 120–135.
6. Roger Olson, *Reformed and Always Reforming: The Postconservative Approach to Evangelical Theology* (Grand Rapids, MI: Baker Academic, 2007).
7. Olson, *Reformed and Always Reforming*, p. 75; Roger Olson, *Arminian Theology: Myths and Realities* (Downers Grove, IL: InterVarsity Press, 2006).
8. Bruce L. McCormack, "The End of Reformed Theology? The Voice of Karl Barth in the Doctrinal Chaos of the Present," in *Reformed Theology: Identity*

Notes

and Ecumenicity (ed. Wallace M. Alston, Jr., and Michael Welker; Grand Rapids, MI: Eerdmans, 2003), p. 49 fn. 8; cf. Brian Gerrish, "Tradition and the Modern World: The Reformed Habit of Mind," in *Toward the Future of Reformed Theology* (ed. David Willis and Michael Welker; Grand Rapids, MI: Eerdmans, 1999); pp. 3–20.

9. See the perceptive analysis of Matt Jenson, *The Gravity of Sin: Augustine, Luther, and Barth on Homo Incurvatus in Se* (London: T&T Clark, 2006).

10. G. C. Berkouwer, *General Revelation* (Studies in Dogmatics; Grand Rapids, MI: Eerdmans, 1955), p. 277. More recently, see Kevin J. Vanhoozer, *Remythologizing Theology* (Cambridge Studies in Christian Doctrine; Cambridge: Cambridge University Press, 2010).

11. John Webster, *Holy Scripture: A Dogmatic Sketch* (Current Issues in Theology; Cambridge: Cambridge University Press, 2003), p. 13.

12. John Calvin, *Commentary on the Book of Psalms* (trans. James Anderson; Grand Rapids, MI: Eerdmans, 1963), p. 2.

13. The term "imagination" may be used in a wider sense, referring to one's paradigmatic view of the universe, or specifically to refer to vain speculation. It is in this latter, more pejorative, sense that I employ it here, without denying the usefulness of the former meaning for a theological epistemology.

14. John Webster, *Holy Scripture: A Dogmatic Sketch*, pp. 68–106.

15. On the *archetypal/ectypal* distinction, see the illuminating essay by Willem J. van Asselt, "The Fundamental Meaning of Theology: Archetypal and Ectypal Theology in Seventeenth-Century Reformed Thought," *WTJ* 64, no. 2 (2002), pp. 319–335; see also Richard A. Muller, *PRRD*, vol. 1, pp. 126–136.

16. Karl Barth, "The Word of God and the Task of the Ministry," in *The Word of God and the Word of Man* (trans. Douglas Horton; London: Hodder and Stoughton, 1928), p. 186.

17. Carl R. Trueman, *John Owen: Reformed Catholic, Renaissance Man* (Great Theologians; Aldershot: Ashgate, 2007), p. 36.

18. On the culture of Reformation-era communication, see Andrew Pettegree, *Reformation and the Culture of Persuasion* (Cambridge: Cambridge University Press, 2005).

19. Ben Quash, "Revelation," in *The Oxford Handbook of Systematic Theology* (ed. John Webster, Kathryn Tanner, and Iain Torrance; New York: Oxford University Press, 2007), p. 329.

20. For a brief discussion of Barth's doctrine of Holy Scripture, see Paul T. Nimmo, *Being in Action: The Theological Shape of Barth's Ethical Vision* (London: T&T Clark, 2007), pp. 25–40.

21. Edward A. Dowey, Jr., *A Commentary on the Confession of 1967 and An Introduction to The Book of Confessions* (Philadelphia, PA: Westminster, 1968), p. 100.

22. The historiography of McKim and Rogers fails to distinguish between concepts and judgments and how different concepts may be used to express the same theological judgment (Jack B. Rogers and Donald K. McKim, *The Authority and Interpretation of the Bible: An Historical Approach* [San Francisco,

CA: HarperCollins, 1980]). Their flawed account has been ably critiqued by John D. Woodbridge, *Biblical Authority: A Critique of the Rogers/McKim Proposal* (Grand Rapids, MI: Zondervan, 1982).

23. See James M. Boice, "Appendix A: Chicago Statement on Biblical Inerrancy," in *Standing on the Rock: Biblical Authority in a Secular Age* (Grand Rapids, MI: Baker, 1994), pp. 147–160.

24. Dowey, *A Commentary on the Confession of 1967*, p. 237.

25. On the importance of providence and the relationship of divine and human action for understanding the nature of Scripture, see Michael Allen, "Divine Transcendence and the Reading of Scripture," *Scottish Bulletin of Evangelical Theology* 26, no. 1 (2008), pp. 32–56.

26. See especially Brian K. Blount, "Reading Contextually as Reading Reformed," in *Reformed Theology: Identity and Ecumenicity II: Biblical Interpretation in the Reformed Tradition* (ed. Wallace M. Alston, Jr., and Michael Welker; Grand Rapids, MI: Eerdmans, 2007), pp. 43–57.

27. For a spacious account of canonization, see John Webster, "The Dogmatic Location of the Canon," in *Word and Church: Essays in Christian Dogmatics* (Edinburgh: T&T Clark, 2001), pp. 34–42.

Chapter 2

1. I. John Hesselink, *On Being Reformed* (Grand Rapids, MI: Servant Books, 1983), p. 57.

2. See, for example, Ulrich Zwingli, "An Exposition of the Faith," in *Zwingli and Bullinger* (Library of Christian Classics; ed. and trans. Geoffrey W. Bromiley; Louisville, KY: Westminster John Knox, 2006), pp. 276–278.

3. Heinrich Bullinger, "A Brief Exposition of the One and Eternal Testament or Covenant of God," in Charles S. McCoy and J. Wayne Baker, *The Fountainhead of Federalism: Heinrich Bullinger and the Covenantal Tradition* (Louisville, KY: Westminster John Knox, 1991), p. 112.

4. Isa. 24.5 may also refer to a covenant made between YHWH and all humanity. The curse in this chapter (and the surrounding subsection) clearly envelopes all of creation, and it is based on their wrongdoing. That the phrase "everlasting covenant" is used in the account of the Noahic Covenant has led many to take this as a reference to that administration, yet the Noahic Covenant is unbreakable or unilateral. Hence, a deeper, universal reality may be implied here (something akin to natural law).

5. On comparative study between ancient near-Eastern contexts and the biblical covenants, see Meredith G. Kline, *The Treaty of the Great King* (Grand Rapids, MI: Eerdmans, 1963).

6. For a historical survey of Reformed adoption of the distinction between "Law" and "Gospel," see Michael S. Horton, "Law, Gospel, and Covenant: Reassessing Some Emerging Antitheses," *Westminster Theological Journal* 64, no. 2 (2002), pp. 279–287.

Notes

7. For wider engagement of this and related issues, see Michael S. Horton, *God of Promise* (Grand Rapids, MI: Baker, 2006), ch. 3.
8. The third covenant—the "covenant of redemption"—shapes this fellowship only indirectly. Its parties are both divine—Father and Son (and, later, Holy Spirit as well)—so that, strictly speaking, it does not include humanity (though its shape indirectly does include humanity by implication).
9. Richard A. Muller, "John Calvin and later Calvinism: The Identity of the Reformed Tradition," in *The Cambridge Companion to Reformation Theology* (ed. David Bagchi and David Steinmetz; Cambridge: Cambridge University Press, 2004), pp. 140–141.
10. See, for example, David A. Weir, *The Origins of the Federal Theology in Sixteenth-Century Reformation Thought* (New York: Clarendon, 1990).
11. *A Declaration of the Faith and Order Owned and Practiced in the Congregational Churches in England* (London, 1658), viii.1 (cited in Carl R. Trueman, *John Owen*, p. 82 fn. 60).
12. Michael S. Horton, *Covenant and Eschatology: The Divine Drama* (Louisville, KY: Westminster John Knox, 2002); idem, *Lord and Servant: A Covenant Christology* (Louisville, KY: Westminster John Knox, 2005); idem, *Covenant and Salvation: Union with Christ* (Louisville, KY: Westminster John Knox, 2007); idem, *People and Place: A Covenant Ecclesiology* (Louisville, KY: Westminster John Knox, 2008).
13. Karl Barth, "The First Commandment as an Axiom of Theology," in *The Way of Theology in Karl Barth: Essays and Comments* (ed. H. Martin Rumscheidt; Allison Park, PA: Pickwick, 1986), p. 77.
14. According to John D. Godsey, Barth penned the Declaration while his two collaborators napped after enjoying a noontime feast (John D. Godsey, "Epilogue: Barth as a Teacher," in *For the Sake of the World: Karl Barth and the Future of Ecclesial Theology* [ed. George Hunsinger; Grand Rapids, MI: Eerdmans, 2004], pp. 208–209).
15. For a more expansive attempt at comparative dogmatic analysis of Barth and the "federal theology," see R. Michael Allen, *The Christ's Faith: A Dogmatic Account* (Studies in Systematic Theology; London: T&T Clark, 2009), ch. 5.
16. Ryan Glomsrud, "Karl Barth as Historical Theologian: The Recovery of Reformed Theology in Barth's Early Dogmatics," in *Engaging with Barth: Contemporary Evangelical Critiques* (ed. David Gibson and Daniel Strange; Leicester: Apollos, 2008), pp. 86–87, 104, 111–112.
17. Andreas J. Köstenberger and R. Scott Swain, *Father, Son, and Spirit: The Trinity and John's Gospel* (New Studies in Biblical Theology; Downers Grove, IL: InterVarsity, 2008), pp. 170–171.

Chapter 3

1. Auguste Lecerfe, *An Introduction to Reformed Dogmatics* (London: Lutterworth, 1949), p. 379.

Notes

2. Calvin emphasizes that God's infinity and spirituality are what ought to banish our "stupid imaginings" by which we "try to measure him by our own senses" or "imagining anything earthly or carnal of him" (*ICR*, I.xiii.20).

3. Thomas F. Tracy, *God, Action, and Embodiment* (Grand Rapids, MI: Eerdmans, 1984), p. 19.

4. See the description of Jan Rohls, *Reformed Confessions: Theology from Zurich to Barmen* (trans. John Hoffmeyer; Columbia Series in Reformed Theology; Louisville, KY: Westminster John Knox, 1998), pp. 45–48.

5. For a thorough account of recent reductions of divine freedom, see Paul D. Molnar, *Divine Freedom and the Doctrine of the Immanent Trinity* (London: T&T Clark, 2002).

6. John Webster, "Life In and Of Himself: Reflections on God's Aseity," in *Engaging the Doctrine of God: Contemporary Protestant Perspectives* (ed. Bruce L. McCormack; Grand Rapids, MI: Baker Academic, 2008), p. 119.

7. Webster, "Life In and Of Himself," p. 119.

8. See also the proposal of Presbyterian theologian William C. Placher, "The Vulnerable God," in *Narratives of a Vulnerable God: Christ, Theology, and Scripture* (Louisville, KY: Westminster John Knox, 1994), pp. 3–26. Placher's early tendency toward revisionism (*à la* Guthrie) was muted in his later *The Domestication of Transcendence: How Modern Thinking About God Went Wrong* (Louisville, KY: Westminster John Knox, 1996), p. xi.

9. See, for example, Bruce L. McCormack, "The Actuality of God: Karl Barth in Conversation with Open Theism," in *Engaging the Doctrine of God*, pp. 185–242.

10. As the argument goes, this new view was held by the "Cappadocian fathers" of the Greek-speaking "East"—Gregory of Nyssa, Basil the Great, and Gregory Nazianzen—while the classical view was held by Augustine and the Latin-speaking "West."

11. Miroslav Volf, "'The Trinity is Our Social Program': The Doctrine of the Trinity and the Shape of Social Engagement," *Modern Theology* 14, no. 3 (1998), pp. 403–423.

12. See, for example, Lewis Ayres, *Nicaea and Its Legacy: An Approach to Fourth-Century Trinitarian Theology* (New York: Oxford University Press, 2004).

13. In this vein, see Andreas Köstenberger and Scott R. Swain, *Father, Son, and Spirit: The Trinity and John's Gospel* (New Studies in Biblical Theology 24; Downers Grove, IL: InterVarsity, 2008).

14. Gilles Emery, *The Trinitarian Theology of St. Thomas Aquinas* (Oxford: Oxford University Press, 2007).

15. Douglas F. Kelly, "The True and Triune God: Calvin's Doctrine of the Trinity," in *A Theological Guide to Calvin's Institutes: Essays and Analysis* (ed. David W. Hall and Peter A. Lillback; Phillipsburg, NJ: Presbyterian & Reformed, 2008), p. 76.

16. Robert Bellarmine, *Secunda controversia generalis de Christo*, in *Disputationum de controversiis Christianae fidei adversus haereticos* (Rome, 1832), 1: 307–308.

17. Stephen Edmondson, *Calvin's Christology* (Cambridge: Cambridge University Press, 2004), p. 214.

Notes

18. For introduction to this debate, see Kelly M. Kapic, "The Son's Assumption of a Human Nature: A Call for Clarity," *International Journal of Systematic Theology* 3, no. 2 (2001), pp. 154–166. For a mediating proposal, see R. Michael Allen, *The Christ's Faith: A Dogmatic Account*, ch. 4.

19. For a good analysis of the Reformed revision to creedal interpretation, see G. C. Berkouwer, *The Work of Christ* (Studies in Dogmatics; trans. Cornelius Lambregtse; Grand Rapids, MI: Eerdmans, 1965), pp. 174–180.

20. John Calvin, *A Harmony of the Gospels: Matthew, Mark, and Luke*, vol. 1 (Calvin's New Testament Commentaries; ed. David W. Torrance and Thomas F. Torrance; trans. A. W. Morrison; Grand Rapids, MI: Eerdmans, 1972), p. 106.

21. Owen and other classical Reformed theologians, however, are not affirming the project of modern liberal "Spirit-Christology," wherein Jesus is portrayed as a spiritual human but merely a human. In other words, revisionist "Spirit-Christology" substitutes a spiritual (yet human) experience for the deity of Christ; Owen would sharply demur here.

22. George Hunsinger, *How to Read Karl Barth: The Shape of His Theology* (Oxford: Oxford University Press, 1991), pp. 185–188. For criticism of the way Hunsinger uses this analogy (with reference to Karl Barth's theology), see Paul C. Nimmo, "Karl Barth and the *Concursus Dei*: A Chalcedonianism Too Far?" *International Journal of Systematic Theology* 9, no. 1 (2007), pp. 58–72.

23. Stephen R. Holmes has recently argued that Owen's great achievement is showing that "hypostatic union does not require a single psychological centre . . . In our culture which conflates the personal and the psychological, this is difficult to grasp, but it is surely also necessary to grasp" ("Reformed Varieties of the *Communicatio Idiomatum*," in *The Person of Christ* [ed. Stephen R. Holmes and Murray A. Rae; London: T&T Clark, 2005], p. 86).

24. "The Christ" translates "Messiah," the Old Testament term for "the anointed one(s)."

25. Berkouwer, *The Work of Christ*, p. 63.

26. Furthermore, major sources from the classical tradition (e.g., Thomas Aquinas' *Summa Theologiae*) made use of the *munus triplex* for explaining the person and work of Christ. Reformed theologians did their work within this exegetical tradition, cognizant of this approach to the unity of the Scriptures.

27. This is not to say that Jesus does not also condemn violence in certain respects, on which see Hans Boersma, *Violence, Hospitality, and the Cross: Reappropriating the Atonement Tradition* (Grand Rapids, MI: Baker Academic, 2004).

28. See especially Michael S. Horton, *Lord and Servant: A Covenant Christology* (Louisville, KY: Westminster John Knox, 2005), chs. 8–9; Robert Sherman, *King, Priest, and Prophet: A Trinitarian Theology of Atonement* (Theology for the Twenty-First Century; London: T&T Clark, 2004); and the more lay-accessible accounts of William C. Placher, *Jesus the Savior: The Meaning of Jesus Christ for Christian Faith* (Louisville, KY: Westminster John Knox, 2001), chs. 7, 16, 25; Robert Letham, *The Work of Christ* (Contours of Christian Theology; Downers Grove, IL: InterVarsity, 1993).

Notes

1. G. C. Berkouwer, *Faith and Justification* (Studies in Dogmatics; trans. Lewis B. Smedes; Grand Rapids, MI: Eerdmans, 1954), pp. 32–33.
2. John Murray, *Redemption Accomplished and Applied* (Grand Rapids, MI: Eerdmans, 1955), p. 87. Murray also lists "union with Christ" (immediately prior to glorification); however, his basic argument is that this reality encompasses the whole order. It is still worth consulting the elaborate, yet exegetically derived *ordo* found in William Perkins, "A Golden Chaine," in *The Works of William Perkins* (ed. I. Breward; London: Sutton Courteney, 1970), vol. 3, pp. 169–259.
3. It is quite possible that the genitive "of the Son of God" in v. 20 should be rendered subjectively, so that it speaks instead of "the faith of the Son of God" rather than the Christian's "faith in the Son of God." This only heightens the Reformed emphasis on life "in Christ."
4. While maintaining that practice changes here from Old to New Covenant, Reformed theologians have emphasized that the Old Testament spoke of this New Covenant prophetically, suggesting that changes loomed on the horizon, however mysterious they may seem before the coming of the Messiah.
5. John Webster, *Holiness* (Grand Rapids, MI: Eerdmans, 2003), pp. 86–87.
6. For a trenchant study of biblical and historical terminology, as well as a lucid and well proportioned account of the Reformed approach to the doctrine, see James Buchanan, *The Doctrine of Justification* (Edinburgh, 1867; repr. Edinburgh: Banner of Truth Trust, 1961).
7. Buchanan, *Justification*, p. 153.
8. There arose a fervent controversy among various Puritan and Reformed pastors, when some suggested that imputation was not double. The so-called *neonomians* taught that Jesus died for the forgiveness of our sins, but that our feeble yet persevering obedience was accepted positively as a fulfillment of the law. There was, therefore, no imputation of Christ's righteousness or "active obedience." James Buchanan offers a very helpful summary of this controversy (*Justification*, pp. 176–178). Certain revisions to the Protestant doctrine of justification in the last 20 years, many under the banner of the "new perspective on Paul," offer renewed versions of *neonomianism*.
9. On the nature of the distinction, see William Cunningham, *The Reformers and the Theology of the Reformation* (Edinburgh: Banner of Truth Trust, 1967), pp. 402–406; Buchanan, *Justification*, p. 307. There was debate on this distinction at the Westminster Assembly, notably because William Twisse and Thomas Gataker opposed the maneuver. The distinction is not found in the Confession *per se*, though it is implied in QQ. 70–73 of the Larger Catechism.
10. Though Barth at times seems to say very little of the "more and more" of salvation, on which see George Hunsinger, "Baptized into Christ's Death: Karl Barth and the Future of Roman Catholic Theology," in *Disruptive Grace: Studies in the Theology of Karl Barth* (Grand Rapids, MI: Eerdmans, 2000), pp. 273–274.

Notes

11. H. Richard Niebuhr, *Christ and Culture* (New York: Harper & Row, 1956).

12. J. I. Packer, *Knowing God* (Downers Grove, IL: InterVarsity, 1973), p. 201.

13. Webster, *Holiness*, pp. 93–94.

14. Thomas Manton, *Works of Thomas Manton*, vol. 12: *Sermons on Romans 8 and 2 Corinthians 5* (London: Nisbet 1870), pp. 116–117.

15. Karl Barth, *The Theology of the Reformed Confessions* (trans. Darrell L. Guder and Judith J. Guder; Columbia Series in Reformed Theology; Louisville, KY: Westminster John Knox, 2002), pp. 151–152.

16. There has been a consistent line of dissenters, however, from John McLeod Campbell to Karl Barth to Thomas F. Torrance and his brother James B. Torrance.

17. For a helpful analysis of the "reflex act" and the "practical syllogism," see Paul Helm, *John Calvin's Ideas* (New York: Oxford University Press, 2004), p. 416; *Contra* R. T. Kendall, *Calvin and English Calvinism until 1649* (New York: Oxford University Press, 1979).

18. Of course, there is the qualification in WCF 18.7, that many "unregenerate men" may do things that (1) "God commands," and that (2) are "of good use to themselves and others." Here one should think of religiously agnostic celebrity generosity, for example, the adoption of orphans in poor countries by otherwise thoroughly hedonistic celebrities, such as Madonna or Angelina Jolie. Such mercies are (1) obedient to God's commands to show mercy, and (2) eminently useful. Motivation is another issue, however, and ultimately limits the value of such works of mercy.

19. See Mark A. Noll, *The Rise of Evangelicalism: The Age of Edwards, Whitefield, and the Wesleys* (History of Evangelicalism; Downers Grove, IL: InterVarsity, 2004). I am inclined to see more discontinuity between the First and Second Great Awakenings than Noll posits. It should also be noted that Noll helpfully shows the real beginnings of the Second Great Awakening to lie a decade earlier than often thought, stirring in the work of Methodist preachers in the mid-1780s. The piety of revivalistic Methodism, however, spread to Reformed churches quickly.

20. See especially George Hunsinger, "The Harnack/Barth Correspondence: A Paraphrase with Comments," in *Disruptive Grace: Studies in the Theology of Karl Barth* (Grand Rapids: Eerdmans, 2000), pp. 319–337.

21. American Intellectual Culture; Lanham, MD: Rowman & Littlefield, 2002.

22. As revivalistic methods arose in the nineteenth century, the "New Side" and "New School" tolerated and even supported such novelties, while the "Old Side" and "Old School" protested.

23. With regard to Reformed theologians who base progressive politics upon their Reformed theological commitments, see especially Hunsinger, *Disruptive Grace*, chs. 1–5.

24. For a penetrating jeremiad against such psychologizing, see Michael S. Horton, *Christless Christianity: The Alternative Gospel of the American Church* (Grand Rapids, MI: Baker, 2008).

25. Friedrich Schleiermacher, *The Christian Faith* (ed. H. R. Mackintosh and J. S. Stewart; Philadelphia, PA: Fortress, 1976), p. 456.

26. See especially Walter E. Wyman, Jr., "Sin and Redemption," in *The Cambridge Companion to Friedrich Schleiermacher* (ed. Jacqueline Mariña; Cambridge: Cambridge University Press, 2005), p. 130.
27. Schleiermacher, *The Christian Faith*, p. 54.
28. Buchanan, *Justification*, p. 366.

Chapter 5

1. Serene Jones, *Feminist Theory and Christian Theology: Cartographies of Grace* (Guides to Theological Inquiry; Minneapolis, MN: Fortress, 2000), ch. 5.
2. For a survey of the earlier history of interpretation on this key text, see John Murray, *The Imputation of Adam's Sin* (Grand Rapids, MI: Eerdmans, 1959).
3. See R. Michael Allen, "Calvin's Christology: A Dogmatic Matrix for Discussion of Christ's Human Nature," *International Journal of Systematic Theology* 9, no. 4 (2007), pp. 383–391.
4. The key term is *eph ho*, which may mean "in which" or "with the result that." For exegetical discussion of this key term and its effect on this *locus classicus*, see Joseph Fitzmyer, *Romans: A New Translation with Introduction and Commentary* (Anchor Bible 33; New York: Doubleday, 1993), on Rom. 5.12.
5. See Ian McFarland, "The Fall and Sin," in *The Oxford Handbook of Systematic Theology* (ed. John Webster, Kathryn Tanner, and Iain Torrance; New York: Oxford University Press, 2007), p. 151 fn. 11.
6. Although certain persons in the Reformed tradition have argued this point in various modern contexts: see, for example, Karl Barth, *CD* IV/1.
7. Ian McFarland, "The Fall and Sin," p. 148.
8. Jones, *Feminist Theory and Christian Theology*, p. 117.
9. Charles Matthewes, *A Theology of Public Life* (Cambridge Studies in Christian Doctrine; Cambridge: Cambridge University Press, 2007), p. 61.
10. The key exegetical basis for the doctrine of prevenient grace has been Jn. 1.9—"the true light, which enlightens everyone, was coming into the world."
11. R. A. Markus, "A Defense of Christian Mediocrity," in *The End of Ancient Christianity* (Cambridge: Cambridge University Press, 1990), pp. 45–62.
12. For a contemporary Reformed proposal suggesting that we dare to hope for an empty hell (a perspective styled "reverent agnosticism"), see George Hunsinger, "Must Christians Believe in Hell?" in *Why are We Here? Everyday Questions and the Christian Life* (ed. Ronald F. Thiemann and William C. Placher; Harrisburg, PA: Trinity Press International, 1998), pp. 143–155; a more detailed account is "Hellfire and Damnation: Four Ancient and Modern Views," in Hunsinger, *Disruptive Grace*, pp. 226–249.
13. John Owen, *Works of John Owen*, volume 10: *The Death of Christ* (Edinburgh: Banner of Truth Trust, 1967), pp. 140–429.
14. Idem, *Works of John Owen*, volume 10: *The Death of Christ*, pp. 482–624. See Carl R. Trueman, "John Owen's *A Dissertation on Divine Justice*: An Exercise

in Christocentric Scholasticism," *Calvin Theological Journal* 33, no. 1 (1998), pp. 87–103.

15. See Carl R. Trueman, *John Owen: Reformed Catholic, Renaissance Man* (Great Theologians; Aldershot: Ashgate, 2007), pp. 116–117.

16. Robert W. Jenson, "Triune Grace," *Dialog* 41, no. 4 (2002), p. 291.

17. J. I. Packer, *Evangelism and the Sovereignty of God* (Downers Grove, IL: InterVarsity, 1961), p. 27.

18. The other exegetical difficulty in this text involves making sense of the term "foreknew" in v. 29: does it refer to God's foresight of faith, on the basis of which he predestines? Or does it refer to God's intimate love for those whom he then predestines?

19. The elect community surely encompasses persons from the Reformed, Arminian, and other camps. The question here, however, regards whether or not each of these theological positions adequately allows for biblical assurance of one's salvation in a coherent manner.

20. Most Reformed theologians, both Continental and Puritan, have affirmed both sources and have emphasized the Christological primacy of assurance. See Randall Zachman, *The Assurance of Faith: Conscience in the Theology of Martin Luther and John Calvin* (Louisville, KY: Westminster John Knox, 1993), p. 246. While Zachman wrongly construes Calvin's doctrine of reconciliation as "universal," he rightly argues that "Luther and Calvin also agree that the faith of believers must be confirmed by the testimony of a good conscience that grows out of sanctification by Christ and the Holy Spirit, and that the lack of such confirming testimony falsifies any claim to faith."

21. "Conscience" is not an unproblematic term, however, given the moral and epistemological autonomy encouraged by Enlightenment modernity; for a cultural diagnosis and dogmatic reconfiguration, see John Webster, "God and Conscience," in *Word and Church: Essays in Christian Dogmatics* (Edinburgh: T&T Clark, 2001), pp. 233–262.

22. R. T. Kendall, *Calvin and English Calvinism until 1649* (New York: Oxford University Press, 1979).

23. On the relationship of Christ's work to the doctrines of election and assurance, see Richard A. Muller, *Christ and the Decree: Christology and Predestination in Reformed Theology from Calvin to Perkins* (Grand Rapids, MI: Baker Academic, 2008).

24. David Fergusson, "Divine Providence and Action," in *God's Life in Trinity* (ed. Miroslav Volf and Michael Welker; Minneapolis, MN: Fortress, 2006), p. 162.

25. For contemporary reflection in New Testament and early Jewish studies on this dynamic of grace and human action, see the essays in John M. G. Barclay and Simon J. Gathercole, *Divine and Human Agency in Paul and His Cultural Environment* (LNTS 335; London: T&T Clark, 2006). The essay by Barclay supports the traditional Reformed approach in its consideration of 5 key texts (1 Cor. 15.10; Phil. 2.12–14; Gal. 2.19–21; Rom. 15.15–19; 2 Cor. 9.8–10): "In all cases, the logical sequence (whatever its grammatical expression) places divine grace anterior to human action, and affirms the

Notes

continuation of that grace in human ability. But in no case does that human actor become passive or inactive in the face of divine grace, but is rather energized by that grace to action" ("'By the Grace of God I am What I am': Grace and Agency in Philo and Paul," p. 153).

26. Kathryn Tanner, *Jesus, Humanity, and the Trinity: A Brief Systematic Theology* (Minneapolis, MN: Fortress, 2001), pp. 2–3. For Tanner's account of Aquinas and Barth, see her earlier book, *God and Creation in Christian Theology: Tyranny or Empowerment?* (Oxford: Blackwell, 1988; repr. Minneapolis, MN: Fortress, 2005), chs. 2–3.

27. Tanner, *Jesus, Humanity, and the Trinity*, pp. 12, 13.

28. See Barth, *CD*, III/3, pp. 94–107.

29. This has tremendous import when considering the dual authorship of Holy Scripture. Sadly, the Reformed dogmatic tradition has not yet emphasized this link between noncompetitive divine and human relations and the inspiration of Scripture.

30. Of course, Barth has been maligned as giving too little attention to human agency. But see John Webster, *Barth's Ethics of Reconciliation* (Cambridge: Cambridge University Press, 1995); idem, *Barth's Moral Theology: Human Action in Barth's Thought* (Edinburgh: T&T Clark, 1998); Paul Dafydd Jones, *The Humanity of Christ: Christology in Karl Barth's* Church Dogmatics (London: T&T Clark, 2008). While agreeing with the arguments of Webster and Jones, I remain convinced that Barth's universal doctrine of reconciliation does threaten to undo the reality of human agency (constituting what G. C. Berkouwer called "the triumph of grace"). This is a more specific concern than the altogether misleading yet all-too-frequent charge that he gives short shrift to Christ's humanity and that of others. Such criticisms operate from the assumption that divine freedom and human freedom relate in a competitive manner.

31. See, for example, Katherine Sonderegger, "Election," in *The Oxford Handbook of Systematic Theology* (ed. John Webster, Kathryn Tanner, and Iain Torrance; Oxford: Oxford University Press, 2007), pp. 105–120.

32. A good beginning can be found in D. A. Carson, "The Wrath of God," in *Engaging the Doctrine of God: Contemporary Protestant Perspectives* (ed. Bruce L. McCormack; Grand Rapids, MI: Baker Academic, 2008), pp. 37–63; Oliver Crisp, "Karl Barth and Jonathan Edwards on reprobation (and hell)," in *Engaging with Barth: Contemporary Evangelical Critiques* (ed. David Gibson and Daniel Strange; Nottingham: Apollos, 2008), pp. 300–322.

33. On Barth's doctrine of providence, see George Hunsinger, *How to Read Karl Barth: The Shape of His Theology* (New York: Oxford University Press, 1991), pp. 185–224; as well as the essays by Caroline Simon and Randall Zachman in George Hunsinger (ed.), *For the Sake of the World: Karl Barth and the Future of Ecclesial Theology* (Grand Rapids, MI: Eerdmans, 2004), pp. 115–142.

34. See George Hunsinger, *How to Read Karl Barth*, pp. 85, 185–188. For a criticism of Hunsinger's widespread use of this "Chalcedonian pattern," see Paul T. Nimmo, "Karl Barth and the *concursus Dei*: A Chalcedonianism Too Far?" *International Journal of Systematic Theology* 9, no. 1 (2007), pp. 58–72.

Notes

35. George Weigel, *The Cube and the Cathedral: Europe, America, and Religion without God* (New York: Basic, 2006).

36. See J. B. Schneewind, *The Invention of Autonomy: A History of Modern Moral Philosophy* (Cambridge: Cambridge University Press, 1998).

37. Webster, *Holiness*, p. 103 (cf. Michel Foucault, *The Uses of Pleasure: The History of Sexuality*, volume 2 [London: Penguin, 1992], pp. 26–28).

38. Cynthia L. Rigby, "What Does God Have to Do With Us?" in *Conversations with the Confessions: Dialogue in the Reformed Tradition* (ed. Joseph D. Small; Louisville, KY: Geneva, 2005), p. 123.

39. Webster, *Holiness*, p. 86.

40. Webster, *Holiness*, p. 103.

41. Margit Ernst-Habib, "'Chosen by Grace': Reconsidering the Doctrine of Predestination" in *Feminist and Womanist Essays in Reformed Dogmatics* (ed. Amy Plantinga Pauw and Serene Jones; Columbia Series in Reformed Theology; Louisville, KY: Westminster John Knox, 2005), p. 77.

42. Regina Schwarz, *The Curse of Cain: The Violent Legacy of Monotheism* (Chicago, IL: University of Chicago Press, 1997); cf. Rodney Stark, *One True God: Historical Consequences of Monotheism* (Princeton, NJ: Princeton University Press, 2001).

43. Amy Plantinga Pauw, "The Graced Infirmity of the Church," in *Feminist and Womanist Essays in Reformed Dogmatics* (ed. Amy Plantinga Pauw and Serene Jones; Columbia Series in Reformed Theology; Louisville, KY: Westminster John Knox, 2005) p. 195.

44. Hunsinger, *Disruptive Grace*, pp. 16–17.

Chapter 6

1. Cited by David Wells, *God in the Wasteland: The Reality of Truth in a World of Fading Dreams* (Grand Rapids, MI: Eerdmans, 1994), p. 118.

2. For analysis of the biblical-theological development of temple and worship, see G. K. Beale, *The Temple and the Church's Mission: A Biblical Theology of the Dwelling Place of God* (New Studies in Biblical Theology; Downers Grove, IL: InterVarsity, 2004).

3. James B. Torrance, *Worship, Community, and the Triune God of Grace* (Downers Grove, IL: InterVarsity, 1996). On the importance of mediation in worship, see texts as diverse as Exod. 20.18–21; Heb. 12.19–20; Col. 1.15; Jn. 1.17; 2 Cor. 4.6.

4. For an account of sacrifice and worship within contemporary Roman Catholic theology, see the exceptional book by Matthew Levering, *Sacrifice and Community: Jewish Offering and Christian Eucharist* (Illuminations; Oxford: Blackwell, 2005).

5. See, for example, Torrance, *Worship, Community, and the Triune God of Grace*, pp. 95–120 ("Gender, Sexuality and the Trinity").

6. For a savvy yet brief approach, see William C. Placher, "A Note on Language," in *Jesus the Savior: The Meaning of Jesus Christ for the Christian Faith* (Louisville,

KY: Westminster John Knox, 2001), pp. 199–200. For a recent and controversial effort to deal with the issue of language for God, see the report "The Trinity: God's Love Overflowing," found on the website of the Presbyterian Church (USA.).

7. For a fascinating concern about the (in)ability of recent liturgical resources to honor the full breadth of the biblical witness, see Kathryn Greene-McCreight, "What's the Story? The Doctrine of God in *Common Order* and in the *Book of Common Worship*," in *To Glorify God: Essays on Modern Reformed Liturgy* (ed. Bryan D. Spinks and Iain R. Torrance; Grand Rapids, MI: Eerdmans, 1999), pp. 99–114.

8. For a wider account of Reformed efforts to shape worship by Scripture, see the many writings of Hughes Oliphant Old, perhaps especially his introductory book, *Worship* (Guides to the Reformed Tradition; Atlanta, GA: John Knox, 1984).

9. While the Reformed have insisted on the value of the other five practices identified by the Roman Catholic Church as sacraments, they have insisted that only those practices mandated by Christ can be called "sacraments." See, for example, HC 68, in *BC*, p. 69.

10. George Hunsinger, "Baptism and the Soteriology of Forgiveness," *International Journal of Systematic Theology* 2, no. 3 (2000), p. 261; see also his *The Eucharist and Ecumenism: Let Us Keep the Feast* (Current Issues in Theology; Cambridge: Cambridge University Press, 2008), part 2. For a confessional statement of similar import, see HC 67, in *BC*, p. 69.

11. Martha L. Moore-Keish, "How Shall We Worship?" in *Conversations with the Confessions* (ed. Joseph D. Small), p. 192.

12. For a promising attempt to bridge the gaps between Reformed Eucharistic theology and that of the Roman Catholic, Eastern Orthodox, Lutheran, and Anglican churches regarding the presence of Christ, see George Hunsinger, *The Eucharist and Ecumenism*, part 1. Hunsinger suggests that Reformed churches "follow Vermigli, Bucer, and Cranmer (and possibly Calvin)" (p. 315) regarding Christ's presence, and that they espouse the notion of "transelementation" (*metastomichaicheiosis*), though he insists that transelementation is not a metaphysical theory (as is transubstantiation).

13. Annie Dillard, *Teaching a Stone to Talk* (New York: Harper & Row, 1982), pp. 58–59.

14. For a catalog of concerns regarding infant baptism, see David F. Wright, *What Has Infant Baptism Done to Baptism? An Enquiry at the End of Christendom* (Milton Keynes: Paternoster, 2005).

15. By "pure" and "fully regenerate," of course, they speak quantitatively, not qualitatively. They mean that every individual person is a true Christian, not that every or even any person is sinlessly perfect.

16. For the most compelling baptistic account available, see Henri Blocher, "Old Covenant, New Covenant," in *Always Reforming: Explorations in Systematic theology* (ed. Andrew T. B. McGowan; Leicester: Apollos, 2006), pp. 240–270.

Notes

17. Richard Pratt, "Infant Baptism in the New Covenant," in *The Case for Covenantal Infant Baptism* (ed. Gregg Strawbridge; Phillipsburg, NJ: Presbyterian & Reformed, 2003), p. 168.
18. Pratt, "Infant Baptism in the New Covenant," p. 173.
19. Jewish theology maintains a similar doctrine of covenantal membership and covenant breaking; see David Novak, *The Jewish Social Contract* (New Forum Books; Princeton, NJ: Princeton University Press, 2005), ch. 2.
20. B. B. Warfield, "The Polemics of Infant Baptism," in *The Works of B. B. Warfield*, volume 9: *Studies in Theology* (New York: Oxford University Press, 1932), p. 408.
21. See Patrick D. Miller, *The God You Have: Politics, Religion, and the First Commandment* (Facets; Minneapolis, MN: Fortress, 2005), p. 67. For Puritan exegesis of the pertinent Old Testament texts, see Thomas Watson, *The Ten Commandments* (Edinburgh: Banner of Truth Trust, 1958), pp. 59–84.
22. David VanDrunen, "Iconoclasm, Incarnation, and Eschatology: Toward a Catholic Understanding of the Reformed Doctrine of the 'Second' Commandment," *International Journal of Systematic Theology* 6, no. 2 (2004), pp. 130–147.
23. VanDrunen, "Iconoclasm, Incarnation, and Eschatology," p. 145.
24. This nuance is missed by Martha Moore-Keish, "How Shall We Worship?" p. 195, who wrongly construes "worship according to the Word alone" with "worship by words alone." Given that the Dutch and Puritan traditions she criticizes actually emphasized regular sacramental practice, it is odd to characterize them as denigrating the material.
25. J. I. Packer, *Knowing God* (Downers Grove, IL: InterVarsity, 1973), ch. 4.
26. For an exciting account of this emphasis, see the magisterial work of Michael S. Horton, *People and Place: A Covenant Ecclesiology* (Louisville, KY: Westminster John Knox, 2008), ch. 2 ("*Creatura Verbi*: The Sacramental Word"); see also Stephen Webb, *The Divine Voice: Christian Proclamation and the Theology of Sound* (Grand Rapids, MI: Brazos, 2004).
27. Horton, *People and Place*, p. 63. Jon Levenson has shown how Judaism holds to a similar emphasis on the religion of the ear over and against the religions of the eye; see his *Sinai and Zion: An Entry into the Jewish Bible* (San Francisco, CA: HarperCollins, 1985), pp. 147–148. Horton's engagement of the best in contemporary Jewish theology (e.g., Levenson, Michael Wyschogrod) ought to be pursued further in seeking to understand better the Old Testament, from which Reformed theology has always drawn much for dogmatic purposes.

Chapter 7

1. B. B. Warfield, *Calvin and Augustine* (Phillipsburg, NJ: Presbyterian & Reformed, 1956), pp. 484–487.
2. For a perceptive Anglican-Reformed approach to this issue, see Kathryn Tanner, "Workings of the Spirit: Simplicity or Complexity?" in *The Work of*

193

the Spirit: Pneumatology and Pentecostalism (ed. Michael Welker; Grand Rapids, MI: Eerdmans, 2006), pp. 87–106.

3. Reformed theologians have differed over the centuries with regard to the extent to which theological method parallels that of scientific method in a whole host of academic disciplines. Especially in the Enlightenment era, many theologians were tempted to view theology as guided by universal principles that were not constrained or rooted in dogmatic teaching. In reality, this is simply one widespread manifestation of the universal tendency toward idolatry, namely, the human compulsion to think about God in manners of our own choosing.

4. Kevin J. Vanhoozer, *The Drama of Doctrine: A Canonical-Linguistic Approach to Christian Theology* (Louisville, KY: Westminster John Knox, 2005), especially chs. 5–7. The use of drama as a helpful category for thinking about theological method in the church has been employed frequently in recent decades, by Hans Urs von Balthasar, Karl Barth, Michael Horton, and especially now by Vanhoozer. In his book *Covenant and Eschatology: The Divine Drama* (Louisville, KY: Westminster John Knox, 2002), Michael Horton has shown that drama well describes the covenantal nature of theological work, suggesting that it has a particular usefulness in specifically Reformed theological prolegomena.

5. Heiko A. Oberman, *The Dawn of the Reformation: Essays in Late Medieval and Early Reformation Thought* (Grand Rapids, MI: Eerdmans, 1992), especially ch. 12.

6. *Contra* Anna Williams, "Tradition," in *The Oxford Handbook of Systematic Theology* (ed. John Webster, Kathryn Tanner, and Iain Torrance; New York: Oxford University Press, 2007), pp. 364–365.

7. The term "critical traditioning" is drawn from Ellen F. Davis, "Critical Traditioning: Seeking an Inner-Biblical Hermeneutic," in *The Art of Reading Scripture* (ed. Ellen F. Davis and Richard B. Hays; Grand Rapids, MI: Eerdmans, 2003), pp. 163–180.

8. For entry into this thorny subject, see Richard J. Mouw, "The Problem of Authority in Evangelical Christianity," in *Church Unity and the Papal Office: An Evangelical Dialogue on John Paul II's Encyclical* Ut Unum Sint (ed. Carl Braaten and Robert Jenson; Grand Rapids, MI: Eerdmans, 2001), pp. 124–141.

9. Amy Plantinga Pauw, "The Graced Infirmity of the Church," in *Feminist and Womanist Essays in Reformed Dogmatics*, pp. 189, 190.

10. The Donatists were a sect that believed the moral quality of the priest who made or broke the efficacy of the sacraments; for example, partaking of the eucharist was ineffective if the officiating priest later recanted the faith during a period of persecution. This was a live issue in the early church.

11. On "invisibility," see Michael Allen, "The Church and the Churches: A Dogmatic Essay on Ecclesial Invisibility," *European Journal of Theology* 16, no. 2 (2007), pp. 113–119.

12. John Webster, "On Evangelical Ecclesiology," in *Confessing God* (London: T&T Clark, 2005), pp. 182, 184.

Notes

13. Webster, "On Evangelical Ecclesiology," p. 174.

14. John Webster, "Confession and Confessions," in *Nicene Christianity: The Future for a New Ecumenism* (ed. Christopher R. Seitz; Grand Rapids, MI: Brazos, 2001), p. 129.

15. William Cunningham, "Leaders of the Reformation," in *The Reformers and the Theology of the Reformation* (ed. James Buchanan and James Bannerman; Edinburgh: Banner of Truth Trust, 2000), pp. 27–28.

16. For a recent example, see John Webster, "The Self-Organizing Power of the Gospel of Christ: Episcopacy and Community Formation," in *Word and Church: Essays in Christian Dogmatics* (Edinburgh: T&T Clark, 2001), pp. 191–210; as well as P. T. Forsyth, *Lectures on the Church and Sacraments* (London: Longmans, Green, 1917), p. 42.

17. For more comprehensive expositions of Reformed ecclesiology, see James Bannerman, *The Church of Christ: A Treatise on the Nature, Powers, Ordinances, Discipline, and Government of the Christian Church* (Edinburgh: Banner of Truth Trust, 1960); G. C. Berkouwer, *The Church* (trans. James E. Davison; Studies in Dogmatics; Grand Rapids, MI: Eerdmans, 1976); and especially Horton, *People and Place*.

18. On the application of Reformed ecclesiology to American republicanism, see Mark A. Noll, *America's God: From Jonathan Edwards to Abraham Lincoln* (New York: Oxford University Press, 2002).

19. Calvin locates this within his discussion of the true church as, primarily, that place where the Word is rightly preached (*ICR* IV.i.5–6); see Philip W. Butin, *Reformed Ecclesiology: Trinitarian Grace According to Calvin* (Studies in Reformed Theology and History; Princeton, NJ: Princeton Theological Seminary, 1994).

20. Webster, "Confession and Confessions," in *Nicene Christianity*, p. 124.

21. Webster, "Confession and Confessions," in *Nicene Christianity*, p. 127.

22. Roger Lundin, *From Nature to Experience: The American Search for Cultural Authority* (American Intellectual Culture; Lanham, MD: Rowman & Littlefield, 2006).

23. See especially Michael Horton, *People and Place,* ch. 2.

24. Phillipsburg, NJ: Presbyterian & Reformed, 2008.

25. See, for example, the argument that modern evangelicalism is so diverse as to be a vacuous identity in D. G. Hart, *Deconstructing Evangelicalism: Conservative Protestantism in the Age of Billy Graham* (Grand Rapids, MI: Baker Academic, 2005). Hart's argument, however, should be compared to the survey of evangelical statements of faith gathered in J. I. Packer and Thomas C. Oden, *One Faith: The Evangelical Consensus* (Downers Grove, IL: InterVarsity, 2004).

26. On the "new Calvinism," see Collin Hansen, *Young, Restless, Reformed*. In March 2009, TIME magazine named "the new Calvinism" one of the ten most influential developments on the contemporary global scene.

27. On this and Barth's approach to the Reformed confessions in his early lectures, see the study by John Webster, "*The Theology of the Reformed Confessions*," in *Barth's Earlier Theology: Four Studies* (London: T&T Clark, 2005), especially

pp. 45, 63. While Webster addresses early and relatively occasional lectures in the broader Barthian corpus, his analysis offers a faithful approach to the mature Barth as well.

28. Karl Barth, *The Theology of the Reformed Confessions* (trans. Darrell L. Guder and Judith J. Guder; Columbia Series in Reformed Theology; Louisville, KY: Westminster John Knox, 2002), p. 16.

29. Philip Schaff, *The Creeds of Christendom*, vol. 1 (New York: Harper & Brothers, 1877; repr. Grand Rapids, MI: Baker, 1983), pp. 389–390.

30. Bern: World Alliance of Reformed Churches, 1982.

31. Andrew T. B. McGowan, "Was Westminster Calvinist?" in *Reformed Theology in Contemporary Perspective: Westminster: Yesterday, Today—and Tomorrow?* (ed. Lynn Quigley; Edinburgh: Rutherford House, 2006), pp. 62–63; see also Scott R. Clark, *Recovering the Reformed Confession: Our Theology, Piety, and Practice* (Phillipsburg, NJ: Presbyterian & Reformed, 2008), p. 181.

32. David F. Wright, "Westminster: Reformed and Ecumenical?" in *Reformed Theology in Contemporary Perspective*, p. 163.

33. See, for example, the historical background of the "Confession of 1967" and various twentieth-century maneuvers to undo the ongoing effect of "federal theology" in the Westminster Standards as described by Jack Rogers, *Reading the Bible and the Confessions: The Presbyterian Way* (Louisville, KY: Geneva, 1999), especially pp. 87–102.

34. William C. Placher, "Contemporary Confessions and Biblical Authority," in *To Confess the Faith Today* (ed. Jack L. Stotts and Jane Dempsey Douglass; Louisville, KY: Westminster John Knox, 1990), pp. 66–74.

35. *BO*, G-14.0207 (cited in Jack Rogers, *Reading the Bible and the Confessions: The Presbyterian Way* [Louisville, KY: Geneva, 1999], p. 67).

36. On the history of debates regarding the explicit naming of "essential tenets," see Rogers, *Reading the Bible and the Confessions*, pp. 91–102.

37. David Fergusson, "The Confession of Faith in the Life of the Church of Scotland," in *Reformed Theology in Contemporary Perspective*, p. 210. Debates amongst theologians of the Church of Scotland can be accessed in Alasdair C. Heron (ed.), *The Westminster Confession in the Church Today: Papers Prepared for the Church of Scotland Panel on Doctrine* (Edinburgh: Saint Andrew Press, 1982).

38. John McIntyre, "Confessions in Historical and Contemporary Setting," in *The Presumption of Presence: Essays in Honor of D. W. D. Shaw* (ed. Peter McEnhill and G. B. Hall; Edinburgh: Scottish Academic Press, 1996), pp. 22–40.

39. Colin Gunton, "Confessions, Dogmas, and Doctrine: An Exploration of Some Interactions," in *Reformed Theology in Contemporary Perspective*, p. 224.

40. For a helpful introduction to the history and exegesis of this creedal statement, see James F. Kay, "He Descended into Hell," in *Exploring and Proclaiming the Apostles' Creed* (ed. Roger E. Van Harn; Grand Rapids, MI: Eerdmans, 2004), pp. 117–129. A more advanced work well worth consulting is David Lauber, *Barth on the Descent into Hell: God, Atonement and the Christian Life* (Barth Studies; Aldershot: Ashgate, 2004). His account is

superior to the influential work of the late Presbyterian theologian, Alan Lewis, *Between Cross and Resurrection: A Theology of Holy Saturday* (Grand Rapids, MI: Eerdmans, 2001).

41. Lauber offers an excellent account of the biblical argument here, in his *Barth on the Descent into Hell*, ch. 3.

42. Cunningham, "Leaders of the Reformation," in *The Reformers and the Theology of the Reformation*, p. 2. As noted earlier, Roger Lundin has described eloquently the extension of *sola Scriptura* into a thoroughgoing (and secular) iconoclasm; most recently, see his *Believing Again: Doubt and Faith in a Secular Age* (Grand Rapids, MI: Eerdmans, 2009).

43. Webster, *Barth's Earlier Theology*, p. 11.

Chapter 8

1. Max Weber, *The Protestant Ethic and the Spirit of Capitalism* (New York: Charles Scribner's Sons, 1958).

2. David W. Hall, "Calvin on Human Government and the State," in *A Theological Guide to Calvin's Institutes*, pp. 438–439.

3. John Webster, "Eschatology and Anthropology," in *Word and Church*, p. 266.

4. For a helpful survey of "the non-negotiables of biblical theology" as related to culture (from a "Reformed Baptist" perspective), see D. A. Carson, *Christ and Culture Revisited* (Grand Rapids, MI: Eerdmans, 2008), pp. 44–59.

5. While Caroline Walker Bynum's *The Resurrection of the Body in Western Christianity, 200–1336* (New York: Columbia University Press, 1995) argues that the early church did not downplay material existence, her argument is not altogether successful. Still, she does show significant suggestions early in the tradition of greater appreciation for embodiment.

6. Charles Mathewes, *A Theology of Public Life*; on this modern tendency, see also the historical analysis of Roger Lundin, *From Nature to Experience: The American Search for Cultural Authority* (Lanham, MD: Rowman & Littlefield, 2006), part 1.

7. See especially Reinhold Niebuhr, *The Nature and Destiny of Man* (2 vols.; New York: Charles Scribner's Sons, 1964). For analysis of Niebuhr within his twentieth-century context, see William Werpehowski, "Reinhold Niebuhr," in *The Blackwell Companion to Political Theology* (ed. Peter Scott and William Cavanaugh; Blackwell Companions to Religion; Oxford: Blackwell, 2004), pp. 180–193.

8. John Murray, "Common Grace," in *The Collected Works of John Murray*, volume 2: *Systematic Theology* (ed. Iain Murray; Edinburgh: Banner of Truth Trust, 1977), p. 93.

9. Murray, "Common Grace," p. 96.

10. Marilynne Robinson, *Gilead* (New York: Farrar, Strauss, and Giroux, 2004), p. 245.

11. Most bluntly argued in Jürgen Moltmann, *Theology of Hope* (trans. J. W. Leith; New York: Harper & Row, 1967), p. 16: "Christianity is eschatology." There

Notes

are exceptional precursors to this type of cosmic history (e.g., Joachim of Fiore).

12. Mark A. Noll, *The Scandal of the Evangelical Mind* (Grand Rapids, MI: Eerdmans, 1995), ch. 5.

13. Perhaps the sharpest criticism of this tendency occurs in Justo L. González, *Mañana: Christian Theology from a Hispanic Perspective* (Nashville, TN: Abingdon, 1990), pp. 164–167.

14. On Bebbington's "quadrilateral" and its usefulness as a way of describing modern evangelicalism, see Timothy Larsen, "Defining and Locating Evangelicalism," in *The Cambridge Companion to Evangelical Theology* (ed. Timothy Larsen and Daniel J. Treier; Cambridge: Cambridge University Press, 2007), pp. 1–14.

15. See, for example, Richard A. Muller, "How Many Points?," *Calvin Theological Journal* 28, no. 2 (1993), p. 427.

16. Samuel T. Logan, "The Context and Work of the Assembly," in *To Glorify and Enjoy God: A Commemoration of the Westminster Assembly* (ed. John L. Carson and David W. Hall; Edinburgh: Banner of Truth Trust, 1994), p. 29.

17. For an introduction to the debate regarding theonomy, see T. David Gordon, "A Critique of Theonomy: A Taxonomy," *Westminster Theological Journal* 56, no. 1 (1994), pp. 24–45.

18. Richard B. Gaffin, "Theonomy and Eschatology: Reflections on Postmillenialism," in *Theonomy: A Reformed Critique* (ed. William S. Barker and W. Robert Godfrey; Grand Rapids, MI: Zondervan, 1990), pp. 197ff.

19. Horton, *People and Place*, p. 274.

20. D. A. Carson, *Christ and Culture Revisited* (Grand Rapids, MI: Eerdmans, 2008), especially ch. 2: "Niebuhr Revised: The Impact of Biblical Theology"; cf. George Hunsinger, *The Eucharist and Ecumenism*, pp. 249–253.

21. Hunsinger, *The Eucharist and Ecumenism*, pp. 248–249.

22. James Henley Thornwell, *Collected Writings of James Henley Thornwell*, volume 4: *Ecclesiastical* (Edinburgh: Banner of Truth Trust, 1986), p. 469.

23. Thornwell, *Collected Writings*, vol. 4, p. 473.

24. James Henley Thornwell, "An Address to All Churches," delivered to the Southern Presbyterian Church in 1859.

25. For analysis of the exegetical debates regarding slavery, see especially E. Brooks Holifield, *Theology in America: Christian Thought from the Age of the Puritans to the Civil War* (New Haven, CT: Yale University Press, 2005), pp. 496–497; Mark A. Noll, *The Civil War as a Theological Crisis* (Chapel Hill, NC: University of North Carolina Press, 2006), ch. 3: "The Crisis over the Bible."

26. Morton H. Smith, *Studies in Southern Presbyterian Theology* (Phillipsburg, NJ: Presbyterian & Reformed, 2004), p. 178; Holifield, *Theology in America*, p. 502.

27. Holifield, *Theology in America*, pp. 391–392.

28. Smith, *Studies in Southern Presbyterian Theology*, p. 174.

29. Thornwell, *Collected Writings*, vol. 4, pp. 163–164.

30. Smith, *Studies in Southern Presbyterian Theology*, p. 176.

31. For the January 7, 2009 statement on the Israeli-Palestinian conflict, see: www.pcusa.org/pcnews/2009/09010.htm

32. For the December 5, 2007 story about supporting migrant workers at Burger King, see: www.pcusa.org/pcnews/2007/07793.htm

33. For a helpful analysis, see Mark R. Lindsay, *Covenanted Solidarity: The Theological Basis of Karl Barth's Opposition to Nazi Anti-Semitism and the Holocaust* (Issues in Systematic Theology 9; New York: Peter Lang, 2001); Katherine Sonderegger, *That Jesus Christ Was Born a Jew: Karl Barth's 'Doctrine of Israel'* (University Park, PA: Penn State University Press, 2002). For a pastoral meditation on Barmen that offers cogent and careful analysis of its opposition to any confusion of Christianity with any ideology, see Patrick D. Miller, *The God You Have: Politics, Religion, and the First Commandment* (Facets; Minneapolis, MN: Fortress, 2005).

34. For the most cogent proposal of "political theology" following in Barth and Barmen's wake, see the provocative essays by George Hunsinger, *Disruptive Grace*, part 1.

35. On Reformed use of the two kingdom theology (which has been oftentimes seen as exclusively Lutheran, especially due to Niebuhr's typology), see D. G. Hart, *A Secular Faith: How Christianity Favors the Separation of Church and State* (Chicago, IL: Ivan R. Dee, 2006), especially ch. 9: "A Secular Faith."

36. For a contemporary reassertion of the spirituality of the church, see D. G. Hart, "The Spirituality of the Church," in *Recovering Mother Kirk: The Case for Liturgy in the Reformed Tradition* (ed. D. G. Hart; Grand Rapids, MI: Baker Academic, 2003), pp. 64–65. Hart rightly shows that both the spiritual-church and the activistic approaches were used by Christians to affirm economic and political practices that they already held on other (nonreligious) grounds.

37. Horton, *People and Place*, p. 304.

Conclusion

1. Phillipsburg, NJ: Presbyterian & Reformed, 2006.

Bibliography

Allen, Michael. "Calvin's Christology: A Dogmatic Matrix for Discussion of Christ's Human Nature," *International Journal of Systematic Theology* 9, no. 4 (2007): 383–391.

Allen, Michael. *The Christ's Faith: A Dogmatic Account*. Studies in Systematic Theology. London: T&T Clark, 2009.

Allen, Michael. "The Church and the Churches: A Dogmatic Essay on Ecclesial Invisibility," *European Journal of Theology* 16, no. 2 (2007): 113–119.

Allen, Michael. "Divine Transcendence and the Reading of Scripture," *Scottish Bulletin of Evangelical Theology* 26, no. 1 (2008): 32–56.

Alston, Wallace M., and Michael Welker (eds.). *Reformed Theology: Identity and Ecumenicity*. Grand Rapids, MI: Eerdmans, 2000.

Ayres, Lewis. *Nicaea and Its Legacy: An Approach to Fourth-Century Trinitarian Theology*. New York: Oxford University Press, 2004.

Bannerman, James. *The Church of Christ: A Treatise on the Nature, Powers, Ordinances, Discipline, and Government of the Christian Church*. Edinburgh: Banner of Truth Trust, 1960.

Barclay, John M. G., and Simon J. Gathercole. *Divine and Human Agency in Paul and His Cultural Environment*. LNTS 335. London: T&T Clark, 2006.

Barth, Karl. "The First Commandment as an Axiom of Theology." Pages 63–78 in *The Way of Theology in Karl Barth: Essays and Comments*. Ed. H. Martin Rumscheidt. Allison Park, PA: Pickwick, 1986.

Barth, Karl. *The Theology of the Reformed Confessions*. Columbia Series in Reformed Theology. Trans. Darrell L. Guder and Judith J. Guder. Louisville, KY: Westminster John Knox, 2002.

Barth, Karl. "The Word of God and the Task of the Ministry." Pages 183–217 in *The Word of God and the Word of Man*. Trans. Douglas Horton. London: Hodder and Stoughton, 1928.

Beale, G. K. *The Temple and the Church's Mission: A Biblical Theology of the Dwelling Place of God*. New Studies in Biblical Theology. Downers Grove, IL: InterVarsity, 2004.

Bellarmine, Robert. *Secunda controversia generalis de Christo*, in *Disputationum de controversies Christianae fidei adversus haereticos* (Rome, 1832), 1:307–308.

Berkouwer, G. C. *The Church*. Studies in Dogmatics. Trans. James E. Davison. Grand Rapids, MI: Eerdmans, 1976.

Berkouwer, G. C. *Faith and Justification*. Studies in Dogmatics. Trans. Lewis B. Smedes. Grand Rapids, MI: Eerdmans, 1954.

Bibliography

Berkouwer, G. C. *General Revelation*. Studies in Dogmatics. Grand Rapids, MI: Eerdmans, 1955.

Berkouwer, G. C. *The Work of Christ*. Studies in Dogmatics. Trans. Cornelius Lambregtse. Grand Rapids, MI: Eerdmans, 1965.

Blocher, Henri. "Old Covenant, New Covenant." Pages 240–270 in *Always Reforming: Explorations in Systematic Theology*. Ed. Andrew T. B. McGowan. Leicester: Apollos, 2006.

Brian K. Blount, "Reading Contextually as Reading Reformed." Pages 43–57 in *Reformed Theology: Identity and Ecumenicity II: Biblical Interpretation in the Reformed Tradition*. Ed. Wallace M. Alston, Jr., and Michael Welker. Grand Rapids, MI: Eerdmans, 2007.

Boersma, Hans. *Violence, Hospitality, and the Cross: Reappropriating the Atonement Tradition*. Grand Rapids, MI: Baker Academic, 2004.

Boice, James M. *Standing on the Rock: Biblical Authority in a Secular Age*. Grand Rapids, MI: Baker, 1994.

Brueggemann, Walter. "Foreword," *Journal for Preachers* 26 (Easter 2003): 1.

Buchanan, James. *The Doctrine of Justification*. Edinburgh, 1867. Reprint. Edinburgh: Banner of Truth Trust, 1961.

Butin, Philip W. *Reformed Ecclesiology: Trinitarian Grace According to Calvin*. Studies in Reformed Theology and History. Princeton, NJ: Princeton Theological Seminary, 1994.

Calvin, John. *Commentary on the Book of Psalms*. Trans. James Anderson. Grand Rapids, MI: Eerdmans, 1963.

Calvin, John. *A Harmony of the Gospels: Matthew, Mark, and Luke*. Volume 1. Calvin's New Testament Commentaries. Ed. David W. Torrance and Thomas F. Torrance. Trans. A. W. Morrison. Grand Rapids, MI: Eerdmans, 1972.

Calvin, John. *The Institutes of the Christian Religion*. Two Volumes. Library of Christian Classics. Ed. John T. McNeill. Trans. Ford Lewis Battles. Louisville, KY: Westminster John Knox, 2005.

Calvin, John. *Sermons on the Ten Commandments*. Ed. Benjamin W. Farley. Grand Rapids, MI: Baker, 1980.

Carson, D. A. *Christ and Culture Revisited*. Grand Rapids, MI: Eerdmans, 2008.

Carson, D. A. "The Wrath of God." Pages 37–63 in *Engaging the Doctrine of God: Contemporary Protestant Perspectives*. Ed. Bruce L. McCormack. Grand Rapids, MI: Baker Academic, 2008.

Clark, R. Scott. *Recovering the Reformed Confession: Our Theology, Piety, and Practice*. Phillipsburg, NJ: Presbyterian & Reformed, 2008.

Cochrane, Arthur C. (ed.). *Reformed Confessions of the Sixteenth Century*. Louisville, KY: Westminster John Knox, 2003.

The Constitution of the Presbyterian Church (U.S.A.). Part I: Book of Confessions. Louisville, KY: Geneva, 1996.

Crisp, Oliver. "Karl Barth and Jonathan Edwards on reprobation (and hell)." Pages 300–322 in *Engaging with Barth: Contemporary Evangelical Critiques*. Ed. David Gibson and Daniel Strange. Nottingham: Apollos, 2008.

Bibliography

Cunningham, William. *The Reformers and the Theology of the Reformation*. Edinburgh: Banner of Truth Trust, 1967.

Davis, Ellen F. "Critical Traditioning: Seeking an Inner-Biblical Hermeneutic." Pages 163–180 in *The Art of Reading Scripture*. Ed. Ellen F. Davis and Richard B. Hays. Grand Rapids, MI: Eerdmans, 2003.

Dillard, Annie. *Teaching a Stone to Talk*. New York: Harper & Row, 1982.

Dowey, Edward A. *A Commentary on the Confession of 1967 and An Introduction to The Book of Confessions*. Philadelphia, PA: Westminster, 1968.

Edmondson, Stephen. *Calvin's Christology*. Cambridge: Cambridge University Press, 2004.

Emery, Gilles. *The Trinitarian Theology of St. Thomas Aquinas*. Oxford: Oxford University Press, 2007.

Ernst-Habib, Margit. "'Chosen by Grace': Reconsidering the Doctrine of Predestination." Page 77 in *Feminist and Womanist Essays in Reformed Dogmatics*. Columbia Series in Reformed Theology. Ed. Amy Plantinga Pauw and Serene Jones. Louisville, KY: Westminster John Knox, 2005.

Fergusson, David. "The Confession of Faith in the Life of the Church of Scotland." Pages 201–214 in *Reformed Theology in Contemporary Perspective: Westminster: Yesterday, Today—and Tomorrow?* Ed. Lynn Quigley. Edinburgh: Rutherford House, 2006.

Fergusson, David. "Divine Providence and Action." Pages 153–165 in *God's Life in Trinity*. Ed. Miroslav Volf and Michael Welker. Minneapolis, MN: Fortress, 2006.

Fitzmyer, Joseph. *Romans: A New Translation with Introduction and Commentary*. Anchor Bible 33. New York: Doubleday, 1993.

Forsyth, P. T. *Lectures on the Church and Sacraments*. London: Longmans, Green, 1917.

Foucault, Michel. *The Uses of Pleasure: The History of Sexuality*. Volume 2. London: Penguin, 1992.

Gaffin, Richard B. "Theonomy and Eschatology: Reflections on Postmillenialism." Pages 97–226 in *Theonomy: A Reformed Critique*. Ed. William S. Barker and W. Robert Godfrey. Grand Rapids, MI: Zondervan, 1990.

Glomsrud, Ryan. "Karl Barth as Historical Theologian: The Recovery of Reformed Theology in Barth's Early Dogmatics." Pages 84–112 in *Engaging with Barth: Contemporary Evangelical Critiques*. Ed. David Gibson and Daniel Strange. Leicester: Apollos, 2008.

Godsey, John D. "Epilogue: Barth as a Teacher." Pages 202–214 in *For the Sake of the World: Karl Barth and the Future of Ecclesial Theology*. Ed. George Hunsinger. Grand Rapids, MI: Eerdmans, 2004.

González, Justo L. *Mañana: Christian Theology from a Hispanic Perspective*. Nashville, TN: Abingdon, 1990.

Gordon, T. David. "A Critique of Theonomy: A Taxonomy," *Westminster Theological Journal* 56, no. 1 (1994): 24–45.

Greene-McCreight, Kathryn. "What's the Story? The Doctrine of God in *Common Order* and in the *Book of Common Worship*." Pages 99–114 in

Bibliography

To Glorify God: Essays on Modern Reformed Liturgy. Ed. Bryan D. Spinks and Iain R. Torrance. Grand Rapids, MI: Eerdmans, 1999.

Gunton, Colin. "Confessions, Dogmas, and Doctrine: An Exploration of Some Interactions." Pages 215–227 in *Reformed Theology in Contemporary Perspective: Westminster: Yesterday, Today—and Tomorrow?* Ed. Lynn Quigley. Edinburgh: Rutherford House, 2006.

Guthrie, Shirley C. *Always Being Reformed: Faith for a Fragmented World.* Louisville, KY: Westminster John Knox, 1996.

Hall, David W. "Calvin on Human Government and the State." Pages 411–440 in *A Theological Guide to Calvin's Institutes.* Ed. David W. Hall and Peter A. Lillback. Phillipsburg, NJ: Presbyterian & Reformed, 2008.

Hansen, Collin. *Young, Restless, Reformed: A Journalist's Journey with the New Calvinists.* Wheaton, IL: Crossway, 2008.

Hart, D. G. *Deconstructing Evangelicalism: Conservative Protestantism in the Age of Billy Graham.* Grand Rapids, MI: Baker Academic, 2005.

Hart, D. G. *The Lost Soul of American Protestantism.* American Intellectual Culture. Lanham, MD: Rowman & Littlefield, 2002.

Hart, D. G. *A Secular Faith: How Christianity Favors the Separation of Church and State.* Chicago, IL: Ivan R. Dee, 2006.

Hart, D. G. "The Spirituality of the Church." Pages 51–68 in *Recovering Mother Kirk: The Case for Liturgy in the Reformed Tradition.* Grand Rapids, MI: Baker Academic, 2003.

Helm, Paul. *John Calvin's Ideas.* New York: Oxford University Press, 2004.

Heron, Alasdair (ed.). *The Westminster Confession in the Church Today: Papers Prepared for the Church of Scotland Panel on Doctrine.* Edinburgh: Saint Andrew Press, 1982.

Hesselink, I. John. *On Being Reformed.* Grand Rapids, MI: Servant Books, 1983.

Holifield, E. Brooks. *Theology in America: Christian Thought from the Age of the Puritans to the Civil War.* New Haven, CT: Yale University Press, 2005.

Holmes, Stephen R. "Reformed Varieties of the *Communicatio Idiomatum.*" Pages 70–86 in *The Person of Christ.* Ed. Stephen R. Holmes and Murray A. Rae. London: T&T Clark, 2005.

Horton, Michael S. *Christless Christianity: The Alternative Gospel of the American Church.* Grand Rapids, MI: Baker, 2008.

Horton, Michael S. *Covenant and Eschatology: The Divine Drama.* Louisville, KY: Westminster John Knox, 2002.

Horton, Michael S. *Covenant and Salvation: Union with Christ.* Louisville, KY: Westminster John Knox, 2007.

Horton, Michael S. *God of Promise: An Introduction to Covenant Theology.* Grand Rapids, MI: Baker, 2006.

Horton, Michael S. *Lord and Servant: A Covenant Christology.* Louisville, KY: Westminster John Knox, 2005.

Horton, Michael S. "Law, Gospel, and Covenant: Reassessing Some Emerging Antitheses," *Westminster Theological Journal* 64, no. 2 (2002): 279–287.

Bibliography

Horton, Michael S. *People and Place: A Covenant Ecclesiology*. Louisville, KY: Westminster John Knox, 2008.

Hunsinger, George. "Baptism and the Soteriology of Forgiveness," *International Journal of Systematic Theology* 2, no. 3 (2000): 247–269.

Hunsinger, George. *Disruptive Grace: Studies in the Theology of Karl Barth*. Grand Rapids, MI: Eerdmans, 2000.

Hunsinger, George. *The Eucharist and Ecumenism: Let Us Keep the Feast*. Current Issues in Theology. Cambridge: Cambridge University Press, 2008.

Hunsinger, George. *How to Read Karl Barth: The Shape of His Theology*. New York: Oxford University Press, 1991.

Hunsinger, George. "Must Christians Believe in Hell?" Pages 143–155 in *Why are We Here? Everyday Questions and the Christian Life*. Ed. Ronald F. Thiemann and William C. Placher. Harrisburg, PA: Trinity Press International, 1998.

Jenson, Matt. *The Gravity of Sin: Augustine, Luther, and Barth on Homo Incurvatus in Se*. London: T&T Clark, 2006.

Jenson, Robert W. "Triune Grace," *Dialog* 41, no. 4 (2002): 291.

Jones, Paul Dafydd. *The Humanity of Christ: Christology in Karl Barth's* Church Dogmatics. London: T&T Clark, 2008.

Jones, Serene. *Feminist Theory and Christian Theology: Cartographies of Grace*. Guides to Theological Inquiry; Minneapolis, MN: Fortress, 2000.

Kapic, Kelly M. "The Son's Assumption of a Human Nature: A Call for Clarity," *International Journal of Systematic Theology* 3, no. 2 (2001): 154–166.

Kay, James F. "He Descended into Hell." Pages 117–129 in *Exploring and Proclaiming the Apostles' Creed*. Ed. Roger E. Van Harn. Grand Rapids, MI: Eerdmans, 2004.

Kelly, Douglas F. "The True and Triune God: Calvin's Doctrine of the Trinity." Pages 65–89 in *A Theological Guide to Calvin's Institutes: Essays and Analysis*. Ed. David W. Hall and Peter A. Lillback. Phillipsburg, NJ: Presbyterian & Reformed, 2008.

Kendall, R. T. *Calvin and English Calvinism until 1649*. New York: Oxford University Press, 1979.

Kline, Meredith G. *The Treaty of the Great King*. Grand Rapids, MI: Eerdmans, 1963.

Köstenberger, Andreas J., and R. Scott Swain, *Father, Son, and Spirit: The Trinity and John's Gospel*. New Studies in Biblical Theology 24. Downers Grove, IL: InterVarsity, 2008.

Larsen, Timothy. "Defining and Locating Evangelicalism." Pages 1–14 in *The Cambridge Companion to Evangelical Theology*. Cambridge Companions to Religion. Ed. Timothy Larsen and Daniel J. Treier. Cambridge: Cambridge University Press, 2007.

Lauber, David. *Barth on the Descent into Hell: God, Atonement and the Christian Life*. Barth Studies. Aldershot: Ashgate, 2004.

Lecerfe, Auguste. *An Introduction to Reformed Dogmatics*. London: Lutterworth, 1949.

Bibliography

Letham, Robert. *The Work of Christ*. Contours of Christian Theology. Downers Grove, IL: InterVarsity, 1993.

Levenson, Jon. *Sinai and Zion: An Entry into the Jewish Bible*. San Francisco, CA: HarperCollins, 1985.

Levering, Matthew. *Sacrifice and Community: Jewish Offering and Christian Eucharist*. Illuminations; Oxford: Blackwell, 2005.

Lewis, Alan. *Between Cross and Resurrection: A Theology of Holy Saturday*. Grand Rapids, MI: Eerdmans, 2001.

Lindsay, Mark R. *Covenanted Solidarity: The Theological Basis of Karl Barth's Opposition to Nazi Anti-Semitism and the Holocaust*. Issues in Systematic Theology 9. New York: Peter Lang, 2001.

Lucas, Sean Michael. *On Being Presbyterian: Our Beliefs, Practices, and Stories*. Phillipsburg, NJ: Presbyterian & Reformed, 2006.

Lundin, Roger. *Believing Again: Doubt and Faith in a Secular Age*. Grand Rapids, MI: Eerdmans, 2009.

Lundin, Roger. *From Nature to Experience: The American Search for Cultural Authority*. American Intellectual Culture. Lanham, MD: Rowman & Littlefield, 2006.

Manton, Thomas. *Works of Thomas Manton*. Volume 12: *Sermons on Romans 8 and 2 Corinthians 5*. London: Nisbet, 1870.

Markus, R. A. "A Defense of Christian Mediocrity." Pages 45–62 in *The End of Ancient Christianity*. Cambridge: Cambridge University Press, 1990.

Matthewes, Charles. *A Theology of Public Life*. Cambridge Studies in Christian Doctrine. Cambridge: Cambridge University Press, 2007.

McCormack, Bruce L. "The Actuality of God: Karl Barth in Conversation with Open Theism." Pages 185–242 in *Engaging the Doctrine of God: Contemporary Protestant Perspectives*. Ed. Bruce L. McCormack. Grand Rapids, MI: Baker Academic, 2008.

McCormack, Bruce L. "The End of Reformed Theology? The Voice of Karl Barth in the Doctrinal Chaos of the Present." Pages 46–64 in *Reformed Theology: Identity and Ecumenicity*. Ed. Wallace M. Alston, Jr., and Michael Welker. Grand Rapids, MI: Eerdmans, 2003.

McCoy, Charles S., and J. Wayne Baker. *The Fountainhead of Federalism: Heinrich Bullinger and the Covenantal Tradition*. Louisville, KY: Westminster John Knox, 1991.

McFarland, Ian. "The Fall and Sin." Pages 140–159 in *The Oxford Handbook of Systematic Theology*. Ed. John Webster, Kathryn Tanner, and Iain Torrance. New York: Oxford University Press, 2007.

McGowan, Andrew T. B. "Was Westminster Calvinist?" Pages 46–65 in *Reformed Theology in Contemporary Perspective: Westminster: Yesterday, Today—and Tomorrow?* Ed. Lynn Quigley. Edinburgh: Rutherford House, 2006.

McIntyre, John. "Confessions in Historical and Contemporary Setting." Pages 22–40 in *The Presumption of Presence: Essays in Honor of D. W. D. Shaw*. Ed. Peter McEnhill and G. B. Hall. Edinburgh: Scottish Academic Press, 1996.

Bibliography

Miller, Patrick D. *The God You Have: Politics, Religion, and the First Commandment*. Facets; Minneapolis, MN: Fortress, 2005.

Molnar, Paul D. *Divine Freedom and the Doctrine of the Immanent Trinity*. London: T&T Clark, 2002.

Moltmann, Jürgen. *Theology of Hope*. Trans. J. W. Leith. New York: Harper & Row, 1967.

Moore-Keish, Martha L. "How Shall We Worship?" Pages 187–206 in *Conversations with the Confessions: Dialogue in the Reformed Tradition*. Ed. Joseph D. Small. Louisville, KY: Geneva, 2005.

Mouw, Richard. *Calvinism at the Las Vegas Airport*. Grand Rapids, MI: Zondervan, 2004.

Mouw, Richard J. "The Problem of Authority in Evangelical Christianity." Pages 124–141 in *Church Unity and the Papal Office: An Evangelical Dialogue on John Paul II's Encyclical* Ut Unum Sint. Ed. Carl Braaten and Robert Jenson. Grand Rapids, MI: Eerdmans, 2001.

Muller, Richard A. *Christ and the Decree: Christology and Predestination in Reformed Theology from Calvin to Perkins*. Grand Rapids, MI: Baker Academic, 2008.

Muller, Richard A. "How Many Points?" *Calvin Theological Journal* 28, no. 2 (1993): 425–433.

Muller, Richard A. "John Calvin and later Calvinism: The Identity of the Reformed Tradition." Pages 130–149 in *The Cambridge Companion to Reformation Theology*. Cambridge Companions to Religion. Ed. David Bagchi and David Steinmetz. Cambridge: Cambridge University Press, 2004.

Muller, Richard A. *Post-Reformation Reformed Dogmatics: The Rise and Development of Reformed Orthodoxy, ca. 1520 to ca. 1725*. 4 Volumes. Grand Rapids, MI: Baker Academic, 2003.

Murray, John. *The Collected Works of John Murray*. Volume 2: *Systematic Theology*. Ed. Iain Murray. Edinburgh: Banner of Truth Trust, 1977.

Murray, John. *The Imputation of Adam's Sin*. Grand Rapids, MI: Eerdmans, 1959.

Murray, John. *Redemption Accomplished and Applied*. Grand Rapids, MI: Eerdmans, 1955.

Niebuhr, Reinhold. *The Nature and Destiny of Man*. 2 volumes. New York: Charles Scribner's Sons, 1964.

Niebuhr, H. Richard. *Christ and Culture*. New York: Harper & Row, 1956.

Nimmo, Paul T. *Being in Action: The Theological Shape of Barth's Ethical Vision*. London: T&T Clark, 2007.

Nimmo, Paul T. "Karl Barth and the *Concursus Dei*: A Chalcedonianism Too Far?" *International Journal of Systematic Theology* 9, no. 1 (2007): 58–72.

Noll, Mark A. *America's God: From Jonathan Edwards to Abraham Lincoln*. New York: Oxford University Press, 2002.

Noll, Mark A. *The Civil War as a Theological Crisis*. Chapel Hill, NC: University of North Carolina Press, 2006.

Bibliography

Noll, Mark A. *The Rise of Evangelicalism: The Age of Edwards, Whitefield, and the Wesleys.* History of Evangelicalism. Downers Grove, IL: InterVarsity, 2004.

Noll, Mark A. *The Scandal of the Evangelical Mind.* Grand Rapids, MI: Eerdmans, 1995.

Novak, David. *The Jewish Social Contract.* New Forum Books; Princeton, NJ: Princeton University Press, 2005.

Oberman, Heiko A. *The Dawn of the Reformation: Essays in Late Medieval and Early Reformation Thought.* Grand Rapids, MI: Eerdmans, 1992.

Old, Hughes Oliphant. *Worship.* Guides to the Reformed Tradition. Atlanta, GA: John Knox, 1984.

Olson, Roger. *Arminian Theology: Myths and Realities.* Downers Grove, IL: InterVarsity Press, 2006.

Olson, Roger. *Reformed and Always Reforming: The Postconservative Approach to Evangelical Theology.* Grand Rapids, MI: Baker Academic, 2007.

Owen, John. *Works of John Owen*, volume 10: *The Death of Christ.* Edinburgh: Banner of Truth Trust, 1967.

Packer, J. I. *Evangelism and the Sovereignty of God.* Downers Grove, IL: InterVarsity, 1961.

Packer, J. I. *Knowing God.* Downers Grove, IL: InterVarsity, 1973.

Packer, J. I., and Thomas C. Oden. *One Faith: The Evangelical Consensus.* Downers Grove, IL: InterVarsity, 2004.

Pauw, Amy Plantinga. "The Graced Infirmity of the Church." Pages 189–203 in *Feminist and Womanist Essays in Reformed Dogmatics.* Columbia Series in Reformed Theology. Ed. Amy Plantinga Pauw and Serene Jones. Louisville, KY: Westminster John Knox, 2005.

Pauw, Amy Plantinga, and Serene Jones (eds.). *Feminist and Womanist Essays in Reformed Dogmatics.* Columbia Series in Reformed Theology. Louisville, KY: Westminster John Knox, 2005.

William Perkins, "A Golden Chaine." Pages 169–259 in *The Works of William Perkins.* Volume 3. Ed. I. Breward. London: Sutton Courteney, 1970.

Pettegree, Andrew. *Reformation and the Culture of Persuasion.* Cambridge: Cambridge University Press, 2005.

Placher, William C. "Contemporary Confessions and Biblical Authority." Pages 66–74 in *To Confess the Faith Today.* Ed. Jack L. Stotts and Jane Dempsey Douglass. Louisville, KY: Westminster John Knox, 1990.

Placher, William C. *The Domestication of Transcendence: How Modern Thinking About God Went Wrong.* Louisville, KY: Westminster John Knox, 1996.

Placher, William C. *Jesus the Savior: The Meaning of Jesus Christ for Christian Faith.* Louisville, KY: Westminster John Knox, 2001.

Placher, William C. *Narratives of a Vulnerable God: Christ, Theology, and Scripture.* Louisville, KY: Westminster John Knox, 1994.

Pratt, Richard. "Infant Baptism in the New Covenant." Pages 156–174 in *The Case for Covenantal Infant Baptism.* Ed. Gregg Strawbridge. Phillipsburg, NJ: Presbyterian & Reformed, 2003.

Bibliography

Rigby, Cynthia L. "What Does God Have to Do With Us?" Pages 121–134 in *Conversations with the Confessions: Dialogue in the Reformed Tradition*. Ed. Joseph D. Small. Louisville, KY: Geneva, 2005.

Robinson, Marilynne. *Gilead*. New York: Farrar, Strauss, and Giroux, 2004.

Rogers, Jack. *Reading the Bible and the Confessions: The Presbyterian Way*. Louisville, KY: Geneva, 1999.

Rogers, Jack, and Donald K. McKim. *The Authority and Interpretation of the Bible: An Historical Approach*. San Francisco, CA: HarperCollins, 1980.

Rohls, Jan. *Reformed Confessions: Theology from Zurich to Barmen*. Columbia Series in Reformed Theology. Trans. John Hoffmeyer. Louisville, KY: Westminster John Knox, 1998.

Schaff, Philip. *The Creeds of Christendom*. Volume 1. New York: Harper & Brothers, 1877. Reprint. Grand Rapids, MI: Baker, 1983.

Schleiermacher, Friedrich. *The Christian Faith*. Ed. H. R. Mackintosh and J. S. Stewart. Philadelphia, PA: Fortress, 1976.

Schneewind, J. B. *The Invention of Autonomy: A History of Modern Moral Philosophy*. Cambridge: Cambridge University Press, 1998.

Schwarz, Regina. *The Curse of Cain: The Violent Legacy of Monotheism*. Chicago, IL: University of Chicago Press, 1997.

Sherman, Robert. *King, Priest, and Prophet: A Trinitarian Theology of Atonement*. Theology for the Twenty-First Century. London: T&T Clark, 2004.

Smith, Morton H. *Studies in Southern Presbyterian Theology*. Phillipsburg, NJ: Presbyterian & Reformed, 2004.

Sonderegger, Katherine. "Election." Pages 105–120 in *The Oxford Handbook of Systematic Theology*. Ed. John Webster, Kathryn Tanner, and Iain Torrance. Oxford: Oxford University Press, 2007.

Sonderegger, Katherine. *That Jesus Christ Was Born a Jew: Karl Barth's 'Doctrine of Israel'*. University Park, PA: Penn State University Press, 2002.

Stark, Rodney. *One True God: Historical Consequences of Monotheism*. Princeton, NJ: Princeton University Press, 2001.

Tanner, Kathryn. *God and Creation in Christian Theology: Tyranny or Empowerment?* Oxford: Blackwell, 1988. Reprint. Minneapolis, MN: Fortress, 2005.

Tanner, Kathryn. *Jesus, Humanity, and the Trinity: A Brief Systematic Theology*. Minneapolis, MN: Fortress, 2001.

Tanner, Kathryn. "Workings of the Spirit: Simplicity or Complexity?" Pages 87–106 in *The Work of the Spirit: Pneumatology and Pentecostalism*. Ed. Michael Welker. Grand Rapids, MI: Eerdmans, 2006.

Thornwell, James Henley. *Collected Writings of James Henley Thornwell*. Volume 4: *Ecclesiastical*. Edinburgh: Banner of Truth Trust, 1986.

Torrance, James B. *Worship, Community, and the Triune God of Grace*. Downers Grove, IL: InterVarsity, 1996.

Torrance, T. F. *The Hermeneutics of John Calvin*. Edinburgh: Scottish Academic Press, 1988.

Tracy, Thomas F. *God, Action, and Embodiment*. Grand Rapids, MI: Eerdmans, 1984.

Bibliography

Trueman, Carl R. *John Owen: Reformed Catholic, Renaissance Man*. Great Theologians. Aldershot: Ashgate, 2007.

Trueman, Carl R. "John Owen's *A Dissertation on Divine Justice*: An Exercise in Christocentric Scholasticism," *Calvin Theological Journal* 33, no. 1 (1998): 87–103.

van Asselt, Willem J. "The Fundamental Meaning of Theology: Archetypal and Ectypal Theology in Seventeenth-Century Reformed Thought," *WTJ* 64, no. 2 (2002): 319–335.

Van Drunen, David. "Iconoclasm, Incarnation, and Eschatology: Toward a Catholic Understanding of the Reformed Doctrine of the 'Second' Commandment," *International Journal of Systematic Theology* 6, no. 2 (2004): 130–147.

Vanhoozer, Kevin J. *The Drama of Doctrine: A Canonical-Linguistic Approach to Christian Theology*. Louisville, KY: Westminster John Knox, 2005.

Vanhoozer, Kevin J. *Remythologizing Theology*. Cambridge Studies in Christian Doctrine. Cambridge: Cambridge University Press, 2010.

Vischer, Lukas (ed.). *Reformed Witness Today: A Collection of Confessions and Statements of Faith*. Bern: World Alliance of Reformed Churches, 1982.

Volf, Miroslav. "'The Trinity is Our Social Program': The Doctrine of the Trinity and the Shape of Social Engagement," *Modern Theology* 14, no. 3 (1998): 403–423.

Walker Bynum, Caroline. *The Resurrection of the Body in Western Christianity, 200–1336*. New York: Columbia University Press, 1995.

Warfield, B. B. *Calvin and Augustine*. Phillipsburg, NJ: Presbyterian & Reformed, 1956.

Warfield, B. B. *The Works of B. B. Warfield*, volume 9: *Studies in Theology*. New York: Oxford University Press, 1932.

Watson, Thomas. *The Ten Commandments*. Edinburgh: Banner of Truth Trust, 1958.

Webb, Stephen. *The Divine Voice: Christian Proclamation and the Theology of Sound*. Grand Rapids, MI: Brazos, 2004.

Weber, Max. *The Protestant Ethic and the Spirit of Capitalism*. New York: Charles Scribner's Sons, 1958.

Webster, John. *Barth's Earlier Theology: Four Studies*. London: T&T Clark, 2005.

Webster, John. *Barth's Ethics of Reconciliation*. Cambridge: Cambridge University Press, 1995.

Webster, John. *Barth's Moral Theology: Human Action in Barth's Thought*. Edinburgh: T&T Clark, 1998.

Webster, John. "Confession and Confessions." Pages 119–132 in *Nicene Christianity: The Future for a New Ecumenism*. Ed. Christopher R. Seitz. Grand Rapids, MI: Brazos, 2001.

Webster, John. *Holiness*. Grand Rapids, MI: Eerdmans, 2003.

Webster, John. *Holy Scripture: A Dogmatic Sketch*. Current Issues in Theology. Cambridge: Cambridge University Press, 2003.

Bibliography

Webster, John. "Life In and Of Himself: Reflections on God's Aseity." Pages 107–124 in *Engaging the Doctrine of God: Contemporary Protestant Perspectives.* Ed. Bruce L. McCormack. Grand Rapids, MI: Baker Academic, 2008.

Webster, John. "On Evangelical Ecclesiology." Pages 182 and 184 in *Confessing God.* London: T&T Clark, 2005.

Webster, John. *Word and Church: Essays in Christian Dogmatics.* Edinburgh: T&T Clark, 2001.

Weigel, George. *The Cube and the Cathedral: Europe, America, and Religion without God.* New York: Basic, 2006.

Weir, David A. *The Origins of the Federal Theology in Sixteenth-Century Reformation Thought.* New York: Clarendon, 1990.

Wells, David. *God in the Wasteland: The Reality of Truth in a World of Fading Dreams.* Grand Rapids, MI: Eerdmans, 1994.

Werpehowski, William. "Reinhold Niebuhr." Pages 180–193 in *The Blackwell Companion to Political Theology.* Blackwell Companions to Religion. Ed. Peter Scott and William Cavanaugh. Oxford: Blackwell, 2004.

Williams, Anna. "Tradition." Pages 362–377 in *The Oxford Handbook of Systematic Theology.* Ed. John Webster, Kathryn Tanner, and Iain Torrance. New York: Oxford University Press, 2007.

Willis, David, and Michael Welker (eds.). *Toward the Future of Reformed Theology: Tasks, Topics, Traditions.* Grand Rapids, MI: Eerdmans, 1999.

Woodbridge, John D. *Biblical Authority: A Critique of the Rogers/McKim Proposal* Grand Rapids, MI: Zondervan, 1982.

Wright, David F. "Westminster: Reformed and Ecumenical?" Pages 162–177 in *Reformed Theology in Contemporary Perspective: Westminster: Yesterday, Today—and Tomorrow?* Ed. Lynn Quigley. Edinburgh: Rutherford House, 2006.

Wright, David F. *What Has Infant Baptism Done to Baptism? An Enquiry at the End of Christendom.* Milton Keynes: Paternoster, 2005.

Wyman, Walter E. "Sin and Redemption." Pages 129–150 in *The Cambridge Companion to Friedrich Schleiermacher.* Cambridge Companions to Religion. Ed. Jacqueline Mariña. Cambridge: Cambridge University Press, 2005.

Zachman, Randall. *The Assurance of Faith: Conscience in the Theology of Martin Luther and John Calvin.* Louisville, KY: Westminster John Knox, 1993.

Zwingli, Ulrich. "An Exposition of the Faith." Pages 245–282 in *Zwingli and Bullinger.* Library of Christian Classics. Ed. and trans. Geoffrey W. Bromiley. Louisville, KY: Westminster John Knox, 2006.

Index of Scriptures

Genesis

1:1	18
1:4	158
1:10	158
1:12	158
1:18	158
1:21	158
1:25	158
1:26-30	71
1:28-30	159
1:31	158
2:7	134, 159
2:17	42, 100
3	42
3:4-5	28
3:14-19	42
3:15	43
3:21	42
3:22	42
3:24	43
4:12	162
4:15	162
6:5	98
8:21	98
8:21-22	162
9:9-11	162
15:10-11	122
20:6	162
37-50	110
50:20	110

Exodus

3:12	117
3:14	20
3:18	117
7:16	117
8:1	117
8:20	117
8:25-28	117
9:1	117
9:13	117
10:3	117
10:7-11	117
10:24-26	117
12:31	117
13:3-10	122
20:2	14
20:3	19
20:4-6	128
20:5-6	15
32:1	12
32:5	13
32:6	12
32:9	12
32:20	12
32:28	12
32:34	12
33:19	101

Leviticus

10:1-2	117

Index of Scriptures

Numbers

16	117

Deuteronomy

4	130
4:15-20	129
7:7	100
18:18	72
29:29	18, 19

1 Samuel

15:22	117

2 Samuel

6:3	117
6:13	117

2 Kings

14:6	98
19:27-28	162

2 Chronicles

26:16-19	117

Nehemiah

8:1-6	122

Job

14:4	98
15:14-16	98

Psalms

1	19
3:8	40, 43
14:1-3	98
30:11	154
65:9-10	162
104:14-15	162
104:24	162
104:27-30	162
110:1	71
145:9	162

Isaiah

53:6	17
55:10-11	32
64:6	87

Jeremiah

19:5	117
31	37, 126, 127
31:3	43
31:29-30	98
32:35	117

Ezekiel

18:20	98

Hosea

6:7	41
11:9	58

Matthew

11:9	72
13:24-30	113
15:1-4	117
25:31-46	102, 142

Mark

15:34	154

John

1:1-3	18
1:1-4	23
1:14	24, 68, 69
1:17	18
1:18	18
1:29	23, 145
2:19	117
2:21	117

Index of Scriptures

5:7 130
5:20 67

Galatians
2–3 174
2:14 79
2:16 79
2:19-20 76–77
3:10-12 82

Ephesians
1:5 115
1:12 115
1:14 115
2:1 98
2:3 98
2:8-9 102
2:10 102
2:11 176

Philippians
1:6 105
1:29 104
2 108
2:12-13 108

Colossians
1:15 18

2 Timothy
1:13-14 131
3:16 29
3:16-17 26

Hebrews
1:1 24
1:1-2 72

1:2-3 23
1:3-4 37
4:12 26
7:27 72
9:12 72
9:26 72
10:1-4 120
10:11-15 120
10:25 122
11:1 77
11:6 88, 116
13:15-16 120

James
1:17 162

1 Peter
1:8 130
1:12 24
1:14 24
1:15 24
1:20 40
1:20-21 24
2:9 115, 117

2 Peter
1:10 107
3:16 26

1 John
3:2 130

Revelation
20 4, 166
20-21 116
21:3 117
21:22-27 150

Index of Names

Aquinas, Thomas 55, 68, 108–9, 158

Arminius, Jacob 99

Augustine of Hippo 2, 3, 17, 62, 64, 96, 102, 138–9, 175

Ayers, Lewis 62

Barth, Karl 8, 9, 17, 20, 22, 24, 28, 35, 46–51, 58, 60–1, 66, 67, 84, 87, 90, 108–10, 113, 144, 146, 148–9, 151, 173, 179

Baur, F. C. 27, 29, 52

Bavinck, Herman 21, 90, 91–2

Bebbington, David 165

Bellarmine, Robert 64

Berkouwer, G. C. 18, 70, 76

Brueggemann, Walter 14

Bucer, Martin 77

Buchanan, James 80, 94

Bullinger, Heinrich 4, 39, 77, 149

Burman, Franz 44

Calvin, John 3, 4, 5, 8, 12, 13, 18, 19, 25, 27, 29, 30, 38, 44, 54, 63–6, 67, 68, 76, 77, 80, 83, 87, 97, 116, 124, 133, 138, 141, 143, 153–4, 163, 164, 168, 169

Carson, D. A. 168–9

Clark, R. Scott 147–8

Cocceius, Johannes 4, 44, 164

Culp, Kristine 14

Cunningham, William 143, 154

Dillard, Annie 125

Dowey, Edward 29, 30

Edmondson, Stephen 66

Edwards, Jonathan 4, 46, 51, 89, 164

Emery, Gilles 63

Ernst-Habib, Margit 112

Fergusson, David 108, 152

Finney, Charles 89–90

Forsyth, P. T. 115

Foucault, Michel 111

Gabler, J. P. 52

Gaffin, Richard 53, 167

Gallie, W. B. 2

Gerrish, Brian 16–17

Glomsrud, Ryan 50

Grenz, Stanley 62

Gunton, Colin 153

Guthrie, Shirley 56–8, 60–1, 149, 158, 162, 178

Hall, David 156

Handel 71

Hart, Darryl G. 90

Hauerwas, Stanley 169

Heidegger, Martin 57

Index of Names

Index of Names